The Appraisal
of Investments
in Educational Facilities

ORGANISATION FOR ECONOMIC CO-OPERATION AND DEVELOPMENT

ORGANISATION FOR ECONOMIC CO-OPERATION AND DEVELOPMENT

Pursuant to Article 1 of the Convention signed in Paris on 14th December 1960, and which came into force on 30th September 1961, the Organisation for Economic Co-operation and Development (OECD) shall promote policies designed:

- to achieve the highest sustainable economic growth and employment and a rising standard of living in Member countries, while maintaining financial stability, and thus to contribute to the development of the world economy;
- to contribute to sound economic expansion in Member as well as non-member countries in the process of economic development; and
- to contribute to the expansion of world trade on a multilateral, non-discriminatory basis in accordance with international obligations.

The original Member countries of the OECD are Austria, Belgium, Canada, Denmark, France, Germany, Greece, Iceland, Ireland, Italy, Luxembourg, the Netherlands, Norway, Portugal, Spain, Sweden, Switzerland, Turkey, the United Kingdom and the United States. The following countries became Members subsequently through accession at the dates indicated hereafter: Japan (28th April 1964), Finland (28th January 1969), Australia (7th June 1971), New Zealand (29th May 1973), Mexico (18th May 1994), the Czech Republic (21st December 1995), Hungary (7th May 1996), Poland (22nd November 1996) and Korea (12th December 1996). The Commission of the European Communities takes part in the work of the OECD (Article 13 of the OECD Convention).

Publié en français sous le titre :
L' ÉVALUATION DES INVESTISSEMENTS EN ÉQUIPEMENTS ÉDUCATIFS

EUROPEAN INVESTMENT BANK

The European Investment Bank (EIB), the European Union's financing institution, was established in 1958 by the Treaty of Rome. Owned by the European Union's Member States, the EIB enjoys its own legal personality and financial autonomy.

As an EU institution, the EIB's mission is to finance investment projects which contribute towards economic integration and greater social cohesion of the Member States. The Bank's financing activities focus on supporting the following EU policy objectives:

- Regional development: areas lagging behind in their development (Objective I areas, as classified under European Structural Funds), areas faced with industrial decline (Objective 2), rural areas encountering conversion problems (Objective 5(b)) and Arctic areas with an extremely low population density (Objective 6).
- Creation of trans-European transport, telecommunications and energy transfer networks.
- Protection of the rural and urban environment.
- Increased energy self-sufficiency and more efficient use of existing energy resources.
- Health and education development.
- Reinforcement of the competitiveness of European industry and support for small and medium-sized enterprises (SMEs).

The Bank raises funds for lending by issuing bonds on the international capital markets. Their first-class "AAA" credit rating enables the EIB to borrow on the finest terms available. Operating on a non-profit basis, the Bank lends the proceeds of these borrowings on highly favourable terms, adding only a small margin to cover its operating costs. The EIB works in close co-operation with the banking community, both when borrowing and lending.

The Bank applies a selective approach to its financing decisions. Each investment proposal must meet one or more of the above mentioned EU policy objectives. In addition, each project is thoroughly scrutinised for financial, technical and economic viability and also for compliance with EU legislation on environmental issues and procurement.

OECD 2000

Although the main thrust of Bank activity is necessarily within the European Union, which accounts for 90% of aggregate lending, the EIB also helps to implement the EU's development aid and co-operation policy towards third countries, financing projects in some 120 non-member countries with which the EU has concluded co-operation agreements, notably in : Africa, the Caribbean and the Pacific (ACP), the Republic of South Africa, the southern-rim Mediterranean countries, Central and Eastern Europe, Asia and Latin America.

PROGRAMME ON EDUCATIONAL BUILDING

The Programme on Educational Building (PEB: *Programme pour la construction et l'équipement de l'éducation*) operates within the Organisation for Economic Co-operation and Development (OECD). PEB promotes the international exchange of ideas, information, research and experience in all aspects of educational building.

The overriding concerns of the Programme are to ensure that the maximum educational benefit is obtained from past and future investment in educational buildings and equipment, and that the building stock is planned and managed in the most efficient way.

The three main themes of the Programme's work are:

- improving the quality and suitability of educational facilities and thus contributing to the quality of education;

- ensuring that the best possible use is made of the very substantial sums of money which are spent on constructing, running and maintaining educational facilities;

- giving early warning of the impact on educational facilities of trends in education and in society as a whole.

OECD 2000

FOREWORD

The OECD Programme on Educational Building (PEB) in collaboration with the Projects Directorate of the European Investment Bank (EIB) organised an international conference on the evaluation of investment in educational facilities in Luxembourg on 16 and 17 November 1998. The conference brought together 90 researchers, education planners and policy-makers, managers and architects. For the EIB this was a new field of activity, since until recently it has not been involved in financing education projects. A resolution adopted by Heads of Government of the countries of the European Union in June 1997, aimed at encouraging economic growth and reducing unemployment, specified that the EIB would henceforth devote a part of its loans to educational projects. The Bank has as a result broadened its eligibility rules and is encouraging research into the evaluation of investments in education at an international level.

The introduction and the conclusions of this book were written by Isabelle Etienne, Consultant, OECD Programme on Educational Building.

This book is published on the responsibility of the Secretary-General of the OECD.

TABLE OF CONTENTS

Introduction 9

Chapter 1. **Economic Analysis of Educational Projects**... 15

Building Human Capital in Europe: Issues and Methods
George Psacharopoulos.. 17
Cost-benefit Analysis in Education Projects: Internal Rates of Return,
Methodologies and Theoretical Objections
Tom Healy.. 33
Externalities, Non-Market Effects, and Trends in Returns
to Educational Investments
Walter W. McMahon 51

Chapter 2. **Performance Indicators for Educational Projects**............................... 85

Investment in Education in OECD Countries, Finance and Ownership
Andreas Schleicher... 87
What Do Develop Countries Today Demand from their Educational Systems ?
Torsten Husén.. 113
What Do Develop Countries Expect of their Educational Systems ?
Reflections on the French Experience
François Louis... 127

Chapter 3. **Management of Physical Resources for Education** 155

Making Better Use of School Buildings: School as Social Capital
Kenn Fisher 157
The Impact of School Building Conditions, Student Achievement,
and Behaviour
Glen I. Earthman.. 181

OECD 2000

Chapter 4. **Design and Equipement of Physical Facilities for Education** 195

Environmental Appraisal of Education Facilities
Christopher French 197
Patterns and Design Strategies for New School Buildings
Rodolfo Almeida 205
Investing for Flexibility
Sam Cassels and Peter McLennan 219

Conclusion 225

Notes 232

INTRODUCTION

In an environment in which knowledge increasingly forms the basis of economic growth, education assumes strategic significance. It is central to the continued development of societies and represents one major solution to the unemployment issue. The development of a skilled labour force essentially affects the supply side of the labour market, and must be associated with other policies that improve the ability of the labour market to adjust to structural change and foster sustainable economic growth.

The European Investment Bank (EIB) is the financing institution of the European Union (EU). It was created by the Treaty of Rome in 1958 and its mission is to further EU objectives, including the promotion of economic development and employment, by making long-term finance available for technically sound investment and economically viable projects. In this context, as part of the European Union's 1997 Amsterdam Special Action Programme (ASAP) initiative, the EIB has broadened the scope of its lending activities to include projects in the education and health sectors.

One year after the launch of ASAP, the EIB's Board of Directors approved lending totalling nearly three billion Euro in these sectors. The funds are directed towards 26 projects, or investment schemes, in 14 of the 15 EU Member States. The majority of these are in assisted areas where the need for modernising and extending the health and education infrastructure is most pressing. By November 1998, finance contracts had been signed worth 1.5 billion Euro.

The OECD, for its part, has developed a range of indicators in order to provide a comparative picture of investments in education in OECD countries, focusing on educational finance and ownership. The aim is threefold: to enhance individual and collective economic performance through education, to promote the efficiency of educational systems, and to identify additional resources to meet increasing demands for education.

Within the OECD, the Programme on Educational Building (PEB) has undertaken research on strategies for managing the educational infrastructure, on the role of design in improving the effectiveness of schools, as well as on management and the development of indicators for evaluating educational facilities. This places PEB in a strategic position to examine the question of the appraisal of investments in education.

9

In such a perspective, international indicators should inform the process of policy formation, reinforce the public accountability of educational systems, and provide insight into the comparative functioning of educational systems, focusing both on the human and financial resources invested in education and on returns to these investments. To be useful, such indicators should not only describe features of education but also facilitate analysis and explanation. They must also provide timely and relevant information for policy makers who face, for example, the competing demands of capital investment for school buildings and current expenditure.

Comparative examination of cost patterns addresses several issues:

• How countries compare with respect to the levels of national resources invested in education.

• How the relative share of public and private investments in education have evolved at different levels of education. Education is still a largely public enterprise; however, the private sector is a significant source of funds, albeit more so in some countries than in others.

• How education resources are used and how spending allocation can affect the quality of instruction, the condition of educational facilities, and the ability of the educational system to adjust to changing demographic and enrolment trends.

The distinction between capital expenditure and current expenditure is highly significant in this context. Capital expenditure encompasses outlays for assets that last longer than one year and includes spending on the construction, renovation, and major repairs of buildings. Current expenditure includes financial outlays for school resources used each year to operate schools. It can be divided into three functional categories: compensation of teachers, compensation of other staff, and current expenditure other than on compensation of personnel. The proportion of capital expenditure is generally larger at the tertiary level, because there are more differentiated and advanced teaching facilities. The central question is how supply and demand patterns translate into unit costs.

This report is the result of a conference jointly organised by the Projects Directorate of the EIB and by the OECD Programme on Educational Building. The aim of the conference was to address issues covering basic aspects of investment in physical educational facilities and important issues in the economics of education. How are the economic rates of return of an educational investment to be evaluated? How is cost-effectiveness in such a sector measured? How can we be reasonably certain that the right sort of projects are financed, given the educational policy implemented in each country?

More specifically, this report is structured around four thematic chapters. The first theme aims at presenting a state of the art of the economic analysis of educational projects. The second theme focuses on the contribution of performance indicators in the evaluation of education systems. The third theme concerns the management of physical resources for education, especially the relationship between school environment and student achievement. The last theme addresses the design and equipment of physical facilities for education. These arguments warrant some development here.

* * *

Chapter One examines the economic analysis of educational projects. It argues that building human capital is the key to European well-being in the next millennium. Where investment in physical capital was the key in the past, today the emphasis seems to have shifted towards investment in human capital. Therefore, the stock of human capital in Europe should be much higher than the physical capital stock.

Human capital means a more educated and healthy population, a situation that leads to higher productivity. Education is a major component of human capital. Assuming three major phases in establishing an educational facility - building a school, operating a school, and building human capital - the human capital effect is certainly the most problematic and difficult to document. Within this framework, project appraisal methodology can be based on cost-effectiveness analysis or cost-benefit analysis. For investments in education, positive externalities, such as reduced crime or enhanced social cohesion, also bear careful study.

People have become extremely important in knowledge- and competence-based economies. In considering the rates of return to investments in education, the value of human capital investment is examined in terms of production rather than consumption. Estimating the benefits of investment in education applied to human capital entails estimating the additional benefits over a lifetime for all individuals of investing in more human capital. "While there is clear evidence that investment in human capital yields benefits, it remains difficult to calculate precise rates of return from particular investments" (Healy). Chapter One provides tools for analysing and calculating these rates of return, thereby demonstrating their importance for future investments in the educational sector.

Education is crucial not only to economic growth but also to the broader process that supports this growth. It plays a vital role in sustaining economic development in all countries and by "generating non-market returns and externalities that are also vital to human welfare. It is the identification and measurement of these externalities and non-market effects of investments in education and their implications, including cur-

11

rent trends for the planning and investment in education facilities" (McMahon) that are examined later in this chapter. The non-market social benefits of education are carefully examined in no fewer than 78 countries. The major net outcomes of education include: increased earnings; better private and public health; lower fertility rates; democratisation; greater political stability; reduced poverty and inequality; improved environmental quality; and lower crime rates.

* * *

Chapter Two examines specific performance indicators for educational projects, the recent evolution of educational systems, and the current demands on them. As noted above, the OECD education indicators aim at providing governments and policy makers relevant information on the efficiency of educational systems. Indicators on effectiveness, efficiency and quality facilitate the measurement of educational services in OECD countries. A comparative, international quantitative perspective lets countries view their own performances in the light of other countries' performance. This chapter addresses the relevance of such measurements as well as the difficulties that they imply. Effectiveness reflects the link between the outcomes of educational services and previously-defined objectives. Quality indicators aim at identifying and measuring how schools function, and at reflecting the different ways in which school systems are organised. The measurement of efficiency, perhaps the most important indicator in the present context, relates to the ways in which educational systems make use of their resources to produce educational outcomes. "Although the optimal volume of resources required to prepare each student for life and work in the modern economy is not known, international comparisons of the investment per student in education can provide a starting point for evaluating the effectiveness of different models of educational provision" (Schleicher).

Next, the chapter examines the evolution of educational systems and the recent changes and current trends affecting them in OECD countries. Structural and didactic changes and new modes of pedagogical production will undoubtedly have to occur, in terms of teacher training and the core curriculum. A number of questions are thus raised:

• What tasks should teachers be assigned in the first place? What should the core curriculum be like in a system of lifelong learning? What kind of skills will be called for in a society that requires lifelong learning and relearning?

• The structure of the curriculum in a changing society must be considered differently in the perspective of lifelong education than in the perspective of a relatively static society. Curricular content would have to move from providing encyclopaedic knowledge of more or less disconnected items to providing intellectual instruments that help students orient themselves in an expanding knowledge society.

- Analysing the impact of a rapidly changing society on schooling will also lead to certain policy conclusions about both the structure and the curricula of the formal educational system. This reminds us that educational provision, reforms, and outcomes must be seen in a socio-economic context.

- The role of formal education will have to be reconsidered. The changes needed to enhance the quality of formal schooling within the framework of the learning society have to be contemplated. In developing countries, particular attention must be paid to the tension between quality and equality or quality and opportunity.

Recent trends in the French system of education have shown the necessity of improving the measurement of public service performance and quality. This chapter examines the specific obstacles as a response to specific systemic features. "Public service values are sometimes put forward as an argument against looking into the cost-effectiveness of education systems, but should these values not be viewed, on the contrary, as a requirement that lends impetus to action by all those who work in education?" (Louis).

The validity of analysing the cost-effectiveness of education is viewed against the context of the underachievement of the system in an original manner. The educational system must be effective and subject to evaluation. In the French example, various indicators have been established to determine how the system functions and performs but a cautionary note is sounded: "Evaluation cannot be conceived as an end in itself, but must serve a double key objective: the improvement of the management of the system and sound investments".

* * *

Chapter Three deals with the management of physical resources for education. The question is crucial for determining the degree of influence of schools as built environments upon student, teacher, and general system performance. This chapter presents some of the results from the abundant, recent research on assessing the possible relationship between student performance and the built environment. How can this influence be accurately measured? Student achievement and student behaviour are the main variables measured. If, indeed, building factors influence learning, then funds spent to improve the built environment will also have a direct impact on student achievement. The chapter makes some suggestions about possible measurements of these factors. The physical environment is examined in its relationship to criteria such as student achievement, health, attendance and behaviour, and parental involvement. The claim is then put forth that spending funds on the built environment may directly affect student performance and results in a positive way.

13

Schools can be viewed as "social capital" and understood as part of society as a whole. Making better use of school buildings implies understanding their role as learning environments within the community. A good analysis of the different ways in which these environments relate to the community might have a direct impact on the quality of investments. The concept of social capital is defined, and then foreseen as complementing financial and human capital. The subsequent question is whether performance measures indicating the level of health and performance of society can be measured. School design has reflected social evolution and "a greater understanding of how social capital works in the physical sense is likely to come from qualitative measures" (Fisher).

* * *

Chapter Four focuses on the design and equipment of physical facilities for education. Their appraisal is an important step in the overall process of educational building assessment. From designing and building new facilities to renovating older buildings, project proposals must be carefully evaluated before any investment strategy decisions are made.

Design appraisal involves a series of elements: building quality and its relevance to the pedagogical project; the provision of new information technology and various services; integration within the community; the quality of the architecture, furniture, and other equipment; geographic location; the adequacy of the building materials, etc. Notwithstanding local specificity and variations among countries, national and local authorities, or among projects themselves, the Luxembourg seminar tried to analyse their combination and their impact on the overall quality of an educational building.

The environmental appraisal of educational facilities has become a central issue in all OECD Member countries, as reflected in the work of the Organisation on sustainable development in general, and its research on education and sustainability in particular. The environmental appraisal of a future building directly affects design, by emphasising a range of items from energy savings, insulation, and technology systems to the general level of building comfort.

Finally, this chapter presents some reflections on flexibility. What is a flexible design? Which requirements is it supposed to meet? It seems that today's investment cycle is shortening, and this recasts the question of the time horizon for the economic appraisal of buildings. This issue is even more important in tertiary education where refurbishment or renovation costs are extremely high.

Chapter One

ECONOMIC ANALYSIS
OF EDUCATIONAL PROJECTS

BUILDING HUMAN CAPITAL IN EUROPE: ISSUES AND METHODS

George **Psacharopoulos**
University of Athens

Introduction

The formula for the development prescription has changed since after World War II when investment in physical capital was the key to boosting economic development. Today's emphasis is on investment in human capital thanks to the so-called "investment in human capital revolution in economic thought" of the early 1960s, associated with Nobel Laureates T.W. Schultz and Gary Becker of the University of Chicago. The importance of human capital was reinforced in the 1980s by the new growth theory promulgated by Robert Lucas, among others, also from the University of Chicago.

The United States Office of the Budget (1993) estimates that the stock of human capital in the US far exceeds the stock of physical capital, including the value of land, with education capital at USD 24.4 trillion and physical assets at USD 18.8 trillion. This estimate is based on the replacement value of the years of schooling of the adult population aged 16 and older. Similar estimates have been produced using discounted lifetime earnings (Jorgenson and Fraumeni, 1989). McMahon (1991) found that not only does the stock of education capital exceed that of physical capital in the United States, but overall returns of 12% to investment in education also far exceed the 4% returns to investment in more conventional forms of capital such as housing.

Although similar measurements do not exist for European countries, one could extrapolate that the stock of human capital in Europe should be much higher than the physical capital stock. Moreover, financial markets are increasingly – and rightly – taking over the financing of physical assets, whereas obvious market failures exist in the financing of intangible assets, including human capital. The European Union therefore has a broad margin for enhancing human capital building. *17*

Education and Development

Human capital means a more educated and healthy population, leading to higher productivity in the widest sense of the term, including intangibles such as more informed consumers, less crime and more social cohesion. Building human capital is therefore the key to European well being in the next millennium. This paper focuses on education, a major component of human capital. The easiest way to illustrate the many links between development and education is to consider some evidence with European countries, starting from employment, the most pressing issue in Europe today.

Employment is generated throughout the school process, from building schools to educating the students who learn in them. In the short-term, if not immediately, building a school generates employment; in the longer-term, operating the school generates employment. Education is by nature a labour-intensive sector; despite several advances in the technology of distance education, the teacher remains an indispensable element in the learning process. Indeed, the teaching profession employs more people than any other everywhere in the world. In the much longer term, the employment and earnings-enhancing effect of education by building "human capital" yields returns often higher than those of conventional investment. In any education project, the longer-term, human capital building effect is likely to far outweigh the direct employment effects. At the same time, the human capital effect is the more subtle to document.

One of the most robust findings in labour economics is that the higher the level of education, the higher the chances that a person will be a formal participant in the labour market, and the higher the chances of employment, especially for females. Once in the labour force, more educated persons experience less unemployment. At the European level, the unemployment rate declines rapidly as the level of education rises; within each level of education, the unemployment rate is higher among women than men. In Ireland, for example, more than one half of the unemployed has a level of educational attainment at or below lower secondary. In Germany, the country with the

Table 1. **Unemployment Rate by Educational Level, 15 European countries, 30-59 years old (%)**

Educational Level	Overall	Men	Women
Lower Secondary	11.4	10.3	12.9
Upper Secondary	7.6	6.2	9.4
University	4.7	4.2	5.5

Source: CEDEFOP, INFO, 1/1998, p.3

highest unemployment rate among the 15, the sharpest decline in unemployment is for those with no secondary versus some secondary education.

This apparently contradicts journalistic reports that unemployment concentrates among the more educated. However, adding information on age or length of unemployment reveals that the more educated remain unemployed for the shortest periods, and the young are most unemployed. In Ireland, for example, the unemployment rate among 25 to 34-year olds is about one-half that among 15 to 24-year olds.

If there is a universal finding in the economics of education, it is that the higher the educational level, the higher a person's earnings, especially for females. Females in every country earn less than males in absolute terms; tertiary education has a higher earnings-boosting effect on females relative to males.

Table 2. **Relative Earnings of Persons Aged 30-44 with Income from Employment by Level of Education Attainment and Gender, 1995 (upper secondary education = 100)**

Country	Below Secondary		Non university tertiary		University Level	
	M+F	Females	M+F	Females	M+F	Females
Austria						
Belgium						
Denmark	84	86	101	108	131	129
Finland	91	91	121	123	175	169
France	79	73	132	139	174	170
Germany	87	88	107	114	159	165
Greece	-	-	-		-	-
Ireland	84	61	122	123	183	197
Italy	80	76	-	-	129	120
Luxembourg						
Netherlands	78	71	122	134	159	160
Portugal	64	63	-	-	180	174
Spain	-	-	-	-	-	-
Sweden	89	86	113	111	147	138
United Kingdom	77	76	137	159	190	210

Source: OECD, Education Indicators, 1997.

According to the founders of the notion of human capital, employers recognise the higher productivity of more educated employees and are willing to pay them more. Although several competing theories have been formulated attributing much of the earnings differential to the superior ability of the more educated (e.g., "the screening hy-

19

pothesis," Arrow, 1973), such theories have not been validated empirically. On the contrary, models of the new growth theory point to even higher returns to educational investment by means of externalities (Romer, 1990; Barro, 1995).

Combining data on earnings differentials and on the cost of producing education has led to several estimates of the rate of return to educational investment, both from the viewpoint of the private individual investor - students and their families - and from the social point of view of the country as a whole.

Table 2 presents an OECD compilation of social returns to education for EU countries in the range of those observed for more traditional investments in physical capital. Given the law of diminishing returns, it is not surprising that some of the highest overall returns are observed in Ireland, which has a comparatively lower stock of human capital. Females have a rate of return of approximately 29% to secondary education completion.

Table 3. **Rates of Return to Investment in Different Levels of Education by Gender, 1995**

Country	Upper Secondary		Non-university Tertiary		University-level	
	Males	Females	Males	Females	Males	Females
Austria	-	-	-	-	-	-
Belgium	-	-	-	-	-	-
Denmark	10	12	5	5	11	9
Finland	10	8	11	12	15	14
France	14	14	18	20	14	13
Germany	6	6	17	9	11	8
Greece	-	-	-	-	-	-
Ireland	19	29	12	8	14	17
Italy	10	10	-	-	10	5
Luxembourg	-	-	-	-	-	-
Netherlands	14	24	-	-	11	11
Portugal	-	-	-	-	-	-
Spain	-	-	-	-	-	-
Sweden	11	10	7	4	8	5
United Kingdom	14	19	5	14	13	19

Source: OECD Education at a Glance (1997), Table E 5.1

Regarding vocational education, evidence from Denmark confirms a counter-intuitive finding observed in many other countries, that the returns to general education and training are much higher than returns to investment in narrow vocational training. This is due primarily to the much higher cost of technical/vocational education

Table 4. **Social Rates of Return by Type of Training, Denmark (%)**

Basic vocational technician training	2.2
Clerical worker training	8.6
Civil engineer training	9.5

Source: OECD Economic Surveys, Denmark, 1997: Table 23

relative to general education, and the fact that vocational graduates do not earn so much more than general graduates as to produce a higher rate of return.

Education in the European Union (EU)

Relative to other regions in the world, the EU has a well-developed educational system, at least coverage-wise at the country level. Table 5 shows that the majority of the population aged 5-29 is enrolled in school.

Table 5. **Total Number of Students Enrolled per 100 Persons in the Population by Age Group, 1995**

Country	under 5	5-29	30 and over
Austria	3.6	54.6	1.7
Belgium	9.3	-	-
Denmark	5.3	60.0	2.9
Finland	2.3	62.9	4.9
France	8.8	63.2	1.0
Germany	4.2	58.8	1.5
Greece	2.0	52.6	0.1
Ireland	2.0	64.3	1.1
Italy	-	-	-
Luxembourg	-	-	-
Netherlands	3.7	62.0	3.0
Portugal	2.9	59.0	1.6
Spain	4.7	59.0	1.1
Sweden	4.9	60.3	6.3
United Kingdom	5.7	57.7	8.1

Source: OECD Education at a Glance, 1997.

Note: Refers to enrolments in public and private education
- = not available

In some countries one-quarter of the population aged 25-64 has some form of tertiary education.

Table 6. **Educational Attainment of the Population aged 25-64, 1995 (%)**

Country	Lower Secondary	Upper Secondary	Tertiary Non-University	University
Austria	31	62	2	6
Belgium	47	29	14	11
Denmark	38	42	6	14
Finland	35	45	9	12
France	32	50	8	11
Germany	16	61	10	13
Greece	57	25	6	11
Ireland	53	27	10	10
Italy	65	27	na	8
Luxembourg	71	18	na	11
Netherlands	39	39	na	22
Portugal	80	9	4	7
Spain	72	12	4	12
Sweden	25	46	14	14
United Kingdom	24	54	9	12

Source: OECD, Education at a Glance 1997: Table A2.1

na = not available, or included in next category.

However, many problems exist:

- Pockets of illiteracy.
- Uneven regional coverage.
- Low education quality.
- Cognitive underachievement.
- Insufficient public financing of educational institutions.
- Lack of autonomy/over-regulated private institutions.
- Non employer-linked, often non cost-effective vocational skills training.

The OECD Adult Literacy Survey produced the astonishing finding that nearly one-quarter of the adult population in Ireland and the United Kingdom has "very poor" literacy skills. UNESCO data (1997) reports that one-quarter of the Portuguese population is illiterate[1]. In Greece, 14 % of the rural population does not know how to read and write. In Italy, 23% of females have received no schooling. In Finland, more than one-third of women has not completed primary schooling. Even in a country of the level of industrial development as the UK, "...the educational attainment levels of 16 to 19-year olds still lag its main competitors and greater measures may be needed to close this gap"[2].

Education deficiencies can be quantitative or qualitative, a much subtler notion. Of the many possible measures of educational quality, measuring students' level of cognitive achievement in standardised tests is considered to be the best, and this is the one adopted here, based on a number of surveys conducted by the International Association for the Measurement of Educational Achievement (IEA).

OECD education indicators show that education quality, measured by internationally comparable achievement tests, is very uneven between countries. In Portugal, 7% of 8th grade pupils drop out and nearly one-third of 2nd grade students repeat the grade.[3] In the Netherlands, a country with an apparently excellent educational system, "the functioning of the primary school system is stretched to the limits, particularly among the smaller schools ... the resources are very limited for a system that appears to be so well funded overall"[4]. The system of early streaming in junior secondary "reinforces social inequality". Vocational education at the secondary level (LBO) "produces an alarming number of students who leave the system with no marketable skills. Unemployment is higher among vocational education completers than among those who drop out of other streams with no qualifications at all". In upper secondary education, there is concern "about poor articulation with the labour market". In Denmark, "the dropout rates of the education system is a matter of great concern"[5]. More than a quarter of students do not finish secondary education. The drop out rate of the first year of vocational education and training is 13%. "An increasing number of jobs requires a sound, broad-based, general education that will increasingly be expected to include foreign language competence. Personal and social competencies are increasingly important as employers place more emphasis on workers characterised by flexibility". In Sweden, the Commission on Productivity in Working Life notes that in spite of the fact that the country has one of the most expensive systems of education study results are in some fields mediocre, teachers often lack sufficient subject knowledge, employees in the industrial sector suffer from low education standards"[6].

EU countries spend between 2 and 7% of their GDP on education. Seven to 13% of total public expenditure is devoted to education. Yet the Austrian university system is in a financial crisis because the federal budget is the only source of income for the universities; tuition fees are a taboo that no political party wants to touch. Nearly all take it for granted that fees are a barrier for poor students and there has been no serious debate of contribution schemes that would minimise undesirable social effects. "The highly inflexible way of financing the education system, and the universities in particular, has meant that federal authorities have lost budgetary manoeuvrability. Once an activity has started, it is very difficult to abandon or even modify it"[7].

In Greece, the country with the lowest share of public expenditure on education, universities are severely under-funded and entry is restricted to only 16% of the candidates despite their willingness to pay for higher education, as demonstrated by the record number of Greek students enrolled in foreign universities[8].

Table 7. **Education Expenditures**

	Education expenditure as percentage of GDP	Public education expenditure as a percentage of total public expenditure	Education expenditure from private sources (percentage)	Expenditure per pupil as a percentage of GDP per capita, all educational institutions
Austria	5.6	-	-	34
Belgium	-	10.2	-	23
Denmark	7.0	12.6	6.0	30
Finland	6.6	11.9	-	30
France	6.2	10.8	8.7	24
Germany	5.8	9.4	22.3	30
Greece	2.4	7.0	-	13
Ireland	5.7	13.2	8.5	21
Italy	4.7	8.8	-	27
Luxembourg	-	-	-	-
Netherlands	4.9	9.4	-	22
Portugal	5.3	-	-	-
Spain	5.6	12.6	14.6	23
Sweden	6.7	11.0	1.8	32
United Kingdom	-	11.6	-	25

Source:OECD, Education Indicators 1997

Human Capital Lending: A New Strategy

Article 126 of the Maastricht Treaty states:

The Community shall contribute to the development of quality education by encouraging co-operation between Member States while fully respecting the responsibility of the Member States for the content of teaching and the organisation of education systems and their cultural and linguistic diversity. Community action shall be aimed at: developing the European dimension of education, encouraging mobility of students and teachers, and encouraging the development of distance education.

Article 127 refers to vocational education, and specifies:

The Community shall implement a vocational training policy which shall support and supplement the action of Member States while respecting the responsibility of Member States for the content and organisation of vocational training, aiming among other things, to stimulate co-operation on training between educational or training establishments and firms.

The Commission of the European Communities' 1995 White Paper on Teaching and Learning specifies guidelines for action:

• Treating material investment and investment in training on an equal basis.

• Providing a broad knowledge base.

• Bringing the school and the business sectors closer together.

Such guidelines should be implemented as we move towards an information or learning society, away from standardised physical production towards knowledge-based production of both goods and services. In European economies, service activities are coming to be dominant.

Economic issues are not the sole rationale for operations in education. Promoting social cohesion can take place through education, the medium that best permeates all sectors of economic activity by providing the necessary human/skill complement to operate more efficiently. Cohesive social infrastructure is economically productive.

Some principles should underpin a European strategy:

• Broaden the notion that education projects simply create employment in the Keynesian sense. In fact, many other macroeconomic interventions on employment protection, or changing the minimum wage rate, might be more effective in boosting employment in the short run, relative to education.

• Broaden the notion that education projects have to be mainly for specific labour skills training. In fact, general education might be more conducive to generating employment in the long run, as well as to higher earnings.

The 1994 OECD *Jobs Study* sets out a strategy based on nine recommendations for improving the ability of labour markets to adjust to structural change. These include macroeconomic policy, working-time flexibility, wage and labour cost flexibility, employment protection legislation, and the development of labour force skills.

Employment protection measures vary enormously among EU countries. In Italy, for example, direct wages constitute less than 50% of total labour costs in a firm, whereas in the UK and Ireland, the share of wages exceeds 70% of the labour cost. The protection-against-unfair-dismissal-strictness index ranges from 2% in the UK to 14% in Italy. If politically the minimum wage cannot be reduced, at least non-wage labour costs should be reduced[9].

25

New Skills

Especially since World War II, labour market skills have meant specificity, and vocational schools should be teaching this and development banks lending for it. It took several decades of failed interventions and research to realise that what employers want is flexible, trainable employees who have received a maximum of general rather than narrow vocational training. In a very influential study, Murnane and Levy (1996) show convincingly that in addition to the "soft skills" needed, relative to the old harder skills such as plumbing, welding or carpentry, in a variety of firms, employers look for the ability to:

• Read at ninth-grade level or higher.

• Do math at ninth-grade level or higher.

• Solve semi-structured problems where hypotheses are formed and tested.

• Work in groups with persons of various backgrounds.

• Communicate effectively orally and in writing.

• Use personal computers to carry out simple tasks like word processing.

The recent increase in the earnings of college graduates relative to secondary school graduates in the United States since 1980 (a trend also observed in many other OECD countries) confirms this. "The widening college-high school earnings gap is explained by ...the fact that college graduates had higher command of the new basic skills and they had an easier time learning the details of new products"[10].

In this spirit, the following are projects that could be financed in education:

• Primary school construction in rural areas.

• School quality enhancements by means of teacher training and computer-assisted learning.

• Vocational skill centres linked to industry.

• Tertiary education: universities relative to Fachochschulen; financial innovations, such as a pan-European student loan scheme (see below) that is not likely to be funded otherwise because of the initial capital needed and the risk.

• Any project associated with positive externalities (such as expanding the literacy of the population in rural areas).

Projects that should not be financed include those that:

- would have taken place even without assistance because students and/or their families were willing to pay for educational services;

- would crowd out private sector education initiatives, e.g., the creation of a private university;

- are associated with mainly private benefits (e.g., the expansion of already subsidised university education);

- have not been properly appraised.

Project Appraisal Methodology

Specific investment operations will need *in situ* appraisal along the lines of established practice in the economics of education. Two classes of education projects are to be distinguished: interventions that do not have an immediate link to the labour market, such as improving basic education in rural areas, and projects justified in terms of an expected economic outcome, *e.g.* a skills training project. The first type is appraised on the basis of cost-effectiveness analysis and the second according to cost-benefit analysis by respective methodologies.

Cost-effectiveness analysis, or assessing the "internal efficiency" of a particular intervention estimates the technical efficiency of the project. The key measurement refers to the minimum cost of providing a unit of outcome such as classrooms, teaching materials, or teachers' training. When the project involves improvements in education quality, measured by increased student cognitive achievement in a particular subject, the key measurement is pricing the coefficients of an educational production function that expresses student achievement (A) as a function of different instructional inputs $(X_1, X_2, X_3, \ldots)$.

$$A = f(X_1, X_2, X_3, \ldots \ldots \ldots)$$

By costing the marginal effect of each input on increasing cognitive achievement, *i.e.*

$$\text{Cost of} \quad (\partial A / \partial X_i),$$

a different, less costly, classroom, better teacher training, or a new type of textbooks could be chosen. This kind of analysis has shifted the composition of World Bank lending for education from bricks and mortar to software inputs, such as textbooks (Harbison and Hanushek, 1992).

27

Cost-benefit analysis, or assessing the "external efficiency" of the intervention, amounts to estimating the internal rate of return or the net present value of the project, similar to what is done routinely when appraising projects in the "harder" sectors of the economy. The human capital school at the University of Chicago developed this methodology in the early 1960s, and it is now the established tool for appraising labour-market-related education projects.

The key measurement on the benefits side is the increased productivity of graduates of the target (project's) educational level, over a control group of graduates with less education (e.g., training school over secondary school graduates). The graduates' productivity is proxied by measuring their salaries (W) in the competitive sector of the economy.

Figure 1. **Age-earning Profiles by Educational Level**

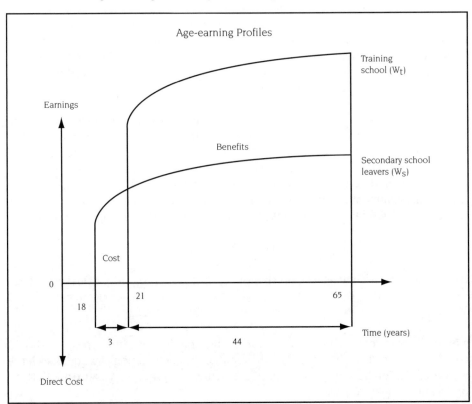

There are two key ingredients on the cost side.

1. The direct cost of providing a student place at the training centre (C_T).

2. The indirect opportunity cost of student time while in training (measured by their forgone salaries, W_s).

Once the costs and benefits have been assessed, they enter the standard cost-benefit formula for estimating the internal rate of return to investment in this particular training school (r). That is, assuming that training lasts 3 years, the estimate involves solving the following equation for r.

$$\sum_{t=1}^{44} \frac{(W_T - W_s)_t}{(1 + r)^t} = \sum_{t=1}^{3} (W_s - W_r)_t (1 + r)^t$$

Estimates such as this shifted the emphasis of World Bank for education from technical education and universities towards basic education and general training, since those showed a much higher rate of return on the investment.

Measuring the profitability of investment in education this way necessarily refers to the project's monetary costs and benefits, like that of any other sector of the economy. However, education investment is associated with a stream of positive externalities - less crime, social cohesion, or more importantly, the radioactive "halo" effect of knowledge becoming a public good - a notion underpinning the new growth theory.

Several attempts notwithstanding (Haveman and Wolfe, 1984), externalities are difficult to measure and must therefore remain an important qualification in educational project appraisal, in the sense that estimated social returns to investment in education underestimate the true returns to society from such investment.

OECD 2000

REFERENCES

ARROW, K. (1973),
"Higher Education as a Filter," *Public Economics*, 2: 113-16.

BARRO, R. (1992),
"Economic Growth in a Cross-section of Countries", *Quarterly Journal of Economics*, CVI(2): May 407-444.

BECKER, G. (1964),
Human Capital. New York: Columbia University Press.

COMMISSION OF THE EUROPEAN COMMUNITIES (1995),
Teaching and Learning - Towards the Learning Society: White Paper. Brussels: European Commission, 1995.

COMMISSION OF THE EUROPEAN COMMUNITIES (1997),
Report from the Commission: Employment in Europe. Brussels: European Commission.

EUROSTAT (1996),
STATISTICAL OFFICE OF THE EUROPEAN COMMUNITIES, *Education across the European Union: Statistics and Indicators*, Luxembourg: Office for Official Publications Communities.

EUROSTAT (1994),
STATISTICAL OFFICE OF THE EUROPEAN COMMUNITIES, *Employment and Unemployment, Aggregates*, 1980-1994, Luxembourg: Office for Official Publications of the European Communities.

HARBISON, R. and HANUSHEK, E. (1992),
Educational Performance in a Poor Country. Baltimore: Johns Hopkins University Press.

HAVEMAN, R. AND WOLFE, B. (1984)
"Schooling and Economic Wellbeing: The Role of Non-market Effects", *Journal of Human Resources* 19 (Summer), 387-407.

IEA (International Association for the Assessment of Educational Achievement),
Science Achievement in the Primary School Years: IEA's Third International Mathematics and Science Study (TIMSS) (1997), Chestnut Hill, MA: Boston College.

LUCAS, R. (1988),
"On the Mechanics of Economic Growth", *Journal of Monetary Economics* (July), 22: 3-42.

JORGENSON, D.W., and B.M. FRAUMENI (1989),
"Investment in Education", *Education Researcher*, (May) 35-44.

McMAHON, W.,
"Relative Returns to Human and Physical Capital in the U.S. and Efficient Investment Strategies", *Economics of Education Review*, 10, no. 4, 1991: 283-296.

Newsweek (1992),
"The Best Schools in the World", December 2.

OECD (1994),
Vocational Training in Germany: Modernisation and Responsiveness. Paris: OECD.

OECD (1994),
Vocational Training in the Netherlands, Reform and Innovation. Paris: OECD.

ROMER, P. (1992),
"Endogenous Technical Change", *Journal of Political Economy*, 95 (5): S71-85.

SCHULTZ, T.W. (1961),
"Investment in Human Capital", *American Economic Review*, 51, May: 1-17.

United States Office of the Budget (1993),
Budget Baselines, Historical Data, and Alternatives for the Future, (January)Table E-3.

31

Cost-benefit Analysis in Education Projects: Internal Rates of Return, Methodologies and Theoretical Objections

Tom **Healy**
OECD

Defining Human Capital Investment

The concept of human capital has been in common currency in economics for at least the past thirty years (*e.g.* Schultz, 1961; Becker, 1964); some trace it back to the work of Adam Smith in the 18th century. In recent decades, the concept powerfully emphasises how important people have become, in knowledge- and competence-based economies. It is useful to distinguish between the different forms of "capital" employed in economic activity - in particular physical and human. Human capital can be defined in many ways. *Human Capital Investment: an International Comparison* adopted the following meaning *"the knowledge, skills, competencies and other attributes embodied in individuals that are relevant to economic activity"*[11].

This particular definition of human capital refers to human attributes broadly, not just in relation to the level to which a person has been educated, but also in relation to the capacity to put a wide range of skills to productive use. It acknowledges attributes that create better health insofar as this has economic or social spin-offs, for example in containing public healthcare spending, but does not regard the intrinsic personal benefit of being healthy as a return to human capital investment. In other words, it looks at the value of human capital investment for production rather than directly for consumption. This focus on the crucial role that human capital plays in economies and societies, which is a central policy concern, is in no way intended to imply that all forms of learning should be directed to economic ends. It is clear that education, for example, has high "consumption" value.

Human capital constitutes an intangible asset that can enhance or support productivity, innovation, and employability and contribute to different types of social benefits such as greater community and social participation, higher social cohesion, lower criminality, and improved health. These "spin-off" benefits in turn feed back into eco-

33

nomic well-being. Human capital may be augmented or may decline or become redundant. It is formed through different influences and in different settings such as the family, the school, the local community and the workplace.

However, human capital as defined here remains an individual characteristic to be distinguished from social capital, which refers to aspects of social life - the existence of networks, norms and relationships - that enable people to act together, create synergies, and build partnerships. Coleman (1990) showed how social capital can influence the ability to acquire human capital, for example when strong communities enhance learning at school. Social capital sets the context in which human capital can be developed.

Costs and Benefits of Human Capital Investment

When individuals and organisations spend time in learning or education, they are investing in human capital. Spending on education through outlays on teachers, classroom materials, and other facilities is not, strictly speaking, investment in human capital. Educational expenditure enables human capital investment to take place. Measured by the proportion of national income devoted to education and training, spending to promote human capital investment accounts for a significant proportion of total national expenditure or GDP. Typically, countries spend over 6% of GDP on initial or formal education, including spending from private sources. Added to this, spending by enterprises on work-based training as well as spending by individuals and families on various learning activities brings the proportion of national income devoted to human capital to well over 10%.

Investment in human capital is a shared enterprise between public and private interests. There is a clear case for public support for some or most of the costs on the grounds that investment in human capital brings about social benefits and some of this investment might not have taken place in the absence of public support. Costs are typically measured by direct spending on education or training such as tuition or educational materials. However, in addition to private direct spending, account should be taken of other costs associated with learning, including transport, student living costs and income and output forgone or lost for those undergoing education or training. Direct and indirect private costs are generally poorly measured and reported across OECD countries, and the most potentially significant portion of private costs relating to time or income forgone while in studying is difficult to estimate.

The effectiveness of investment in human capital depends on a host of factors including the quality of time spent in learning, the quality of teaching, the supply of learning materials, the support of family, community, and society as well as the interaction of economic, labour market, and social influences. More is not necessarily better. However, better targeting of investment, better use of scarce resources, and creating the incentives and economic rewards to learning may have significant impacts on economic growth and social inclusion. A society that under-invests in its own human capital is in danger of undermining the prosperity and social cohesion of the next generation.

Investors in human capital comprise individuals, families, governments, and private organisations. Each actor spends time and money on learning or training to reap a reward in terms of measurable economic benefits, or harder-to-measure benefits such as personal or social well-being. Unlike some other assets, the investor in human capital may not "own" the capital that is the subject of investment. Governments pay for much of the cost of initial education which benefits both individuals and society. Likewise, enterprises spend on the training of their employees, but the skills acquired through enterprise-based training may be taken by trained workers to another enterprise. Defining and measuring a stream of benefits to an investment in human capital poses major challenges, not least because many of the benefits are experienced by others. A more literate or skilled society tends to raise the productivity or social well-being of everyone, including those who have not recently undergone training or education.

To know more about the benefits of investment in education, a wider range of benefits than those which are strictly labour market or economic in nature need to be examined and compared with costs. There is a standard approach in any evaluation of the effectiveness or profitability of a particular investment which compares costs and benefits. If a stream of additional productivity, earnings, or output can be estimated as a result of extra investment in an asset such as a machine or plant, then it is possible to find an "internal rate of return" which equates the present value of a future stream of benefits to the additional cost. As applied to human capital, this entails estimating the additional benefits over a lifetime for all individuals as a result of investing in more human capital. These benefits should also include "spillover" effects such as the impact of higher human capital on the productivity and social well-being of all individuals, including those who have not undergone training. The importance of spillover effects was recognised by the economist Alfred Marshall a century ago:

"We may then conclude that the wisdom of expending public and private funds on education is not to be measured by its direct fruits alone. It will be profitable as a mere investment, to give the masses of the people much greater opportunities than they can generally avail themselves of ... And the economic value of one great industrial genius is sufficient to cover the expenses of the education of a whole town; for one new idea, such as Bessemer's chief invention, adds as much to England's productive power as the labour of a thousand men" [12].

In practice, benefits are measured very restrictedly by the estimated additional earnings from employment as a result of more initial education. This confines the analysis to more readily available data sources, but it neglects important aspects of human capital investment and its impact. On the one hand, it neglects the impact of human capital investment outside and beyond initial or formal education: the skills, aptitudes, and competencies acquired, for example, as a result of work experience or continuing training following the completion of initial education. On the other hand, it neglects the importance of benefits not represented in additional earnings from employment (*e.g.* the effect of caring for young children or elderly persons or the spillover effects mentioned above).

An important distinction is made by analysts between *private* and *social* benefits of education. The latter includes the wider impact of education on society including the spillover effects. Private benefits appropriated by individuals may be monetary or non-monetary, such as better health or higher personal satisfaction. Corresponding to each of these two types of benefits, it is necessary to distinguish between private and public costs.

Estimates of the Social Returns to Education

Macroeconomic growth and performance is a crucial area of the social returns to education. The impact of education and training in this area has been the subject of considerable analysis and measurement in recent decades. The debate about the impact of education and training revolves around the respective roles of various inputs in contributing to growth. In particular, the theories try in various ways to distinguish the contributions of the quantity of physical capital, the quantity of labour, the quality of labour defined, for example, by the average educational level of the population, and the technological capacity of the economy. An underlying difficulty is disentangling the impact of these last two factors, since the characteristics of workers closely interact with their technological or organisational work environment.

The balance of evidence indicates that both human capital and technological know-how are vitally important in growth even if there is an observed feedback effect in the way income growth stimulates demand for education and facilitates higher social spending on education. The evidence indicates that the effect of human capital investment is not uniform. Strategies for investing in education, training, and know-how need to be highly discerning if the desired impact on growth is to be realised. It is vital to understand the national, regional, and institutional context in which human capital investment takes place.

Since the 1960s, economists have been seeking to account for the growth in aggregate output by looking at the rate at which various inputs are growing. The starting point of many economists (Denison, 1962) was that output had grown faster than would be implied by the rate of expansion of the two main economic inputs, capital and labour. This unaccounted-for growth was attributed to a "residual" factor, assumed to represent technical progress or the "quality of labour". Early models of growth accounting found this factor to be large, but they were unable to say precisely what it consisted of, as it was simply calculated as the difference between observed output growth and the growth in measurable inputs. More recent approaches have sought to explain more precisely the contribution of inputs such as labour quality and technical know-how, by building measures of these inputs into growth models and testing whether this reduces the residual or unknown factor. Education and such by-products as research and innovation are of prime importance, as are internally-generated technical change, increasing returns to scale, the know-how acquired in the course of technology-intensive production, and the spillover effect of a growing, "leading-edge" export sector on knowledge throughout the economy.

The evidence from the analysis of educational attainment and earnings indicates a strong positive relationship, on average, between educational attainment and labour market outcomes. These positive effects of education are, in many individual cases, confounded, however, by differences in post-school experiences, by innate ability, by family background, and by other social factors. Studies that attempt to control for such underlying factors tend to find strong evidence of improved productivity, earnings, and employment chances associated with both education and work-based training. However, a frequently-asked question is whether these benefits are the direct result of education and training itself (through investment in skills and competencies), or whether educational attainment acts mainly as a screening or sorting device that enables employers to allocate individuals to high-status or high-productivity occupations.

Models that give undue weight to educational attainment as a motor of growth have been vulnerable to criticism by those who see education as a way of allocating jobs through "screening" (Spence, 1974). Moreover, differences in income by educational attainment can be explained partially by the correlation of attainment with innate ability (Denison, 1964), and so do not guarantee that higher overall attainment will contribute to growth. Research evidence (reviewed by Psacharopoulos, 1994) confirms that education appears to play a significant role in human capital formation, over and above any role it plays as a screening device. However, it shows that productivity-enhancing factors other than education and training play a parallel role.

Recent empirical analysis (Altonji and Pierret, 1996) has examined how quickly employers learn about the true productivity of workers, and adjust their relative wages accordingly. This work suggests that the value of education in predicting future wages does not decline over time, because the increased information about individuals' productivity that employers acquire by observing them on the job confirms the

37

expected relationship between productivity and education levels. Over time, they claim that the "signalling component" of educational qualifications accounts for a relatively small part of the wage differential associated with education.

Studies of identical twins such as that of Ashenfelter and Krueger (1994) have shown that the effects of controlling for ability, race, social class, and family background are to lower estimated returns to education by about 25%. However, other studies such as that by Ashenfelter and Rouse (forthcoming) show that error in the measurement of human capital acquired may lead to an under-estimation of rates of return by as much as 30% (through for example omission of quality of education in the use of years of schooling as an explanatory variable). Therefore, measurement error and the omission of control variables in less sophisticated estimations of returns to education may tend to roughly cancel each other out.

Recent studies have therefore tested the relative importance of educational and non-educational factors. Even though they have not produced a single new theory, some interesting results have emerged. For example:

• The marginal impact of increases in various levels of education appears to vary greatly according to the state of a country's development. A study by Mingat and Tan (1996) for the World Bank found that the level of higher education is most important in high-income countries, and primary education levels are a significant motor of growth in developing countries. While this result is not surprising, it confirms the possibility that over time, the expansion of any one level of education may yield diminishing returns.

• There is a strong identifiable relationship between human capital growth and the growth not just in output but also in labour productivity. This relationship is strongest however when comparing less and more developed countries (Lau, Jamison, and Louat, 1991) than when comparing OECD countries, where it is obscured by the importance of other factors. Nevertheless, a study by Englander and Gurney (1994) looking simultaneously at the effect on productivity of growth in the capital to labour ratio, the size of the labour force, and the enrolment rate in secondary education, found that the latter had contributed 0.6% to annual productivity growth in OECD countries between 1960 and 1985.

• When spending on research and development is included in the model, the independent effect of human capital appears to be reduced. Nonneman and Vanhoudt (1996) used research and development spending relative to GDP as an approximation for technological know-how, adding it to an earlier model (Mankiw-Romer-Weil, 1992). They found that some of the attribution of growth to education was instead associated with research and development spending.

The evidence of additional economic output attributable to education needs to be set against the cost of the investment. Mingat and Tan (1996) have attempted to use estimates of costs and benefits to calculate a "social" rate of return to education. On the basis of economic growth performance, they have calculated that the estimated "social" rate of return was well over 10% per year in the case of tertiary level education between 1960 and 1995 in OECD countries. If such estimates prove robust, they will provide important confirmation that investment is paying off for whole economies and not just for individuals.

Contrasting Rates of Return by Level of Education

This section presents one approach which has been developed in recent years at the OECD to measure rates of return. While the concepts of social and private rates of return have been distinguished by economists, measurements of rates of return have tended to blur this distinction, relying on gross earnings of individuals as the proxy of total or social benefits and leaving aside externalities and non-market benefits. Moreover, data sets have been inadequate for the estimation of public and private costs and benefits - even where the benefits refer in a restricted way to gross earnings and the stream of tax benefits to public authorities. An approach adopted for the OECD INES education indicators project in 1995 (Alsalam and Conley, 1995) based on estimating "social" rates of return where no distinction is made between public and private costs or benefits is described below.

The main driving variables are *i*) cost and *ii*) additional income as a result of higher levels of education. The additional cost of graduating at university higher education over the cost of graduating at upper secondary level is compared with the additional lifetime income as a result of graduating at university higher level compared to upper secondary level. The estimated rate of return to university level education is calculated by finding the rate of discount that equates *i*) the present value of an estimated future stream of *additional* income over a lifetime (from ages 16 to 64), to *ii*) the present value of the *additional* total cost of graduating (including forgone earnings). Formally, this calculation consists of estimating, for educational attainment level i, the rate of interest (r) that equates the present value of a stream of additional benefits $(B_i\text{-}B_{i-1})$ over a working lifetime with the discounted additional costs $(C_i\text{-}C_{i-1})$ of producing a graduate at ISCED level i compared to level i-1:

$$\sum(\mathbf{B}_{i,t}\text{-}\mathbf{B}_{i-1,t})/(1+\mathbf{r})^t = \sum(\mathbf{C}_{i,t}\text{-}\mathbf{C}_{i-1,t})/(1+\mathbf{r})^t$$

The value of t is the time at which each observation of earnings or cost is estimated. On the benefits side, t relates to the working lifetime following exit from schooling. On the cost side, t refers to the duration of a given level of education. Cost per graduate is obtained by taking the average annual spending per student in a recent year at a

OECD 2000

given level of ISCED and multiplying by the *theoretical* average number of years required to graduate at this level. In this case, costs exclude spending on student living expenses. Only spending on tuition (by public and private sources) is included. In practice, there is considerable variation in costs per graduate due to variations in duration of studies and in the <u>annual</u> average spending per student. This is especially the case at tertiary level where costs vary considerably by field of study. However, no distinction is made in this estimation by field of study within ISCED level. In the case of tertiary level, the annual average cost per student is assumed to be equal at university and non-university levels (although differences in cost per <u>graduate</u> at university and non-university levels is allowed for because of differences in the estimated or assumed total duration of studies.)

The results shown in Table 1 suggest that annual rates of return for upper secondary level are generally high (typically above 10%) for both men and women; they are particularly high for women and men in Ireland, the Netherlands, Portugal, Switzerland, and the United States. Rates of return on tertiary education tend to be lower on aver-

Table 1. **Annual Rates of Return to Education[a], 1995**

	Men			Women			
	Upper secondary education	Non-university tertiary	University education	Upper secondary education	Non-university tertiary	University education	Rate of return on business capital[b]
Australia	7.5	9.7	10.4	12.5	7.9	6.7	13.6
Canada	12.5	23.0	16.5	16.1	28.1	28.5	19.3
Czech Republic	22.0	[c]	8.7	13.8	-	7.0	-
Denmark	10.4	5.2	11.0	11.8	5.1	9.2	10.7
Finland	10.4	10.5	14.8	8.1	12.2	14.3	9.4
France	14.2	17.6	14.1	14.1	20.1	12.7	15.0
Germany	5.7	16.6	10.9	5.5	8.7	8.2	13.7
Ireland[d]	18.6	11.7	14.0	28.8	8.2	17.4	14.4
Italy	10.4	-	9.9	9.5	-	4.6	15.9
Netherlands	14.1	-	10.8	24.4	-	10.5	17.9
New Zealand	12.8	-11.5	11.6	11.2	-0.5	10.3	18.5
Norway	11.3	9.4	11.6	17.3	7.8	13.3	7.6
Portugal	33.3	-	27.3	32.4	-	28.3	-
Sweden	10.9	6.5	8.2	9.9	4.2	5.3	14.2
Switzerland	19.0	27.1	5.5	22.1	17.7	5.2	4.2
United Kingdom	14.3	4.8	12.7	19.1	13.7	19.1	11.8
United States	26.3	8.9	12.6	22.9	10.5	12.6	18.3
Average of above	14.9	10.7	12.4	16.4	11.1	12.5	13.6
Coefficient of Variation for above[e]	0.46	0.89	0.36	0.44	0.68	0.56	0.30

Source: Education Policy Analysis, 1997, pp. 35 and 102; indicator E5.1, Education at a Glance, OECD Indicators, 1997, p. 272.

age than rates on upper secondary. In the case of seven countries, the rates for university education fall below 10% for women, with particularly low returns in Italy, Sweden and Switzerland. Of course, these latter results are related in part to the compressed wage structure in many European countries.

Notes:

a) These rates of return were estimated at different levels of educational attainment on the basis of *i*) earnings over a working lifetime for <u>employed persons only</u> (1995 cross-sectional data from various household surveys), and *ii*) costs of graduation based on expenditure data from *Education at a Glance*, OECD *Indicators*. Since the estimate is based on income observed across different age groups at one point in time, it was necessary to assume different rates of increase in average income over time for each age group. In other words, earnings of university graduates aged 35-44 in 1995 is not the same as earnings of university graduates aged 25-34 in the year 2005. This arises because productivity and earnings are increasing for all groups in the population and at the same time some groups are experiencing faster growth than others (due, for example, to shifts in demands for skills). In estimating lifetime benefits, it was assumed that income will grow over time by a constant 1% per annum for all groups in the population.

b) Data on rates of return to business capital (including housing) were obtained from Table 25, Annex of OECD *Economic Outlook*, n° 61, June 1997.

c) Denotes missing value or category not applicable.

d) Data refer to 1994.

e) The ratio of the standard deviation to the average.

Data used for Table 1 provide an overall indication of broad orders of magnitude but cannot be treated as precise estimates for the following reasons:

• They take no account of broader social or economic benefits flowing from investment in education.

• They do not separate the effect of education from other effects such as experience, informal learning, motivation, or innate ability.

• Differences in earnings and employment by level of educational attainment in the course of a working lifetime compound differences in retirement incomes for different educational groups and are not included in the estimate of lifetime returns.

41

- Estimates of returns are sensitive to assumptions about forgone earnings of students.

- The effects of various underlying assumptions in arriving at the estimates of rates of return may be open to question. For example, lifetime earnings across different age groups at one point in time are not necessarily a reliable guide to the likely future earnings profile of a cohort graduating at a particular level of education today.

- Between-country differences in estimated rates of return are strongly influenced by the overall earnings distribution in each country, which is determined by institutional and non-market factors as well as by those associated with human capital.

- Estimates are for total spending on education at a given level and do not distinguish between different types of spending such as current and capital, spending on teachers and educational materials and facilities.

- Rates of return estimates are based on average earnings and costs. In practice, there can be considerable variation in rates of return for different fields of study or particular social groups. So it should be emphasised that these rates of return are more relevant for governments thinking at the macro level about how to structure investments than for individuals making specific decisions about whether to study.

Two observations are interesting to make about the broad orders of magnitude of estimated social returns to education, based on these calculations. First, considering that these estimates omit some important social benefits, they still compare favourably with rates of return on physical capital for most OECD countries. Second, although tertiary education yields greater marginal benefit in additional earnings than in the case of upper secondary level, it does not necessarily bring a better "social" rate of return as measured here.

Published OECD data on returns to business capital (including housing) indicate a return of around 16% in 1995 across OECD countries on average (or 13.6% in the case of the countries shown in Table 1). Table 1 shows returns to business capital alongside estimates of returns to different levels of education. Returns to investment in upper secondary education tend on average to be at the level of returns to business capital, while returns on tertiary level education tend to be slightly less. However, the differences are relatively small. McMahon (1991) has estimated the rate of return to human, physical, and housing capital for the United States over the period 1967-87. He finds that even in the absence of measures of externalities (including lower crime, better health, greater social cohesion, and research and knowledge in the case of higher education) and non-monetary return, rates of return on education (in the region of 10-15%) compare favourably with those on housing capital (4%) and are about the same as or slightly less than those on non-housing physical capital.

Psacharopolous (1994) reviewed other evidence from international studies mainly from the 1980s that show a slightly higher return to upper secondary compared to tertiary education. It appears that the higher wage premium associated with tertiary education is offset by higher costs associated with this level. This pattern strengthens the case for an equitable sharing of costs at tertiary level between the public purse and the individuals who will eventually reap large benefits. The 1980s studies (and calculations cited below) also showed that private returns are greater than social returns, which is not surprising given that a high proportion of initial investment is public, and only a limited range of social benefits are being measured. The prima facie case that this evidence creates for more costs to be borne privately needs to be considered also in the light of benefits such as greater social cohesion and the impact of knowledge and innovation generated in tertiary education on economic growth that are not being measured. If social returns tend to exceed private returns, then there is a case for public subsidy since there is an incentive for individuals to underinvest in human capital relative to a socially optimum amount.

Trends Over Time in Rates of Return

Long-term evidence seems to indicate a decline in rates of return over time, especially at upper secondary level (Psacharopolous, 1994). This could be explained by a declining wage premium for reaching a level of education that is becoming more commonplace. Tertiary education is more mixed. After falling in the 1970s, rates of return to tertiary education rose in the United States during the 1980s and early 1990s (McMahon, 1991). This may be due to a continuing increase in demand for skills, exceeding the expansion of supply, in an era when many new jobs are in technology-based industries that are hungry for skills (Mincer, 1996). However, other influences on wage dispersion, including declining unionisation, help wider differentials between high and low skilled workers in the United States as well as in the United Kingdom and New Zealand. Rising wage inequality by educational attainment was not observed in other OECD countries, and in the Netherlands for example where the premium to university graduates has declined. So, rates of return to tertiary education may not recently have grown in other countries as they have in the United States.

Contrasting Private and Social Rates of Return

In addition to the *social* rates of return, fiscal and private rates of return to investment at university tertiary level for seven OECD countries which participated in an

43

OECD pilot data collection in 1997 can also be illustrated. The analysis is confined to this level since measurement of private costs, including forgone earnings, was problematic in the case of upper secondary level. Although results calculated so far need to be subjected to further analysis and verification, they start to give an indication of the extent to which returns are shared between public and private interests.

Recent work at the OECD on the estimation of private and social returns to education has drawn on the evidence about the relationship between earnings and initial educational attainment for different age groups in the adult population. The following "rates of return" were defined and estimated:

• The *private* return to education takes account only of privately-borne costs (including forgone earnings) and private gains in terms of higher post-tax earnings.

• The *social* return to education includes both private and public costs. By looking at gross earnings, it includes one element of public benefit - the higher tax revenues paid by people who earn more as a result of their education. However, macroeconomic and wider social gains have not been built into calculations of these returns.

• The *fiscal* return to education looks at the direct implications for the public purse. It compares public costs to extra tax revenues and gains from lower payments of public transfers to those who require them less as a result of being more educated. This last benefit is difficult to measure accurately and has not been used in calculating social returns; estimates of fiscal returns are consequently less reliable.

The private rate of return influences whether individuals decide to undertake education. The social rate of return influences whether societies collectively decide to finance education by voting for taxes and making private contributions. The fiscal rate of return potentially shows governments the extent to which the public expenditure devoted to education will be recouped in long-run benefits to the public purse.

These results take account of all types of income: earnings (*i.e.* income from employment), income from pensions, property income and social transfers. These benefits are averaged over the entire population in each age group, gender group and level of educational attainment. An estimated stream of benefits is determined for each group from the age of 16 to 64. Since the estimate is based on income observed across different age groups at one point in time, it was necessary (as in the case of Table 1 above) to assume different rates of increase in average income over time for each age group. In other words, earnings of university graduates aged 35-44 in 1995 is not the same as earnings of university graduates aged 25-34 in the year 2005 because productivity and earnings are increasing for all groups in the population while at the same time some groups are experiencing faster growth than others (due, for example, to shifts in demands for skills). In estimating lifetime benefits, it was assumed that income will grow over time by a constant 1% per annum for all groups in the population. However, this assumption can be altered.

The results of these experimental calculations are presented in Table 2. These results differ from those shown in Table 1 which referred to earnings of employed persons only. While the results in Table 2 refer to all persons regardless of labour force status and to all types of income. Hence, they begin to measure the impact of unemployment or exclusion from the labour market in estimating lifetime benefits and indicate that in the countries examined, there are positive fiscal and private returns to investing in university-level education. Private returns tend to be higher than the fiscal returns. The estimate of private returns indicates that in Australia, Canada, and France, there are private returns in the region of 15-25% for both men and women. For Belgium, Denmark, Sweden, and the United States, the returns appear to be somewhat lower, notwithstanding the high relative premium in gross earnings for these countries at the university level.

Table 2. **Private, Fiscal and Social Rates of Return to Education (1994/95)[a]**

	Men			Women		
	Private	Fiscal	Social	Private	Fiscal	Social
Australia	14	10	11	21	10	13
Belgium	14	9	9	8	13	9
Canada	14	7	9	22	7	11
Denmark	8	8	8	7	8	8
France	20	11	13	28	9	13
Sweden	-	6	9	-	4	7
United States	11	9	10	12	9	11

Source Human Capital Investment: an International Comparison, OECD, 1998, p. 112

a. Based on the value of all benefits to individuals (earnings from employment, social transfers and other income) averaged over all individuals estimated over a working lifecycle.

High rates of private return to education provide an incentive for individuals to invest in schooling since they themselves reap the benefits of this investment. The case for public subsidies to education appears to be strongest at the lower levels, where the social benefits are highest and the obstacles to private investment largest.

In tertiary education, the sharing of costs is not closely related to consideration of rates of return: subsidies to households and institutions tend to be undifferentiated. One alternative approach to the sharing of costs is the taxing of private benefits   *45* from investment largely financed by the public purse. Further analysis would be needed to distinguish the effects of taxes on different types of educational programmes or learning, and to examine the impact of taxation on human as opposed to physical capital. Liebfritz *et al.* (1997) argue that in most OECD countries, corporate tax regimes generally favour intangible investment (including human capital) relative to physical capital, in that expenditures on such factors as education and training, and research and development receive relatively more favourable tax treatment than investment in plant and equipment. Others have argued that tax regimes tend to work in the opposite direction (Miller and Pincus, 1998). The reduction in income tax progress in some OECD countries in the last decade may have encouraged human capital formation at the tertiary level.

Improving the Knowledge Base

While there is clear evidence that investment in human capital yields benefits, it remains difficult to calculate precise rates of return from particular investments. The central problem lies in attributing specific economic gains to particular human attributes, linking these in confidence with particular learning episodes. It is nevertheless desirable to develop at least some measures that can compare alternative human capital investments in terms of their respective costs and benefits. The alternative is the dangerous assumption that because investment in learning as a whole seems to pay off, it is equally worthwhile in all its forms.

The illustrative rates of return presented in this paper are of value in showing that significant net benefits can accrue from investments in education, but that the return on the publicly and privately borne costs can be highly variable. The main difficulty in looking at rates of return at present is that they can only be constructed with the easiest-to-aggregate data. They leave out the full range of social benefits, and only apply to differences in educational attainment, wholly ignoring aspects of human capital that are not linked to initial qualifications.

While quantifiable rates of return are likely to remain crude and incomplete approximations for some time to come, there is considerable value in seeking better data to fill out the highly incomplete picture of the costs and benefits associated with various types of learning. One priority is to obtain better aggregate information about how much is being invested by individuals and enterprises in various forms of learning. Another is to improve understanding of the individual and wider economic benefits associated with learning in work-based and other non-institutional settings. Another track is to provide better estimates at the international level of private returns to learning, particularly in post-compulsory education and training. This type of information may be easier to obtain than broader social benefits, and when linked to private costs can provide a useful benchmark for comparing the private incentive to take part in learning throughout life and the appropriate level of public subsidy to encourage learning.

In *Human Capital Investment: an International Comparison* (OECD, 1998), it was argued that measures of human capital have been strongly guided by what is possible to measure, rather than by what it is desirable to measure. As a result, much analysis has focused on the benefits of initial educational attainment to individuals, rather than on the more complex relationships between lifetime development of skills and competencies on the one hand, and the multiple advantages conferred by these attributes on the other. The priority now should be to develop more direct measures of life-relevant skills, of the value placed on them in the workplace, and of the benefits to individuals and enterprises of work-related training.

OECD 2000

REFERENCES

ALSALAM, N. and CONLEY, R. (1995),
"The Rate of Return to Education: a Proposal for an Indicator", *Education and Employment*, Centre for Educational Research and Innovation, OECD, Paris.

ALTONJI, J. and PIERRET, C. (1996),
"Employer Learning and the Signalling Value of Education", Working Paper No. 5438, National Bureau of Economic Research, Cambridge, Massachusetts.

BECKER, G. (1964),
Human Capital: A Theoretical and Empirical Analysis, with special reference to education, National Bureau of Economic Research, New York.

COLEMAN, J.S. (1990),
Foundations of Social Theory, Harvard University Press.

DENISON, E.F. (1962),
The Sources of Economic Growth in the United States and the Alternatives before Us, Committee for Economic Development, New York.

DENISON, E.F. (1964),
"Measuring the Contribution of Education", *The Residual Factor and Economic Growth*, OECD, Paris.

ENGLANDER, A.S. and GURNEY, A. (1994),
"Medium-term Determinants of OECD Productivity", OECD *Economic Studies*, No. 22, OECD, Paris.

LAU, L., JAMISON, D. and LOUAT, F. (1991),
"Education and Productivity in Developing Countries: an Aggregate Production Function Approach", Working Paper No. 612, World Bank, Washington, DC.

LIEBFRITZ, W., THORNTON, J. and BIBBEE A., (1997),
"Taxation and Economic Performance, Economics Department", *Working Papers*, No. 176, General Distribution document, OCDE/GD(97)107.

McMAHON, W. (1991),
   "Relative Returns to Human and Physical Capital in the US and Efficient Investment Strategies", *Economics of Education Review*, Vol. 10, No. 4, pp. 283-296.

McMAHON, W. (1997),
   "Recent Advances in Measuring the Social and Individual Benefits of Education",
   International Journal of Educational Research, Vol. 27, No. 6, Chapter 1.

MANKIW, N., ROMER, D. and WEIL, D. (1992),
   "A Contribution to the Empirics of Economic Growth", *Quarterly Journal of Economics*, Vol. CVII , pp. 407-437.

MARSHALL, A. (1992),
   Principles of Economics: An Introductory Volume, (eighth edition).

MILLER, P. W. and PINCUS, J.J. (1998),
   "Funding Higher Education: Performance and Diversity, Evaluations and Investi-
   gations Programme" 97/19, Department of Employment, Education, Training and
   Youth Affairs.

MINGAT, A. and TAN, J. (1996),
   "The Full Social Returns to Education: Estimates Based on Countries' Economic
   Growth Performance", Human Capital Development Working Papers, World Bank,
   Washington, DC.

MINCER, J. (1996),
   "Changes in Wage Inequality, 1970-1990", Working Paper 5823, National Bureau
   of Economic Research, Cambridge, Massachusetts.

NONNEMAN, W. and VANHOUDT, P. (1996),
   "A Further Augmentation of the Solow Model and the Empirics of Economic Growth
   for OECD Countries", *Quarterly Journal of Economics*, pp. 943-953.

OECD, Human Resources Development Canada and Statistics Canada (1997),*Literacy
   Skills for the Knowledge Society - Further Results from the International Adult Literacy Survey*, Paris.

OECD, (1998),
   Human Capital Investment: an International Comparison, Paris.

PSACHAROPOULOS, G. (1994),
   "Returns to Investment in Education: a Global Update", *World Development*, Vol. 22
   (9), pp. 1325-1343, September.

49

SCHULTZ, T.W. (1961),
"Investment in Human Capital", *American Economic Review*, LI:1, pp. 1-22.

SPENCE, M. (1974),
Market Signalling, Harvard University Press, Cambridge, Massachusetts.

WOLFE, B. and ZUVEKAS, S. (1997),
"Non-market Outcomes of Schooling", *International Journal of Educational Research*, Vol. 27, No. 6, Chapter 3.

Externalities, Non-Market Effects, and Trends in Returns to Educational Investments

Walter W. **McMahon**
University of Illinois, United States

Knowledge for development and particularly the role of education, which is crucial if knowledge is to be effectively disseminated, can now be seen as the key to economic growth and to the broader development process that supports it. Within each family, within each OECD nation and world-wide, knowledge that is disseminated by education offers critical improvements in the non-market qualities of life and in externality-type benefits to others in the society that are equally and perhaps even more vital than pure economic growth to human welfare. This paper identifies and measures these externalities and non-market effects of investments in education, and their implications, including current trends for the planning and investment in education facilities[13].

The surge of current interest in education as a key means of disseminating knowledge is probably based on two or three recent developments in research. The first is a wave of new studies of large samples of identical twins (Ashenfelter and Rouse, 1998) that are able to remove the effects on later education outcomes due to innate ability and family factors under these highly controlled conditions. These studies find that ability and family background account for about 31% of net returns, but that the measurement error due to self-reporting of education levels and the omission of the effects of educational quality raises the corrected net return by 28%, which is almost exactly offsetting (op. cit., table III, cols. 6, 9, and 10). Using the data directly without these offsetting corrections gives an accurate estimate of the true causal effect of education (Card, 1998). This is the prevailing, albeit not unanimous, opinion in the field as Tom Healy *et al.* (1998) have pointed out.

The other important development in the 1990s is the new endogenous growth models in economics combined with extensive empirical tests using world-wide data, which has led to a dramatic reawakening of the field of economic growth in economics, which had been largely dormant since the late 1960s. These are summarised in *Education and Development: Measuring the Social Benefits* (McMahon 1998a), and are also a basis for the World Bank World Development Report 1998-1999 that takes "Knowledge for Development" as its theme. Together, these new sources develop very extensive empirical evidence that education plays a central role for achieving faster economic growth by means of the more effective dissemination of knowledge. It is also vital for sustaining continuing economic development in industrialised and poor countries by generating non-market returns and externalities that are also vital to human welfare. These externalities and non-market impacts are likely to be considerably larger than the direct market impacts of education on net earnings impacts.

There have been no systematic attempts to measure the non-market social benefits of education and externalities, however, much less to do so in a comprehensive fashion. Hundreds of research studies have used microeconomic data that deal with isolated aspects of these non-market returns, but they are particularistic and very piecemeal (McMahon, 1998a). This considerable microeconomic research is extremely helpful and has led to a vague general awareness of important non-market returns and externalities. Nonetheless, there is often no specific identification of all of the major net marginal products of education, direct and indirect, instantaneous and lagged, and a general awareness of what is and is not known. The lack of systematic and comprehensive estimates of these returns for each nation led T.W. Schultz to state that there is a tendency to overlook and to discount what has not been measured, not to speak of the misperceptions.

This paper tries to systematically identify and measure econometrically the net contributions of education to each major type of non-market and externality benefits of education using data covering 78 countries and a model that traces each of the major market and non-market impacts of education over time. This can be done for each of 22 OECD Member nations as well as for the other 56 countries in Asia, Africa, and Latin America in the model. The non-market returns to education are always measured after extensive controls for other impacts in order to remove other significant effects, and always after controlling for per capita income to remove the economic effect of education and avoid double counting the market returns.

First, this paper identifies major non-market private and social benefits of education and briefly considers how each is measured. Next, empirical estimates of the non-market and externality impacts of education and the market related economic growth impacts (since there is interdependence) for three OECD Member countries are presented. Following this, the methods used for separating direct from the indirect impacts of education as a means of discussing the measurement and valuation of externalities are presented briefly.

Identifying Non-Market Social Benefits of Education

Investment in educational facilities is part of the investment in human capital formed through education. As such, if the allocation of expenditures between current investment in education services and investment in facilities is internally efficient, the average rates of return and cost effectiveness of total investments in education will be essentially the same as those for investment in facilities. Facilities, however, are even longer-term investments since they involve the question of nature and geographical placement, and, hence, who will receive the benefits. Returns that extend into the more distant future and the implications of those current trends that are likely to endure need to be considered. The impacts of educational investments over the next 40 years, or until 2035, about the amount of time current graduates using existing education facilities will remain in the labour force, can be traced. The useful life of education facilities built today must be added to this since they will continue to produce graduates. The total period over which the non-market and externality effects occur and the time delays, in the form of lagged responses, is about 100 years. The effects of investments identified here therefore have very long-term implications indeed.

Some non-market effects of education are purely private benefits. Those with more education enjoy better health, for example, which is a private benefit. This model measures better health as lower infant mortality, a private benefit within families, and greater longevity; by Grossman's (1997) estimates, a four-year college education adds about 1.4 years to life expectancy. But there are also important social benefit externalities from better health, such as those to public health, and the achievement of lower population growth rates that are critical to sustaining higher per capita economic growth in the poorest countries.

Other non-market effects of education are almost purely externalities that are essentially free goods so that the student and his or her family do not take them into account when they decide how much to invest privately in education (Lucas, 1988). Three examples include the *level of democratisation* and the *level of human rights in the community* as measured by the Freedom House (1997) indices, both of which contribute significantly to *political stability* (as measured by the International Country Risk Guide, 1997). Perhaps these are taken for granted in the OECD Member countries, but the political chaos in sub-Saharan Africa is sustained by over 50% adult illiteracy in most countries[14]. Democratic government is partly the result of state education of those who might not otherwise continue, but it is also a result of the education of past generations which has a lagged externality effect on the present that must be considered when planning long-term education investments. Romer (1990) defines the degrees of democracy, human rights, and political stability in the community as a "non-rivalrous" free good for any student and his or her family. Parents, therefore, will not pay privately for more education for their child to receive or to improve these since they are a free good available to all and are taken for granted when deciding how much to invest privately. This means that there will be underinvestment in education if all education is financed privately and if effective democracy, human rights, and political stability are regarded as social benefits. For some education marginal products, private and social benefits are hard to distinguish.

53

What are the total effects of education, or direct private plus social benefit externalities? In all cases, non-market effects of education are measured as the net marginal product of education, after controlling for other things, as graduates use their human capital during their leisure time hours in "household production" of final satisfactions. So there must always be controls for per capita income to avoid double counting the economic returns to education which arise during the time graduates spend in the labour market. This is the standard basis for defining and measuring non-market outcomes of education originally attributable to pioneering work by Becker (1964, 1976, 1981), Haveman and Wolfe (1984), and Wolfe and Zuvekas (1997).

Nine major net outcomes of education, using the data for 78 countries, include the following:

1. Increments to earnings. Although discussed by others, this cannot be ignored here because there are interactions with the non-market returns for which there must be controls. Here it will include the contribution of education to the family's income from higher interest, rent, and profits. This can be added up across households to get education's net contribution to per capita economic growth.

2. Better private and public health. This largely non-market effect must be measured after controlling for per capita income in order to get the additional non-market effect, and avoid double counting the market effects of education as households spend on better health care and better nutrition. Health effects in the regressions are the net effect of more education in lowering infant mortality rates and in raising longevity. These non-market effects are consistent with hundreds of microeconomic studies as surveyed by Grossman and Kaestner (1997) that also seek to control for per capita income. Some of these report conflicting cross effects, but none seek to measure the net nation-wide impact of education on measures of better health more comprehensively.

3. Lower fertility rates. This is largely a social benefit externality in the poor countries, but it is also a private non-market benefit that contributes to higher per capita income among poor families and hence less poverty. In the developing countries and poorer OECD regions, the evidence is that the education of women beyond the ninth grade leads to lower population growth rates as the effect of education in lowering fertility eventually swamps the population-increasing effects of education on infant mortality and longevity. This effect is apparent within the OECD where population growth rates have noticeably slowed. If education investments in facilities are now planned for the poorest regions, however, the further education of females is likely to reduce the social problems connected with higher population growth rates and the resulting emigration to urban ghettos and Northern Europe.

4. Democratisation. This is measured as the attainment of higher degrees of political rights measured by Freedom House (1997) as mentioned. Democratisation does not contribute to economic growth directly (Barro and Sala-I-Martin, 1995) but does contribute significantly to higher degrees of human rights (McMahon, 1999). Both are non-market externalities with highly significant lagged relationships to past education levels after controlling for per capita GDP in the world-wide data.

5. Social benefit of education. Greater political stability comes about in the regressions largely as the result of democratisation. This is certainly the case in all OECD nations. Political stability exists in some nations with lower levels of democracy such as Singapore or China, which have enjoyed rapid growth but on a broader scale, and in the longer run, the degree of democratisation has a highly significant relation to more permanent political stability. Political stability in turn contributes to higher rates of investment in physical capital, and hence to higher rates of pure economic growth, an indirect marginal product (measured by the cross partial derivatives) of education. The direct and indirect net contributions of education to democratisation, human rights, and political stability are all externalities that begin to be realised only after 15 or 20 years, a period outside the scope of many politicians but within that of the planning of investment in educational facilities whose impacts extend about 100 years. So a longer run perspective is needed. The widespread illiteracy and inequality in sub-Saharan Africa where 50-80% of the population often is illiterate, especially in those nations plagued by seemingly endless civil wars, creates widespread instability that scares away investors. It is likely to be many years, and only after substantial investment in educational facilities in the rural areas, before this settles down. Within Latin America, where democracy and greater political stability are now widespread, economic growth has noticeably accelerated. Within the OECD, this process has also occurred in Spain, for example, over the last 40 years, and per capita growth has noticeably accelerated.

6. The reduction of poverty and inequality, as measured by a poverty index and the Gini coefficient, is partly private benefits of education to poor families, but also partly social benefits as it reduces the strain on the social welfare and criminal justice systems. To receive these social benefits, however, requires that education facilities at the secondary level and especially at the two-year college levels be planned, built, and sustained in the poor neighbourhoods and rural areas. Spatial externalities of education arise within and among the OECD Member countries when poorly educated immigrants from the lower income southern European nations move north and create a burden on the northern education, training, welfare, and criminal justice systems. Planning for more adequate education facilities in the poor regions would be the best solution and should probably stress higher high school completion rates that would both reduce out-migration and also lead to more permanently employable productive citizens among those who do emigrate.

55

7. Improved environmental quality is an important indirect benefit of knowledge and of its diffusion through education. The international data measure environmental impacts by lower rates of deforestation, less water pollution, and reduced air pollution. The net effects of education come through poverty reduction, slower population growth rates, and democratisation after a lag of 15-20 years, but also through the diffusion of new technologies for a sustainable environment (World Bank, 1998)

8. Higher secondary enrolment rates have a strong net relation to lower crime rates. Criminology literature and research on crime published in economics, sociology, and psychology journals, make it clear that keeping young people off the streets and under supervision, especially if more healthy peer group relations can thereby also be formed, is critical for achieving lower crime rates. This can be done by increasing gross secondary schools enrolment rates to 100% or more, and by increasing two-year community colleges enrolment rates; both cases lead to greater employability, and a supervised environment later.

9. Consistent with this, world-wide and US data show that, after controlling for other things, higher secondary education gross enrolment rates and lower unemployment rates both make a significant net contribution to lower violent crime and property crime rates. This is a major externality of the publicly-supported government schools, since in contrast to private education they have a commitment to achieving higher community-wide enrolment rates at each age level, and thereby fewer unemployable drop-outs and less inequality later in life.

Apart from the net contribution of education investments to these nine market and non-market outcomes, two other effects of education are not measured:

1. Changes in private consumption tastes as a result of education. For example, more education increases the tastes for symphony concerts and reduces it for drag racing or boxing. However, new tastes offset those that are displaced, and there is no net increase in social welfare that can be indisputably identified.

2. Broad international externalities, such as Global Warming or the effectiveness of the international community. Undoubtedly higher education helps graduates to be aware of the problems and to organise to do something about them. As yet, there are no usable measures of either for which the data is sufficiently comprehensive.

Estimates of Total Market and Non-Market Effects of Education Projects

What are the empirical estimates of the net effects of education on each of these market and non-market ultimate outcomes? Estimated policy impacts for France, the

UK, and the US or other policy impacts could be calculated and shown for any of the other OECD nations.

Three scenarios show the time form of the lagged responses. Scenario No. 1, the Endogenous Development time path, involves no extraordinary education policy change. It is the continuation of the endogenous growth process developed extensively both theoretically and empirically in recent literature by Romer (1986, 1990), Lucas (1988), and Barro (1992, 1995) and in the augmented Solow models by Mankiw, Romer, and Weil (1992), Kim and Lau (1996), McMahon (1998a, 1998b, 1999), and others. Since population growth, the dissemination of knowledge, and other things keep changing it does not make sense to make zero growth or no endogenous policy change the baseline. Instead, an "endogenous development" path merely projects past policies on all the market and non-market outcome measures is projected as the base to which all changes discussed below are compared.

Scenario No. 2 involves a two percentage point increase in investment in education and education facilities as a percent of GNP, a type of policy in which the prime minister and budget bureau are involved. Gross enrolment rates can and often do exceed 100% because they include remedial courses, overage students, and lifelong learning. What are the net effects of increasing the rate of investment in education as a percent of GNP by two percentage points? For the OECD nations, regressions for the market returns to education are discussed in detail (McMahon, 1984). These time paths are all estimates, subject to the usual standard errors; each line represents the central tendency of a distribution even though it is shown as a single line for the sake of simplicity.

Where scenario No. 2 provides more resources to build educational facilities and to increase educational participation at secondary, two-year college, and four-year college levels in other ways, scenario No. 3 traces the net impacts of a 10 percentage point increase in secondary education on gross enrolment rates which involves an internal reallocation of budgets of the type that can be implemented largely within the education ministry. It squeezes the resources available to both secondary and other levels of education since no extraordinary sudden increase in the internal efficiency of the education sector is assumed.

Net Impacts of Additional Education Investments: France, the United Kingdom, the United States

The graphs for France, the UK, and the US reveal a similar pattern to the other OECD Member countries. A two percentage point increase in the GDP invested in education leads to the time paths after the policy change covering the next 40 years, to 2035, the

57

average time during which students now entering secondary or higher education will be in the labour force.

Investment expenditures include those made for new education facilities and their operation and maintenance. Given how the education sector is specified in the model, increased expenditure on education leads to building new or expanding existing school facilities and to the necessary support for increased access. This results in higher gross enrolment rates primarily at the high school and two- and four-year college levels in the OECD Member countries, but primarily at the basic education levels in the poor nations where primary and junior secondary education are not yet universal.

The impacts of this increased investment shown as scenario No. 2 will in all cases be compared to scenario No. 1, the "Endogenous Development" growth path, as the base solution within each time period of the interactive model that assumes the continuation of existing policies. It is important to note that this is not a zero per capita growth or stationary state solution. The estimate of the net impact of the education policy change is the distance between scenario No. 1 and scenario No. 2.

The net impact on enrolments that occurs first is shown in panels 1 and 2 in the graphs for France, the United Kingdom, and the United States. As the two percentage point increase in investment occurs, more education facilities, teachers, and textbooks are supplied, and facilities are also built closer to the students' home. Reflecting price and distance elasticity, this leads to about a 20 percentage point increase in secondary gross enrolment rates and a six or seven percentage point increase in higher education enrolments.

In France, when investment in education is increased from 5.7% of GNP to 7.7% of GNP, secondary education gross enrolment rates eventually increase from their current 90% (M) and 95% (F) to 110% (in panel 2). This occurs as major efforts are made to reduce high school drop out rates to make secondary education universal, and as some over-age students return to finish high school as part of lifelong learning. Gross enrolment rates therefore rise above 100% as is common when 100% net enrolment rates are approached. Higher education enrolments go from their current 31% to 42% by 2035 (panel 1) as more community college facilities are built and trends toward lifelong learning and computerised instruction of place-bound students lead France towards more universal education at this two-year college level as well.

One implication of this for planning education facilities is that to increase the social benefit externalities of education, more and better facilities need to be built in school districts where secondary enrolment rates are lowest. At the tertiary level, two-year community college facilities especially need to be significantly expanded. Other higher education expenditures are crucial to helping develop and disseminate the new knowledge, which also has externality benefits. Given the social problems, however, planning for higher completion rates at these more basic levels would appear to be the most important.

The net economic growth effects for France (panel 3, scenario No. 2) are to raise per capita income about USD 5 000 (in 1985 prices) above where it would otherwise be by 2035. The major part of this is through the direct effects of education in providing higher skill levels and capacities to continue to learn during time spent in the labour market. Another part is due to the indirect effects on growth. Some of these externalities come through higher Gross Domestic Investment rates (panel 4) as human capital investment offsets the diminishing returns to investment in physical capital that would otherwise occur and as appropriate investments in educational facilities and programmes contribute to greater political stability as shown in panel 11.

The degree of democratisation is not substantially affected because France is already at the upper ceiling for this index (panel 10). However, the model predicts further net improvements in human rights, as measured by the Freedom House Index (panel 9). Significant net improvements in the average health accrue to the French population as current dropouts and others go farther with their education. This is measured by further reductions in infant mortality rates, beginning in 2015, and by a two-year net increase in average life expectancy by then, attributable to more widespread education (panels 13 and 14).

At 1.2 murders per 100,000 in the population, homicide rates are already reasonably low in France. These rates fall further (not shown) and property crime rates (panel 16) rise less than would be expected under the base endogenous development scenario, illustrating a unique interaction between pure economic growth and the non-market effects of education on property crime rates. This is why it is important to control for per capita income before the positive non-market direct effects and indirect externality effects of higher gross enrolment rates in reducing crime rates become clear.

Income inequality is reduced by about two percentage points, as measured by the Gini index (panel 8). This is undoubtedly due to the reduction of high school dropouts (panel 2) and to the provision of more two-year community college facilities in lower income areas and wider access to four-year colleges (panel 1). Higher education enrolment rates in France are already 41% (panel 1), so further expansion would not be highly elitist. Public higher education policies that subsidise only a fraction of each generation that tend to be from relatively high income families, such as is done in most African countries where primary education is not yet universal, are well known to contribute to higher rather than lower inequality later. This is less true in the OECD Member countries where K-12 education is virtually universal.

OECD 2000

In the United Kingdom and the United States, economic growth and the non-market effects of more education are similar to those in France. The policy simulations are again approximately relevant, but there are also some differences in the estimated outcomes. In the US, President Clinton tried unsuccessfully to get financial support for making two years of college universal, but did get federal support to put 100 000 new primary teachers in the classrooms in the federal budget that passed the Congress recently. Improving the quality of secondary education, higher high school completion rates are both under active discussion in both the US and the UK.

What are the potential market impacts? In scenario No. 2, increased investment in human resource development through education adds 8% to the growth rate after an initial lag in both the US and the UK. These small percentage point differences become extremely important when compounded over 40 years, leading to GNP per capita that is about 35% above where it would otherwise be by 2035 (panel 3). This should be regarded as a first approximation but will be seen later to be consistent with the approximately 13% of real social rates of return estimated from microeconomic data. Some of this increase can be seen to arise due to higher output per worker (UK, panel 5), some through higher labour force participation rates, especially of women (panel 7), and about 40% is due to delayed indirect externality effects on economic growth.

This suggests a new method for estimating social rates of return that can be used to compare to the standard rates of return calculated from microeconomic earnings data in each country. This is done by using the net increments in per capita GDP attributable to the increased investment in human capital formation through education generated by the model over the next 40 years as an estimate of the total economic benefits of education. These include only those externalities that affect market-based GDP. The total social costs for the calculation are the additional percentage of GDP invested in education plus the additional foregone earnings costs for the increment in enrolments. The standard rate of return formula is then applied to calculate the pure internal rate of return (see note, Table 1). Table 1 shows the increments to GDP and to the investment costs that include the O and M costs for new facilities, all of which must be discounted back to their present value, and the solution for the social rates of return that do this in the US and the UK. This new method gives estimated social rates of return of 15% for the UK and 14% for the US in real terms. This also is a first approximation that may turn out to be slightly higher or lower as the empirical application of the simulation techniques are refined. But it is reasonable when compared to independent estimates of social rates of return using microeconomic earnings data[15].

Incorporating current dynamic trends in social rates of return estimated from cross-section microeconomic earnings data shows the true expected dynamic social rate of return for two- and four-year college graduates to be about three percentage points higher for males, and five percentage points higher for females than the standard rates of return suggest (Arias and McMahon, 1998). To be comparable to the social rates of return based on my growth estimates, standard cross-section social rates of return need to be adjusted to incorporate expected longitudinal trends also.

The data for incorporating dynamic trends in earnings within each age group is available for the US in the cross-section Census Bureau national labour force surveys, since they are annual, but it has not normally been used in this way to obtain all of the information the data contains. In particular, age earnings profiles for two- and four-year college graduates have been shifting upward dramatically since 1980 (Figure 1). So the true dynamic age-earning profile that each graduate experiences over time is the longitudinal path ABCD, since the earnings of older college graduates are also shifting upward as a graduate arrives in each older age cohort, a steeper age earnings profile than what is revealed by the static cross-section data of earnings at different ages at any given point in time, as shown by the standard cross-section age-earning profiles that apply to any given year, such as CS 1995, in Figure 1.

For direct costs, 2% of GNP per capita per annum are summed up over a five-year period to the year 2000, plus a declining fraction of annual costs after that time that phase out to zero on a straight line basis by the year 2040. Graduating students in each successive cohort after 2000 have not completed their time in the labour force before 2040 and therefore their contributions are not fully included in returns prior to that date. Foregone earnings costs based on domestic earnings data at the next lower level of education are handled in the same way and multiplied by 0.75 to remove the

Figure 1. **Dynamic Age-Earning Profile for a Typical Female College Graduate of the 1967 Cohort**

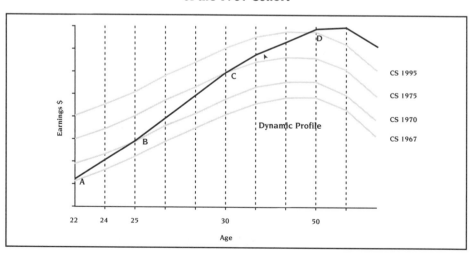

Table 1. **New Social Rates of Return to Education in the UK and US (in USD 1985 prices)**

	2000	2005	2010	2015	2020	2025	2030	2035	2040
UK									
Growth in GNP per Capita	0	72	382	991	1831	2887	4212	5890	5890
Direct + Foreign Earn.Costs	1156	220	189	158	126	95	63	38	0

Social Rate of Return (pure internal rate of return, in real terms): 15%

United States									
Growth in GNP per Capita	0	143	713	1675	2851	4251	5945	8008	8008
Direct + Foreign Earn.Costs	2178	410	351	292	233	174	115	56	0

Source: Arias and McMahon, (1998)

US Social Rate of Return (pure internal rate of return in real terms): 14%

vacation portion of the school year. For the US, they are based on mean earnings of all persons in the labour force aged 18-24 in 1995 from the Current Population Reports of the Census Bureau, 1996, converted to 1985 prices. For new high school enrolments, this is the average earnings of males and females with 9-12 years of education but no diploma; for college level, it is earnings of high school graduates.

On the benefit side, total returns to education are the net increments in GNP per capita for each country after controlling for other sources of economic growth such as investment in physical capital. These increments to GNP are over and above the endogenous development in scenario No. 1 which estimates longer run growth under existing policies. These totals must be converted from a per student to a per capita basis, since the increments to earnings and the increments to direct costs are in these terms. To reflect enrolment increment, 0.20 times high school enrolments and 0.20 times college enrolments from the National Centre for Education Statistics (1996, p. 16) is divided by the total population and used as an adjustment factor at each education level.

In contrast, the real earnings of high school graduates have been shifting downward since 1980; the gap with two- and four-year college graduates is widening, inequality is increasing, and the social rates of return on investment in the education of these college graduates are rising dramatically. There is reason to think that similar trends have been affecting earnings at the different education levels in the UK, and in most other OECD Member countries, based on studies of the Luxembourg international microeconomic earnings panel data (Sullivan and Smeeding (1997); Gottschalk and Smeeding, (1997)).

The result is expected dynamic rates of return in the US for college graduates that are 13.20% for males and 13.42% for females, in 1995, as shown in Table 2 and 11% for both for investment at the high school level. This is not far from the 14% estimate for new investments in education at these levels obtained from the simulations of education impacts shown in Table 1. No expected dynamic rates of return are available for the UK but it is reasonable to assume that the same trends, due to technology premiums for tertiary level graduates and globalisation, are affecting the returns to post secondary education there, so that the trend adjusted rates average three to five percentage points above those reported.

Table 2. **EXPECTED DYNAMIC SOCIAL RATES OF RETURN TO EDUCATION IN THE US, 1980-1995**

	Dynamic Rates of Return*				Cross-section Static Rates				
	1980	1985	1990	1995	1980	1985	1990	1995	1996
High School (M)	10.79	10.29	9.15	10.23	12.62	10.68	12.00	11.00	
High School (F)	13.31	12.48	11.27	12.40	13.38	12.43	11.00	11.00	
College 1-3 (M)	5.75	5.93	5.99	7.05	4.47	5.30	7.19	4.50	
College 1-3 (F)	3.86	2.92	1.85	1.78	4.74	4.99	6.01	1.01	
Assoc.Degree 2(M)				(14.0)*				11.00	15.00
Assoc.Degree 2(F)				(23.0)*				18.00	18.00
College 4 (M)	10.89	13.14	12.21	13.20	8.84	10.78	12.87	10.29	
College 4 (F)	10.36	12.72	11.23	13.42	5.86	7.97	11.47	8.39	
College 5+ (M)	8.73	10.06	11.10	11.11	7.10	7.94	9.63	8.13	
College 5+ (F)	8.05	8.30	6.72	5.56	9.56	8.73	10.24	6.87	

Based on Mean Earnings Data from Current Population Reports, Consumer Income Series P-60, 1967 to 1995. Costs are based on total current fund expenditure per pupil in 4-year institutions of higher education from the Statistical Abstract of Education (1996), NCES.
*Projection of net earnings differentials are made for each age-group using the average annual rate of growth of net earnings differentials during 1981-1995.

Table 3. **INFLATION ADJUSTED TOTAL RETURNS TO FINANCIAL AND HUMAN CAPITAL INVESTMENTS 1975-1995**

	Large Company Stocks	Long-Term Corporate Bonds	Intermediate Government Bonds	High School Education	Associate (2-year) Degree	College (4-Year) Education
1975	-3.2%	-2.4%	-1.8%	10.4%		8.2%
1980	7.0	-10.5	-6.4	12.0		10.6
1985	16.1	19.3	13.3	11.4		12.9
1990	7.4	3.3	3.0	10.2		11.7
1995	11.1	8.1	4.7	11.3	(18.5)*	13.3
Average	7.7%	3.6%	2.6%	11.1%	(18.5)*	11.3%

* (...) = estimate, based on cross-section static rate of return adjusted for the same dynamic trends that apply to 4 year college levels.

OECD 2000

It is reasonable to assume an approximately equal social rate of return to investment in educational facilities as that for all education investment, assuming efficient allocation between facilities and operating budgets, but the rates for females and males must be averaged. The result is a real social rate of return for 1995 of 11.3% for investment in high school facilities, 18.5% at the two-year college level (Table 2). This is reasonably high in relation to an 8.1% inflation adjusted real rate of return on corporate bonds (Table 3). The premium placed on getting more education due to the new technologies and globalisation has every reason to persist indefinitely.

For non-market returns to investments in education in the US and UK, the pattern is somewhat similar to the effects in France. What, then, are the implications of these dynamic trends for the non-market social benefits? Given rising inequality in the income distribution in the US and the UK and high rates of return to expanding high school and college undergraduate gross enrolment rates, increased educational investment leads to significant net reductions in income inequality that are particularly noteworthy (panel 8 for both UK and US). More specifically, with this investment in education, larger percentages within each age group finish high school (panel 2 for both countries) and two- and four-year college enrolments expand from 22% to 35% in the UK and from 56% to 68% in the US (panel 1, scenario 2, for both countries).

In poor countries in the model, a similar percentage increase in education investments produces very different non-market effects. This is primarily because increased investment leads to expansion and improvement at the primary and junior secondary education levels, where there is no universal education, and because of much lower initial levels of political stability and democratisation. This effect on inequality is important not just because inequality has been rising in OECD nations (Gottschalk and Smeeding, 1997) but also because inequality and poverty contribute to higher property crime rates in the regressions (after controlling for other things). This policy will help moderate that trend (panel 16 for both countries).

Homicide rates, which are much higher in the US than elsewhere (9.2 per 100 000 in the US and 1.0 in the UK), are also lowered by one percentage point (11%) in the US by this policy (panel 16). This is significant to consider very seriously since it costs about USD 40 000 per year in the US to incarcerate one person. Using James Heckman's (1998a) estimate, if it costs USD 25 000 per year to keep a high school drop out in school, this is far less than to keep him in prison. If this expenditure is made for four years of high school, after which he earns USD 10 000 per year more than the average eighth grade graduate for the next 40 years in the labour force, there is a significant positive rate of return to society that must be added to the saving in prison costs.

Better health is evident in both the US and UK following the policy change: net reductions in infant mortality rates as females finish high school, and further increases in life expectancy after 2005 in the US and UK (panels 13 and 14). The Wolfe and Zu-vekas (1997) method lets these be valued at the cost of achieving similar results by other means such as expenditures on doctors' visits and drugs. If, instead of higher secondary enrolment rates, this must be done partly for high school dropouts and the uninsured, there is a significant public cost. Additional positive effects on health may accrue, such as reduced smoking, better awareness of low cholesterol diets, etc., that this model considers through effects on longevity.

Democracy, human rights, and political stability effects are small but positive, in sharp contrast to the relative improvements in these in similar simulations for sub-Saharan African nations (US and UK, panels 9, 10, and 11).

Deforestation rates and the rate of destruction of wildlife with which they are cor-related, are eventually reversed in both countries as they gradually respond to the eco-nomic capacity to finance parks and preserves, slower population growth, and more widespread higher education in the electorate (panel 15).

Interactive Simulation of Educational Investments Impacts

What are the impacts on the non-market returns to educational investments in dif-ferent OECD countries (such as Japan for which an East Asian production function has been estimated, or Germany)? What are the 40-year longer run development im-plications of increasing the rate of investment in human capital formation by three per-centage points in Japan, which is being encouraged for other reasons related to its cyclical recession to use a much stronger fiscal stimulus? Overall, these measures of economic growth and non-market impacts of educational investments incorporate the main interactions, dynamic lags, and control for effects not related to the change in education policies. They are a first approximation that inevitably will be refined and broken down further by academic discipline, such as law, political science, public health, or even economics and not just engineering, that make especially important contri-butions to non-market returns and externalities and would be useful to measure more precisely.

Distinguishing Direct and Indirect Externality Effects

Each of the total market and non-market benefits of education will be separated into measures of the direct (or partial) effects and indirect structural effects. All indi-rect effects are externalities as are all total direct and indirect effects of education on certain of the outcomes such as democratisation. The direct effects of education on each outcome will first be separated from the indirect effects that are then expressed

65

as a percent of the total. The United Kingdom will illustrate percentages that reflect a general pattern typical of most OECD Member countries. In poor countries, the pattern is very different, and in interesting ways.

The Conceptual Basis for Measuring Direct vs. Indirect Benefits

How are these separated within the interactive model? The direct (or partial) benefits of education are its marginal products, outcome by outcome, after controlling for "other things". They are closely analogous to those isolated by standard partial equilibrium analysis in economics, which assumes that other things do not change. Measuring them requires enforcing the ceteris paribus condition, which has been done here by multiple regressions techniques used to control statistically for other things that could logically affect each education outcome.

The indirect effects of education arise through community effects that have been heavily influenced by education often through the earlier education of adults in the community. These can also be thought of as structural effects that give measurable feedback effects on each education outcome and augment the direct effects. These are clearly externalities that affect both economic growth and non-market outcomes of education. They are measured, in theory, by cross partial derivatives, and can be obtained empirically from the regression equations: for example, per capita economic growth is determined partly by increasing skill levels in the labour force and by higher labour force participation rates that lead to direct effects from education. They are also affected by higher rates of investment in physical capital, greater longer run political stability following democratisation, and by lower net population growth rates, each of which are measurably affected by education, and therefore generate indirect effects. These are all externality-type effects that do not begin to occur in measurable ways until after 15 to 20 years; they can be expressed as a percent of the total effects of education on economic growth.

A second example of indirect effects is lower property crime rates if a higher percentage of the teenage population is in school under supervision. This is a direct effect of higher secondary education enrolment rates, and can be detected only after controlling for other things among which property crime rates are also lower in the community if poverty rates are lower, if income distribution inequality is lower, and if unemployment rates (two-year lag) are lower. Higher retention rates in school can contribute after a relatively long lag in a recursive relationship to each of these; this suggests indirect effects of education which are positive benefit externalities. However, higher nation-wide per capita income is also associated with higher property crime. A measurable part of this in the simulations is due to increased education, which illustrates how some of the social benefit effects of education can also generate negative externalities. However, it will be seen that the total effects of education which net out the negative indirect effects against the positive direct and indirect effects of education are, on balance, positive in that property crime rates are reduced with higher secondary gross enrolment rates.

To distinguish direct and indirect effects of education and to measure each, a version of the model has been programmed to generate only the direct effects of education on each outcome. Each other variable in each equation takes on the values given by the endogenous development scenario (a "no special education policy change" growth path that contains none of the indirect feedback effects of the education policy change). The endogenous development solution values at each point in time are subtracted from the values generated by the direct effects as the direct effects version of the model is run to get the net direct effects of education which are saved and compared to the net total effects of education. These net total effects of the education policy change net Direct Effects, and the net Indirect Effects as a percent of the Total Effects are shown in the three sets columns in Table 4 for the United Kingdom.

Empirical Measures of Indirect Effects and Externalities

Externality effects from education on pure economic growth and indirect externality effects of education on growth and on the nine major non-market outcomes do not overlap because controls for per capita income have always been enforced when measuring the non-market outcomes.

Effects of Education Externalities on Per Capita GDP

For the UK substantial indirect effects from either increased investment or increased secondary education enrolments on per capita economic growth exist but do not begin to appear until after 15 to 20 years. They reach 56 to 59% of the total effects of education by 2035, typical of the other OECD Member countries.

UNITED KINGDOM

The indirect effects due to increments to political stability and democracy are smaller in the UK than in the African countries. There are, however, positive indirect effects through rates of investment in physical capital as diminishing returns are offset, and through higher education as the new knowledge created through R and D is more rapidly and widely disseminated. The Robbins Commission Report dealt with

67

this earlier, beginning to expand higher education in the UK to larger percentages in each age group in the spirit of the US land-grant institutions. First, higher education was extended to many more applied fields - engineering, agriculture, business administration - and enrolled a larger percent of each college age group. This is thus a part of a continuing trend as higher education embodies the new knowledge and acts as a major vehicle for its transmission to firms as they employ graduates.

Externalities as a percent of Non-Market Effects of Education

The remaining sections report the indirect effects of education as a percentage of the total of each non-market effect of education in the last two columns. Scenario No. 2, the effects of a two percentage point increase in investment in education as a percent of GNP, continues to be the focus.

Inequality

Almost all of the reductions in income distribution inequality in the UK result from the direct effects of increased high school completion rates and expanded access to higher education. Only about 17% of the effects are indirect.

Political Stability, Democratisation, and Human Rights

These indices are already high for the UK so the total effects are relatively small. These community effects of education, albeit after long delays, loom very large in the simulations for Latin America and sub-Saharan Africa. The 52% externality effect on political stability comes largely through education's effect on democratisation, which may be of some significance in terms of British history. In the US, these are major problems in the sense that only 23% of those with less than a high school education vote, and many are primarily influenced by the political advertisements on TV. There is room for improvement in the effectiveness of democracy in political processes.

Health effects are revealed by increased life expectancy of 1.4 years in the UK as well as the 5.5% reduction in the infant mortality rate. These are largely private non-market benefits of education; there is only a small proportion of indirect effects on health: only 13.9% for life expectancy and 18.18% for infant mortality. This is probably an underestimate because the health equations contain regional dummies that pick up some of the community effects. As measured here, 82% of the total contribution of education to reduced infant mortality is due to the direct effects from the mother's more advanced education.

Environmental Effects of Education

These are much more dramatic in places like Brazil where the rapid destruction of forests at 2% a year continues unabated through 2025 in the simulations. Even in the UK, some effects are estimated to be from more widespread environmental education, such as in the continuing reduction of air pollution in the urban areas. Here a relatively small 28% are indirect, but this is not typical of the pattern in developing countries where generally 100% of the effects of education on deforestation and water pollution are indirect, operating through poverty reduction and slower population growth.

Crime

The final panel shows negative indirect effects on property crime rates, which are increased as economic growth raises inequality, and continuing poverty. Higher secondary education enrolment rates are positive, however, as young people stay in high school; this direct effect is larger than the adverse growth effects. Therefore, the net total effects of education are to reduce property crime rates in the UK by 8 to 15 crimes per 100 000 in the population over the next 20 to 40 years.

Conclusion

Summarising the externalities, the indirect and often lagged effects of education are estimated to account for the following:

- 59% of the increments to GNP per capita that are attributable to education in the UK. These increments to GNP do not begin to be substantial until after 20 to 25 years. The percentage that is externalities is lower in the simulations for those OECD Member countries where the initial secondary and higher education gross enrolment rates are higher (*e.g.* 34% of the total effects are externalities in the US).

- 100% of effects of education are externalities for reductions in inequality, improvements in the effectiveness of democracy, human rights, political stability, and environmental quality. This is by definition of these outcomes as "non-rivalrous" public goods.

- 14% of the 1.47 years of increased life expectancy attributable to education investments come from indirect effects - over 18% of the reductions in infant mortality, and 44% of the net reductions in the fertility rate - and hence education externalities as measured by the simulations. Continuing reductions in the fertility rate have a relation to poverty reduction and to reduced welfare costs if secondary education enrolment rates are increased toward 100%.

These estimates, while approximate and subject to the usual standard errors and refinements by others in the specifications, offer a substantial case that over 50% of the market effects and also over 50% of the non-market net benefits of education are externalities. Students and their families have no incentive to finance these privately.

What is the economic value on these outcomes? The effects on per capita GNP including the externalities that affect market returns have a value estimated to be USD 5 890 per person in the UK for example by 2035 (in 1985 USD). The approximately 14% social rate of return that the additional educational investment yields is also in economic value terms. But approximately 59% of this gain in the UK is due to the past education of others and the indirect effects that this generates. The private receipt of this gain by an individual is not contingent on that individual getting more education. Some would regard this as the acid test of whether or not these indirect effects are externalities. The point is that things like democratisation and political stability are free goods available to all that from past investments have raised average productivity in society at all education levels, so that this portion of per capita income is not contingent on the individual having increased his or her education.

The value of the non-market returns to the educational investment is over and above this effect on market-based GNP. Using the cost-based method of valuation, Wolfe and Zuvekas (1997) reaffirm earlier estimates of the value of non-market returns to be "of the same order of magnitude as estimates of the annual marketed earnings-based effects of one more year of schooling". Using this cost-based estimate, non-market returns would double the 14% social rate of return in the UK.

Legislators pay little attention to cost-based estimates by economists and impose their own valuations on both the market and non-market returns. In doing so, they respond to their own constituencies, and how these returns are perceived. The effective electoral base is, however, a relatively small fraction of the voting-age citizens within each constituency since many do not actually vote and there are also influences from special interests. In the US for example, most citizens do not vote, and only 23% of those with less than a high school education vote. Many go to the polls because of televised political advertising and hence the special interests who finance it. This leads to distortions of the non-market returns and externalities. In some developing countries, dictators are not interested at all in some education outcomes such as "democratisation". One result is the tendency to under-investment in education if the cost-based valuations of non-market returns plus market rates of return are used as the criteria for social efficiency.

The implications for financing investments in educational facilities discussed here include specific identifications of non-market returns and externalities, along the lines of the eight categories listed, estimating the non-market and market effects, and making more people in the affected community aware of these. The estimates based on the cost of achieving the same outcomes by alternative means indicate that they are at least as high as the substantial market returns. In many cases, government support will be needed. This requires putting together a coalition of interests aware of the market and non-market benefits and externalities of education.

OECD 2000

ANNEX

OECD 2000

FRANCE
Non-Market Impacts on Economic Development

Scenarios:
#1. Endogeneous Development ; #2. IH/Y=+2Pec't Pts ; #3. GER2T=+10 Pec't Pts

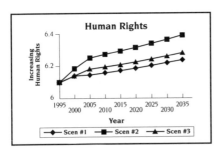

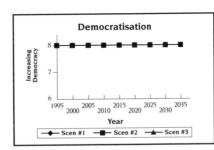

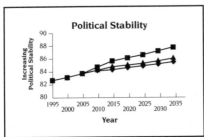

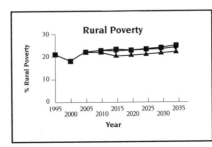

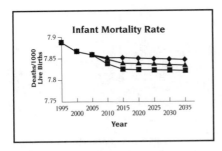

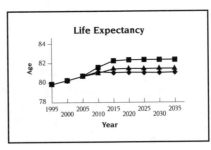

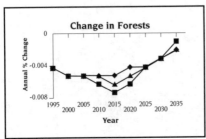

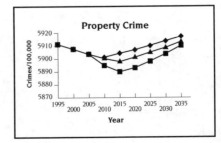

FRANCE
Estimated Policy Impacts on Economic Growth and Equity

Scenarios:
#1. Endogeneous Development ; #2. IH/Y=+2Pec't Pts ; #3. GER2T=+10 Pec't Pts

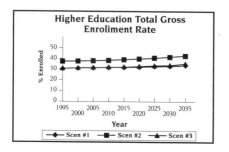

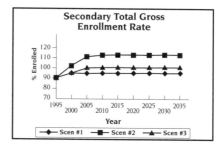

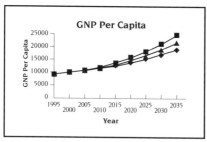

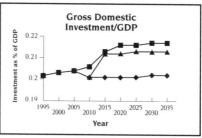

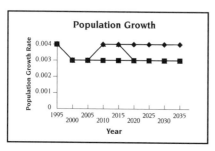

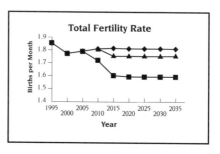

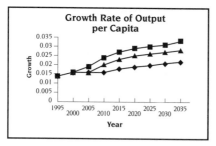

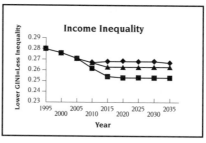

75

UNITED KINGDOM
Non-Market Impacts on Economic Development

Scenarios:
#1. Endogeneous Development ; #2. IH/Y=+2Pec't Pts ; #3. GER2T=+10 Pec't Pts

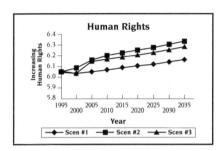

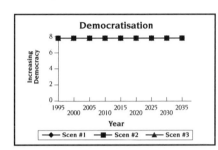

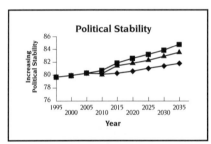

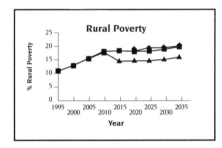

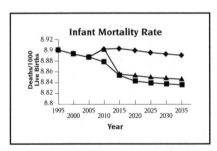

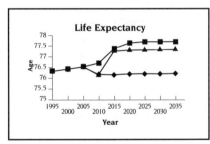

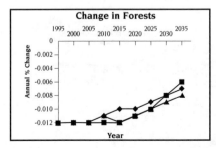

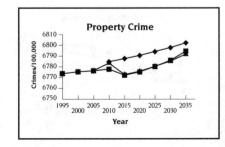

UNITED KINGDOM
Estimated Policy Impacts on Economic Growth and Equity

Scenarios:
#1. Endogeneous Development ; #2. IH/Y=+2Pec't Pts ; #3. GER2T=+10 Pec't Pts

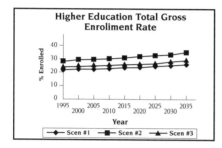

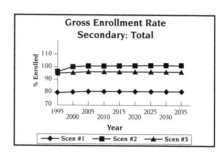

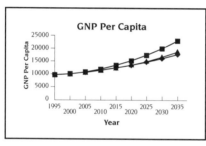

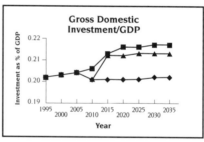

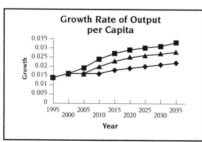

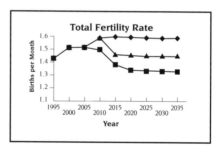

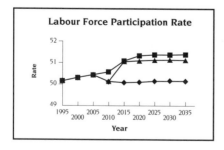

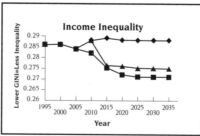

UNITED STATES
Non-Market Impacts on Economic Development

Scenarios:
#1. Endogeneous Development ; #2. IH/Y=+2Pec't Pts ; #3. GER2T=+10 Pec't Pts

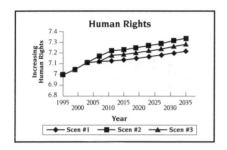

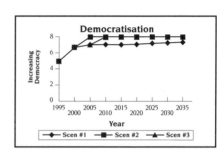

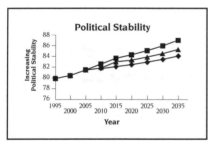

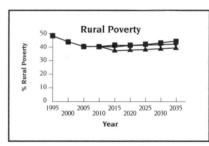

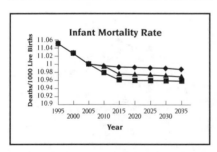

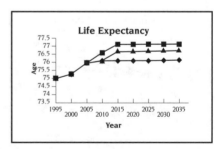

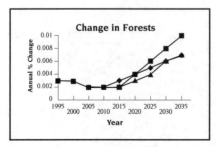

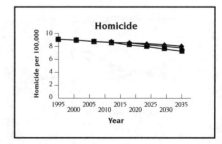

UNITED STATES
Estimated Policy Impacts on Economic Growth and Equity

Scenarios:
#1. Endogeneous Development ; #2. IH/Y=+2Pec't Pts ; #3. GER2T=+10 Pec't Pts

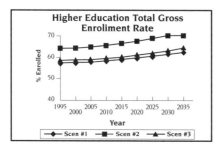

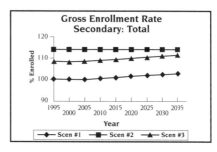

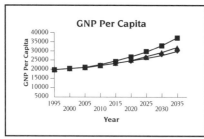

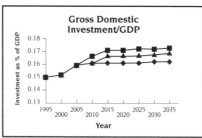

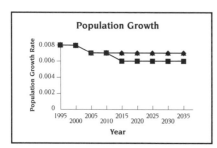

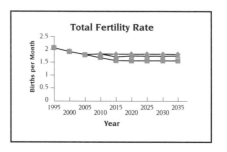

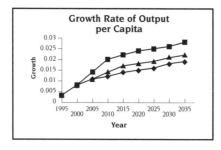

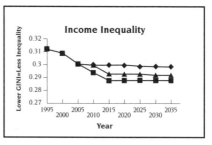

79

REFERENCES

ARIAS, Omar, and Walter McMAHON (1998),
"Dynamic Rates of Return to Education in the US", Working Paper, Department of Economics, University of Illinois at Champaign-Urbana.

ASHENFELTER, Orley and Alan KRUEGER (1994),
"Estimates of the Economic Return to Schooling from a New Sample of Twins", *American Economic Review*, 84 (5), pp. 1157-11.

ASHENFELTER, Orley, and Cecilia ROUSE (1998),
"Income, Schooling, and Ability: Evidence From a New Sample of Identical Twins", *Quarterly Journal of Economics*, Vol. CXIII, No. 1 (February 1998), pp. 253-28.

BARRO, Robert (1997),
"Economic Growth and Convergence", in Barro, *The Determinants of Economic Growth; A Cross Country Empirical Study*, Lionel Robbins Memorial Lectures, London School of Economics, the MIT Press, Cambridge MA.

BARRO, Robert J. (1992),
"Economic Growth in a Cross Section of Countries", *Quarterly Journal of Economics*, CVI(2) (May 1991), pp. 407-444.

ROBERT J. and Xavier SALA-I-MARTIN (1995),
Economic Growth, McGraw Hill, New York.

BECKER, Gary (1965),
"A Theory of the Allocation of Time", *Economic Journal*, 75, pp.493-517.

BECKER, Gary (1993),
Human Capital, 3rd ed., University of Chicago Press, Chicago.

BECKER, Gary (1981),
A Treatise on the Family, Harvard University Press, Cambridge, Massachusetts.

BECKER, Gary (1976),
    The Economic Approach to Human Behaviour, University of Chicago Press, Chicago, Illinois.

BEHRMAN, Jere R. (1997),
    "Conceptual and Measurement Issues", in Behrman and N. Stacey, editors, *The Social Benefits of Education*, Michigan University Press, Ann Arbor.

BEHRMAN and STACEY, editors (1997),
    The Social Benefits of Education, University of Michigan Press, Ann Arbor.

CARD, David (1988),
    "The Causal Effect of Education on Earnings", in *Handbook of Labour Economics*, Vol. 3, Orley Ashenfelter and David Card, editors, forthcoming, and as *Working Paper* No. 2, Centre for Labour Economics, University of California, Berkeley.

CARNOY, Martin (1997),
    "Recent Research on Market Returns to Education", *International Journal of Education Research*, Vol. 27, No.6.

FREEDOM HOUSE (1997),
    Freedom in the World, 1996-97, University Press of America, Lanham, MD and London, England.

GOTTSCHALK, Peter, and Timothy SMEEDING (1997),
    "Cross National Comparisons of Earnings and Income Inequality", *Journal of Economic Literature*, 35, (2), (June).

GROSSMAN, Michael, and Robert KAESTNER (1997),
    "Effects of Education on Health", in Behrman and Stacey, editors, *The Social Benefits of Education*, University of Michigan Press, Ann Arbor.

HAVEMAN, ROBERT, and B. WOLFE (1984),
    "Schooling and Economic Well-being: The Role of Non-Market Effects", *The Journal of Human Resources*, 19, pp. 377-407.

HEALY, Tom, *et al.* (1998),
    Human Capital Investment: An International Comparison, Centre for Educational Research and Innovation, Organisation for Economic Co-operation and Development, Paris.

IBBOTSON and ASSOCIATES (1998).
    Stocks, Bonds, Bills, and Inflation: 1998 Yearbook, Ibbotson and Associates, Chicago.

81

International Country Risk Guide (1997),
"Political, Economic, and Composite Risk", Syracuse, New York.

KIM, Jong Il and Lawrence J. LAU (1996),
"The Sources of Economic Growth of East Asian Newly Industrialised Countries: Some Further Evidence", Faculty Working Paper, Department of Economics, Stanford University, December 1995, summarised in AEA Papers and Proceedings, May 1996.

LUCAS, Robert E. (1988),
"On the Mechanics of Economic Development", Journal of Monetary Economics (July), 22:1, 3-42.

MANKIW, N. Gregory, David ROMER, David N. WEIL (1992),
"A Contribution to the Empirics of Economic Growth", Quarterly Journal of Economics, (May), 107:2, 407-438.

MCMAHON, Walter W. (1992a),
"The Economics of School Expansion and Decline", in Fuller, Bruce and R. Rubinson, The Political Construction of Education, Praeger.

MCMAHON, Walter W. (1984),
"The Relation of Education and R and D to Productivity Growth", Economics of Education Review, Vol. 3, No. 4 (December), pp. 299-314.

MAHON, Walter W. (1987),
"The Relation of Education and R and D to Productivity Growth in the Developing Countries of Africa", Economics of Education Review, Vol. 6, No. 2 (June), pp. 183-194.

MAHON, Walter W. (1991),
"Relative Returns to Human and Physical Capital in the U.S. and Efficient Investment Strategies", Economics of Education Review 10 (4), pp. 283-96.

MAHON, Walter W. (1994),
"Market Signals and Labour Market Analysis", Paper for ILO Workshop on New Trends in Education and Training Policies, Geneva, Switzerland, November 1993.

MAHON, Walter W. (ed. (1997),
"Recent Advances in Measuring the Social and Individual Benefits of Education", Special Issue of the International Journal of Education Research, Vol. 27, No. 7, Pergamon, Elsevier.

MAHON, Walter W. (1998a),
"Conceptual Framework for the Analysis of the Social Benefits of Lifelong Learning", *Education Economics*, Vol.6, No. 3, 307-343.

MAHON, Walter W. (1998b),
"Education and Growth in East Asia", *Economics of Education Review*, Elsevier, June, 1998.

MAHON, Walter W. (1999),
Education and Development; Measuring the Social Benefits, March 1999, Oxford University Press, Oxford.

PSACHAROPOULOS, George (1994),
"Returns to Investment in Education: A Global Update", *World Development*, 22(9), pp. 1325-1343.

ROMER, Paul (1990),
"Endogenous Technical Change", *Journal of Political Economy*, Vol. 98, No. 5, Pt. 2, pp. 571-93.

ROMER, Paul (1986),
"Increasing Returns and Long Run Growth", *Journal of Political Economy*, 94, pp. 1002-37.

SULLIVAN, Dennis, and Timothy SMEEDING (1997),
"Educational Attainment and Earnings Inequality in Eight Nations", *International Journal of Education Research*, (27), 7, 113-134.

U.S. BUREAU OF THE CENSUS. Current Population Reports, Consumer Income Series, Money Income of Households, Families and Persons in the United States, several years 1967-95.

WOLFE, Barbara and Sam ZUVEKAS (1997),
"Non-Market Effects of Education", *International Journal of Education Research*, Vol. 27, No. 6, pp. 491-502.

WORLD BANK (1998),
World Development Report 1998-1999: Knowledge for Development, The World Bank, Washington, DC.

Chapter Two

PERFORMANCE INDICATORS FOR EDUCATIONAL PROJECTS

INVESTMENT IN EDUCATION IN OECD COUNTRIES - FINANCE AND OWNERSHIP

Andreas **Schleicher**
OECD

Introduction

Human capital has become a prime economic resource in OECD Member countries and a key determinant of global competitiveness. Producing human capital is therefore essential and governments are seeking new approaches to enhance individual and collective economic performance, promote the efficiency of education systems, and identify additional resources to meet increasing demands. Education and training are therefore at the forefront of the policy debate at a time of changing demographic and social conditions, shifting demands for skills, and the move towards knowledge-based economies.

To inform the process of policy formation and to reinforce the public accountability of education systems, the OECD develops indicators that elucidate the comparative functioning of education systems, focusing on the investment and returns of human and financial resources. These indicators, published annually in *Education at a Glance*[16] also make it possible to analyse the inter-relationships among the various features of education systems. Countries can compare themselves to other countries' performance, recognise the weaknesses, and identify the strengths of their education systems which are often overlooked in the heat of domestic debate.

This paper compares cost patterns in OECD countries and selected non-member countries and focuses on three aspects of educational spending: national resources invested in education relative to national wealth, numbers of students and size of the public purse; sources of finance and resource-deployment across categories.

National Income Invested in Education

How much to invest in education is a collective public decision. Governments must interpret demands for increased spending for teachers' salaries and educational facilities and assess how effectively existing resources are being used. In primary and secondary education, overall spending is influenced partly by the number of school-age children; class size and teacher salaries create wide differences in how overall investment in education translates into per child spending. In tertiary education, cross-country variations are further accentuated by differences in numbers of participants and by the role of private financing.

Given the variety of influences, it may be surprising that OECD countries spend such similar proportions of their GDP on education: two-thirds spend between 5 and 7% (Table B1.1a)[17]. Despite tight public scrutiny of education budgets, education spending has been less than 5% of GDP in only five of 22 reporting OECD countries. There may be greater discretionary spending on tertiary education, which varies by a factor of over three (Table B1.1c). Considering direct public expenditure together with funds from international sources and all public subsidies to students and households, the share of education in the GDP of OECD countries rises to around 8%. It is higher in Denmark and Sweden, and between 6.5 and 8% in Canada, Finland, France, and the United States. In Greece, Italy, Japan, and Turkey, however, it remains below 5% (Table B1.1a). Many factors come to bear on these relative positions. High-expenditure countries may be enrolling larger numbers of students, while low-expenditure countries may either be very efficient in delivering education or limiting access to higher levels of education. Enrolment distributions between sectors and fields of study may differ, as may length of studies and the scale and organisation of linked research activities.

In nine of the 12 OECD countries for which comparable trend data are available, public and private investment in education has increased since 1990 in real terms. In Australia and Spain, the increase was 20% and in Ireland more than 30%. Spending in Finland, Hungary, and Turkey, however, was lower in 1995 than in 1990. The trend is similar when public investment is considered exclusively: direct public expenditure for institutions and public subsidies to households have increased in 15 of 19 countries since 1990. Only in Hungary, Italy, and Turkey did public expenditure on education decrease substantially between 1990 and 1995, substantial by about 20-25%.

The same table shows that in almost all OECD countries for which comparable trend data are available, education expenditure grew faster than national wealth. In France, Mexico, Norway, Spain, and Switzerland, public expenditure on educational institutions as a percentage of GDP increased by between about 0.5 and 1.4 percentage points from 1990 to 1995. Mexico showed the largest increase, from 3.2% of GDP in 1990 to 4.6% in 1995, reaching the level of spending in the Netherlands and the United

Kingdom. In Finland, the decrease of educational spending in real term followed a decline in GDP between 1990 and 1995, although considering the figures relative to GDP, Finland invests now a larger share of national wealth in education than it did in 1990. In Italy and Turkey, by contrast, public expenditure as a percentage of GDP declined sharply, despite an increase in GDP.

Government Support for Education as a Share of Total Public Expenditure

One way of looking at public investment in education is to examine direct public expenditure on educational services, public subsidies to the private sector, and total public educational expenditure as a percentage of total public expenditure. If the social returns (both private and public benefits) from a particular service are higher than the private benefits alone, markets alone may fail to provide those services adequately. Education is one area where all governments intervene to fund or direct the provision of services, not least to ensure that education is universally accessible. Education, however, is one of many competing areas.

The share of a government's budget that is devoted to education is a function of the perceived value of education relative to other public investments such as health care, social security for the unemployed and the elderly, and defence and security. Governments can fund education primarily through direct transfers to educational institutions or through public subsidies to households and other private entities. The volume of public spending on education is also influenced by the volume of private funding.

OECD countries devote 12.6% of total government outlays to support education, with values ranging between 8 and 23%. The educational budget is below 10% in Germany, Greece, Hungary, Italy, Japan, and the Netherlands and ranges from 16 to 23% in Korea, Mexico, and Norway. These figures cover direct expenditure on educational institutions and public subsidies to households and to other private entities (subsidies to firms or labour organisations that operate apprenticeship programmes).

In most OECD countries, public institutions organise and deliver publicly funded education although in some countries the final funding is transferred to government-dependent private institutions or given directly to households to spend in the institution of their choice. In the former case, the final spending and delivery of education could be considered to be subcontracted by governments to non-governmental institutions, whereas in the latter, students and their families choose the institution that best meets their requirements.

The relative size of public budgets (as measured by public spending divided by GDP) is inversely related to the relative proportion of public expenditure devoted to

89

education. For example, in Korea and Mexico, where public spending is low relative to overall GDP, the proportion dedicated to education is relatively high. Likewise, in countries such as Italy or the Netherlands, where education accounts for a relatively low proportion of total public spending, total public spending relative to GDP is high. Clearly, public funding of education is a priority in all countries, even those with little public involvement in other areas.

The relative size of a country's population of young people, a second issue, determines the potential demand for initial education and training. The larger the proportion, the more resources have to be devoted to education. In Denmark, Finland, Germany, Italy, Sweden, and Switzerland, the proportion of youth is below the OECD average where in Mexico and Korea, the proportion of young people is above the OECD average. Were this proportion equal to the OECD average, public spending on education would decrease by 2.9 and 10 percentage points respectively.

The degree of private sector involvement in the funding of education also affects government allocations (Table B3.1). In general, countries that require students to pay tuition fees and/or to fund most or all of their living expenses appear to devote a smaller percentage of total public funds to tertiary education than countries that provide "free" education and/or generous public subsidies to students. Similarly, where private enterprises contribute substantially to the education of students (*e.g.* in countries with the dual system of apprenticeship), governments also devote a comparatively smaller proportion of public expenditure to education.

Finally, variations in the proportion of total public spending on education tend to reflect differences in the scope of the education sector between countries and differences in the breadth and depth of public-sector involvement in areas outside education. Austria, Denmark, France, Germany, and Sweden spend relatively large amounts on their social-security and national health-care systems, and may appear to be spending relatively small proportions of their public budget on education, although both students and educational institutions may still benefit directly or indirectly from other forms of public expenditure. Some countries provide tax reductions, tax subsidies, or other special tax provisions to students and households unaccounted for in the educational expenditure shown here.

Relative Shares of Public and Private Investment in Education

Cost-sharing between the participants in education and society as a whole is a vigorously debated issue in some countries. The issue is especially relevant at the beginning and ending stages of education where the practice of full or near-full public funding is less common in some countries. As new client groups increase their participation, and as the choices of what, when, how, and where to learn expand, governments are forging new partnerships to mobilise the necessary resources, encourage efficiency, and introduce flexibility to permit everyone to pursue the pathways and learning opportunities which best meet their requirements. New policies are designed to allow the different actors and stakeholders to participate more fully and to share the costs and benefits more equitably. Public funding is consequently seen increasingly as providing only a part, albeit an important part, of the investment in education; private sources are playing an increasingly important role. Many countries are concerned that this balance should not become so tilted as to lead potential learners away from, instead of towards, learning.

Education remains a mainly public enterprise with a substantial and growing degree of private financing for "visible costs". Table B3.1 shows the relative proportions of funds for educational institutions from public and private sources. The first set of columns shows the distribution of the source of expenditures before public-to-private or private-to-public transfers have occurred, or the original source of funds.

The second set of columns shows expenditures after transfers, or final sources. Among the 12 OECD countries reporting data, the proportion of private sector funding for educational institutions ranges from 3% or below in Italy, the Netherlands, and Sweden to over 18% in Australia and Germany. Final funds from private sources capture all education fees (e.g. tuition) paid to educational institutions, for example, including the proportion supported by public subsidies to households. Taking into account public-to-private transfers of funds changes the picture for some countries. In Australia, Canada, Ireland, Italy, and the Netherlands public-to-private transfers of funds raise the share of the private sector in educational funding by between 2.4 and 7.3 percentage points. In these countries, student tuition subsidies account for most public-to-private transfers. Data on both private expenditure and on the share of public subsidies spent on educational institutions are unavailable for many countries. It can be assumed that for all countries that report final funds but not initial sources, public-to-private transfers play an important role in financing education. In Korea and the United States, private sector expenditure is comprised mainly of household expenditure for tuition and fees in tertiary institutions; in Germany almost all private expenditure is accounted for by contributions of the enterprise sector to the dual system of apprenticeship at the upper secondary level.

Countries vary most with respect to tertiary education. The individual, business, and other private sources' share of expenditure, net of public financial aid to students, ranges from less than 2% in Denmark and the Netherlands to over 25% in Argentina, Australia, Chile, the Czech Republic, and Israel. In Hungary, Ireland, and Spain the private share of initial funds still exceeds 20%. In Japan, Korea, and the United States, private sources provide final funds of over 50%.

91

Taxation, spending policies, and the willingness of governments to support students affects the amounts incurred by students and their families for tuition and other education-related expenditures. These vary by country and by student age, domicile, and enrolment (full or part time). To some extent, however, the patterns which have helped establish these subsidy patterns are breaking down. Increasing numbers of more mature students (Indicator C3) are more likely to have established their own households and to prefer part-time and distance learning to full-time, on-campus study.

Considering the public and private shares of educational spending jointly with total education spending as a percentage of GDP shows that some of the countries with the highest total spending relative to national income - the United States, Australia, and Korea - muster these resources with substantial help from private sources. Conversely, in countries with relatively low overall spending such as Italy and Austria, private individuals tend to contribute relatively little. There are exceptions to this pattern.'

In many countries, families are becoming increasingly important for financing education. In Australia, Canada, Denmark, Hungary, and Ireland, direct private expenditure on educational institutions has increased by between 38 and 115%, whereas the increase in direct public funds to educational institutions was not more than 31%. Changes are most striking in tertiary education. In many countries, the growth in tertiary participation represents a strong response to individual and social demand, but the financing mechanisms are outdated. Notwithstanding the major financial role for governments, tertiary education costs learners more in many countries.

Individual data on countries show that where private household spending on tuition fees, education-related services, and living costs has increased, the increase has been due to one or more of four factors: increased enrolments; increased or new fees, charges, or contributions; increased costs of education-related goods and services other than institutions; or increasing enrolments in private institutions with higher fees. It is noteworthy that increased tuition fees and educational costs have not generally implied that increased private spending is accompanied by lower public expenditure on education. To the contrary, *Education at a Glance* shows that public investment in education has also increased in most countries for which 1990-1995 data are available. Some countries with the highest growth in private spending have also shown the highest increase in public funds for education.

Between 1990 and 1995, public spending on tertiary education institutions and on financial aid for students increased by 26% in Australia, where private spending doubled, and by 33% in Ireland, where private spending increased by more than two-thirds. In Hungary, direct public expenditures declined while private expenditure more than doubled, and in Spain both public and private expenditure increased by about a third. Public spending increases were broadly similar in France and Japan (30 and 23%, respectively), although private spending rose more slowly (23 and 16%). In the Netherlands, public funding remained more or less stable although private spending increased by 24%. There and in Canada, household spending on tertiary education has grown more rapidly than has public support.

In Denmark, Germany, Iceland, Italy, the Netherlands, Sweden, and the United Kingdom, the expansion in tertiary education has been financed mainly from public budgets, with little or negligible private spending (less than 9% of total expenditure on educational institutions).

Governments can purchase educational services directly (for example, by paying teacher salaries), transfer funds to educational institutions through various allocation mechanisms, or give money to students (scholarships, grants, or loans) to spend in educational institutions. By making the funding for educational institutions depend on a student's choice to enrol, governments provide incentives for organising programmes and teaching to better meet student requirements, thereby reducing the costs of failure and mismatches. Tuition subsidies are one method, and direct public funding of institutions based on student enrolments or credit hours, which is practised in most OECD countries, is another.

For primary and secondary education, most public money is spent either directly by governments or transferred to educational institutions to acquire resources, more variation in spending patterns exists at the tertiary level. In 12 of 27 countries, more than 20% of public spending at the tertiary level is transferred to households or to recipients other than educational institutions (enterprises or labour unions) which spend these funds at least partly on educational institutions.

Public funds for students' education costs are provided through scholarships, grants and loans (generally included in these data) or through cash or kind subsidies, such as free or reduced-price public transport travel, and family or child allowances contingent on student status (covered, albeit unevenly, across countries in these data). Private student loans are counted as private expenditure, although any interest rate subsidies or government payments for defaults are captured under public funding. In Denmark, Luxembourg and the United Kingdom, between 28 and 55% of public expenditure at the tertiary level goes to scholarships and household grants. In Iceland, New Zealand, Norway, and Sweden, between 18 and 30% of public expenditure is for student loans (reported on a gross basis, without subtracting or netting out repayments or interest payments from borrowers). In Australia, New Zealand, Norway and the United Kingdom, where tertiary education is expanding, particularly in fee-based institutions, public to private transfers are often seen as a means to expand access for lower-income students.

Educational Expenditure per Student

There is no known optimal volume of resources for preparing a student for life and work in the modern economy. The demand for high-quality education, which can translate into higher costs per student, must be balanced against the need to avoid unduly burdening taxpayers. Policy-makers must also balance the importance of improving the quality of educational services with the desirability of expanding access to educational opportunities. A comparison of evolving trends in per-student expenditure shows how expanding enrolments in many countries, particularly in tertiary education, have affected per-student resource allocations. International comparisons of these allocations can be a starting point for evaluating the effectiveness of different models of educational provision.

OECD countries as a whole spend about USD 5 210 per student each year, all levels of education combined: USD 3 595 at primary level, USD 4 970 at secondary level, and USD 10 440 at tertiary level (Table B4.1)[18]. These totals are heavily influenced by the high expenditure in the United States. The simple mean across all countries amounts to USD 3 545 at the primary level, USD 4 605 at secondary level and USD 8 130 at tertiary level. These averages mask a broad range of expenditure per student across OECD countries. Excluding the countries with the two highest and two lowest expenditures, expenditures range from about USD 2 000 to USD 5 600 at the primary level, from USD 2 000 to USD 6 800 at secondary level, and from less than USD 5 000 to more than USD 13 000 at tertiary level. These comparisons are based on purchasing power parities (PPP) rather than market exchange rates, and therefore reflect the amount of a national currency that will buy the same basket of goods and services in a country as the US dollar will in the United States. These adjustments do not adjust for differences in the cost of educational resources of equivalent quality.

Table B4.1 also shows that expenditure per primary school student in non-member countries for which data are shown ranges from around USD 350 or less in the Philippines, to between USD 1 100 and about USD 1 800 in Argentina, Chile, and Malaysia (roughly comparable to spending levels in the Czech Republic, Hungary, and Mexico), and USD 3 160 in Israel. With USD 710 and USD 870, Jordan and Brazil spend far less than any OECD country. If spending per student is compared to GDP per capita, however, Brazil at 15% and Jordan at 20% reach values around the OECD average of 20%. The same table shows that for secondary education, Greece, Hungary and Mexico spend less than USD 2 000 per student, whereas Austria, Switzerland, and the United States spend more than USD 6 800. Spending among non-member countries ranges from around USD 750 or less in Indonesia, Jordan, and the Philippines to USD 1 570-4 300 in Argentina, Chile, Israel, and Malaysia.

At the tertiary level, expenditure per student varies by almost a factor of six. Greece, Hungary, and Spain report per-student expenditure of less than USD 5 000; Canada,

Sweden, Switzerland, and the United States report spending between USD 11 000 and over USD 16 000 per year. Tertiary spending per student in Chile, Israel and Malaysia exceeds the OECD average. It would be misleading to equate generally lower unit-expenditure with poorer educational services, however. The Czech Republic, the Netherlands, Japan, and Korea have comparatively moderate expenditure per student but the best student performances in mathematics (Indicator F1).

Expenditure per student exhibits a common pattern throughout the OECD: it rises sharply with the level of education in each country, and is dominated by personnel costs. The main determinants of expenditure, particularly the place and mode of educational provision, explain the pattern. The vast majority of education still takes place in traditional school and university settings with similar organisations, curricula, teaching styles, and management.

The labour-intensiveness of the traditional education model accounts for the predominance of teachers' salaries in overall costs. Differences in student/teaching staff ratios (Indicator B7), staffing patterns, teachers' salaries (Indicator E1), teaching materials, and facilities influence cost differences between levels of education, types of programmes, and types of schools. New information technologies may achieve future gains in efficiency by holding down unit costs and maintain, if not improve, learning outcomes. Unit cost savings may also be available by expanding distance education, using technology intensively or not.

Institutional arrangements often adapt to changing demographic conditions only after a considerable lag, and can also influence unit expenditure. For example, a declining number of primary students may lead to higher unit costs if staffing is not reduced and/or schools closed in proportion. Conversely, when enrolment increases, class size may increase and teachers may teach outside their field of specialisation, etc. In addition, different national price levels of educational services, in so far as they deviate from overall price levels accounted for in the PPPs, affect country differences in unit expenditure.

In 10 of the 13 countries for which comparable trend data are available for primary and secondary education, per-student expenditure increased between 1990 and 1995, as did enrolment in many of them (Table B4.1 and B4.2). In Ireland and Spain, expenditure per primary and secondary student rose by 33 and 25%, respectively, even as enrolments declined. Only in Finland and Italy did expenditure per primary and secondary student decrease by more than nine percentage points between 1990 and 1995. In Italy, this was despite a simultaneous decrease in enrolments. In Mexico, expenditure per primary student has more than doubled between 1990-1995, from about USD 400 in 1990 to more than USD 1 000 in 1995 (this increase may be slightly overestimated due to incomplete coverage of 1990 expenditure data). In Austria, Ireland, and Spain, the increase exceeded 34%.

At secondary level, per student expenditure increased by two-thirds in Mexico and by about one-fifth or more in Ireland, Spain, and Switzerland between 1990 and 1995. Finland, Germany (FTFR), Italy, and the United Kingdom show a decline in spending per secondary student.

In seven of 12 OECD countries, tertiary expenditure has kept pace with an often dramatic increase in enrolments: in Australia, Austria, Canada, Finland, France, Germany, Mexico, and Spain, expenditure in 1995 was the same as or higher than in 1990. In Australia and Spain, expenditure increased much faster than enrolments, leading to increases in expenditure per tertiary student of 14 and 34% respectively. Even in Ireland where tertiary enrolment grew by over 50% between 1990 and 1995, educational expenditure has almost kept pace. In the Netherlands and the United Kingdom, enrolments increased faster than total expenditure, and expenditure per student in 1995 was lower than in 1990. In Italy, a decrease in funding for tertiary education coupled with an increase in enrolments has led to a decline of 30% in spending per student.

Expenditure per student relative to GDP per capita is a measure that takes into account the number of students that a country is trying to educate as well as its relative wealth. As education is universal at lower levels, spending per student relative to GDP per capita here can be interpreted as the resources spent on young people relative to a country's ability to pay. For higher levels of education, this measure is affected by a combination of wealth, spending, and enrolment rates. At the tertiary level, for example, countries can be relatively high on this measure if they spend a relatively large portion of their wealth on educating relatively few students. For the OECD as a whole, expenditure per student averages 18% of GDP per capita at the primary level, 25% at the secondary level and 49% at the tertiary level.

Table B4.2 shows the clear, positive relationship between spending per student and per capita GDP, showing that poorer countries tend to spend relatively less per student than richer countries as measured by per capita GDP. However, although the relationship between spending per student and GDP per capita is generally positive, per-student spending varies considerably among both richer and poorer countries. The Czech Republic, Japan, Jordan, the United Kingdom, and the United States, five countries with vastly different levels of per capita wealth, all spend about the OECD country mean of 20% to educate the typical primary student. At the primary level, spending is seven percentage points or more above the country mean in Austria, Denmark, and Sweden, and at least six percentage points below in Ireland and Mexico.

The picture is similar for secondary education. Among the poorest OECD countries, Greece spends a relatively small amount of per capita GDP to educate the average secondary student (16%), while Hungary, Indonesia, and Malaysia spend substantially more (between 22 and 23%). Among the wealthiest OECD countries, Japan and the United States spend only 20 and 26% of per capita GDP to educate the average secondary student, while Switzerland spends 30%.

The range in spending across countries on this measure is much wider for tertiary education than for primary. For example, in Chile, Hungary, Malaysia, Mexico, and Sweden tertiary spending per student relative to GDP per capita is more than 20 percentage points above the OECD country mean of 47%. At the other end of the scale, Greece and Italy spend 20 percentage points or more below the OECD country mean.

Cross-country comparisons of the distribution of expenditure across levels of education are an indication of the relative emphasis on education at different levels, and the relative costs of providing education at those levels. Although expenditure per student rises with the level of education in almost all countries, the relative size of the differences varies markedly across countries. At secondary level, expenditure per student averages 1.38 times more than that at primary level, although the variation ranges from 1.04 times in Hungary to more than 1.75 times in the Flemish community of Belgium, France, Germany, and Mexico. Nearly two-thirds of the countries' expenditure per secondary student is between around 1.10 and 1.60 times that at the primary level.

Although OECD countries spend, on average, 2.54 times more per student at the tertiary level than at the primary level, spending patterns vary widely. Italy only spends 1.07 times more for a tertiary student than for a primary student where Mexico spends five times more. These differentials may even underestimate real differences in costs, as in some countries funding provided for tertiary education by private sources has not been adequately taken into account.

Since the length and intensity of tertiary study vary between countries, international variations in annual expenditure per student on educational services as shown in Table B4.1 do not accurately reflect the variability in the total cost of educating the typical tertiary student. Students can choose from institutions and enrolment options to find the best fit between their objectives, abilities, personal interests, and social and economic circumstances. Many students attend school part-time, while working, or attend sporadically, or attend more than one institution before graduating. These patterns can affect the interpretability of expenditure per student.

Country ranking by annual expenditure per student on educational services is strongly affected by differences in definitions of full-time, part-time, and full-time-equivalent enrolment. Some countries count every participant at the tertiary level as a full-time student while others determine a student's participation by the credits obtained for successful completion of specific course units during a specified reference

97

period. Countries that can accurately account for part-time enrolment will spend more per full-time equivalent student than those that cannot differentiate among modes of student attendance.

Similarly, comparatively low annual expenditure per student may result in comparatively high overall costs of tertiary education where tertiary studies are relatively long. For example, annual spending of USD 12 217 per university, or equivalent, student in Canada is about a third higher than in Germany where the figure is USD 9 001. Differences in the tertiary degree structure (Indicator C4) make the average duration of university-equivalent studies of 6.7 years more than twice as long in Germany which provides only "long university or equivalent programmes", compared with 2.5 years in Canada, which provides mostly "short" university-equivalent programmes. The aggregate expenditure for each university-equivalent student is therefore almost twice as high in Germany at USD 60 271 as in Canada, at USD 30 707.

Although the Netherlands spends 17% more per university student each year than does Austria, tertiary studies in Austria last 6.4 years compared with 3.9 years in the Netherlands: total spending in Austria is USD 57 256 compared with only USD 35 202 in the Netherlands. In Canada, short tertiary studies translate an above-average annual cost into a below-average total cost. Total costs per university student in Austria and Germany of about USD 60 000 are about twice the costs in Australia, Canada, Korea, Italy and Spain. In Switzerland, at USD100 000, the total costs for university studies is even higher. These differences must be interpreted in light of possible cross-country differences in the knowledge-intensity of the qualifications of students leaving university.

Deployment of Resources Across Different Resource Categories

Allocations among different functional categories can affect the quality of instruction (teachers' salaries), the condition of educational facilities (school maintenance), and the ability of the education system to adjust to changing demographic and enrolment trends (building new schools). Comparing national distribution of educational expenditure between resource categories gives some insight into variations in the organisation and operation of educational institutions. System level budgetary and structural resource allocation decisions eventually affect the classroom, the nature of instruction, and the conditions under which it is provided.

Educational expenditure can first be divided into capital expenditure[19], or outlays for assets that last longer than one year and include building, renovation, and major repairs, and current expenditures, the annual outlays for school resources to operate schools. Current expenditure can be further divided into teacher compensation, compensation of other staff, and expenditure other than compensation. The amount allocated to each of these functional categories depends partly on current and projected changes in enrolments, salaries, and facility maintenance and construction costs[20].

Education takes place mostly in school and university settings. Its labour-intensive technology explains the large proportion of current spending in total educational expenditure. In primary and secondary education combined, current expenditure accounts for 92% of total outlays on average across all OECD countries. In terms of expenditure per full-time equivalent student enrolled, this amounts to an average of USD 3 847, using PPP indices. The corresponding figure for capital outlays is USD 315 per student.

Countries vary widely with respect to the relative proportion of current and capital spending: at the primary/secondary level, the capital proportion ranges from less than 5% in Canada, Ireland, Italy, Mexico, and the Netherlands, to 15 and 20%, respectively in Japan and Korea (Table B5.1). The picture is similar among the OECD non-member countries for which data are shown, ranging from 3% in India to 13% in Jordan, Malaysia, and the Philippines.

Teacher and other educational staff salaries comprise the bulk of current expenditure in OECD and non-member countries alike. On average across OECD countries, salaries account for 82% of current expenditure at primary and secondary levels combined (equivalent to USD 3 063 spent per full-time equivalent student). In the Czech Republic and Sweden, only 60% of expenditure is devoted to staff compensation, and in Greece, Korea, Luxembourg, Mexico, Portugal and Turkey, the proportion is above 90%. In Greece, Hungary, Ireland, and Mexico, this commitment leaves around USD 400 or less per full-time student for such expenditures as teaching materials and supplies, building maintenance, preparation of student meals, and rental of school facilities.

OECD countries with relatively smaller education budgets (Greece, Mexico, and Portugal) tend to devote a larger share of current educational expenditure to educational staff compensation and less to other contracted and purchased services such as support services (for maintenance), ancillary services (preparing student meals), and rents for buildings and facilities. The notable exceptions to this pattern are the Czech Republic and Hungary, which spend less than the OECD average (82% of current expenditure) on the compensation of staff (60 and 75% respectively) for primary and secondary education combined. The pattern is less uniform among non-member countries for which data are shown.

Expenditure distribution by resource category and the proportion of expenditure accounted for by educational staff compensation in particular depends on the ratio of

99

students to teaching staff, teachers' salaries, the number of instructional hours, and the division of teachers' time between teaching and other duties.

In Denmark and the United States, around 25% of staff expenditure in primary and secondary education combined goes towards compensating personnel other than teachers; in the Flemish community of Belgium, Ireland and Luxembourg, the figure is 6% or less. These differences are likely to reflect the degree to which educational personnel specialise in non-teaching activities (e.g. principals who do not teach, guidance counsellors, bus drivers, school nurses, janitors, and maintenance workers), and the relative salaries of teaching and non-teaching personnel.

In practice, the allocation of salary expenditure between teaching and non-teaching personnel is not clear-cut because of definitions. Some countries define teachers narrowly as those who teach students in the classroom; others count heads of schools and other professional personnel as teachers. These and other differences in definitions, in addition to differences between countries in the coverage of non-teaching staff, mean that the variation observed in the reported percentages of expenditure on non-teaching staff should be viewed with caution.

Among the 13 OECD countries for which data are available, the average amount of teacher compensation per student ranges from below USD 1 000 in the Czech Republic to over USD 4 400 in Switzerland (Table B5.1). At tertiary level, the proportion of total expenditure spent on capital outlays is larger than at primary/secondary level. In 14 of 25 OECD countries, capital expenditure accounts for more than 10%, and in Greece, Italy, Japan, Korea, and Spain, it is between 20 and 28% (Table B5.1)[21]. Malaysia invests more than 31% of total tertiary expenditure in capital outlays, Brazil, and India, by contrast, invest only 5%.

This difference can also be seen in comparisons of the average capital outlay per student, although the distribution is wide. At the tertiary level, capital outlays per student range from less than USD 460 in the Flemish community of Belgium, Finland, Hungary, and the United Kingdom to more than USD 1 800 in Japan and Switzerland. These wide differences are likely to reflect varying national tertiary education organisation and the degree to which new construction is accommodating growing enrolments.

At the same time, the proportion of current expenditure spent on staff is considerably lower at the tertiary level than at the primary/secondary level: all OECD countries for which data are available spend 16% or more of current expenditure on something other than compensating educational personnel. The proportion is 30% or more in more than half of the countries. This trend is similar among non-member countries for which data are shown, with the share of current expenditure other than for the compensation of personnel reaching as much as 47% in Malaysia.

Educational Investment and Outcomes

Educational spending is at least 5% of GDP in most countries; at this level, education systems must provide good value for money. The factors underpinning economic growth are complex but the OECD education indicators point to a *positive relationship* between expenditure for education and macroeconomic performance. Higher education in particular has significant *private benefits* that create a pressure to shift some of the cost to individuals (Indicators E4 and E5). Despite high investments, however, education outcomes remain uneven. *Education at a Glance* includes some of the more disappointing results:

• Variations in student achievement lead to unequal prospects in adulthood. University education adds most to individuals' earnings: graduates earn typically 20-100% more than upper secondary graduates by mid-career. Adult university graduates also receive, on average, twice as much training as upper secondary graduates, who in turn receive twice as much as those with only lower secondary education. Education thus combines with other influences to make adult learning least common among those who need it most. Male tertiary graduates enjoy, on average across OECD countries, six more years of employment than men who have not completed upper secondary education; for women, the gap is 11 years.

• The gap between high- and low-achieving pupils grows progressively while they are at school and is generally wider at age 13 than at age 9. In Korea, student performance at age 9 is relatively uniform but at age 13 it is more variable than in any other OECD country, although spread around at a very high average achievement level. Schools in some countries succeed in limiting this rise in dispersion. In Scotland and in Greece, student scores do not become significantly more dispersed over the four grade years.

• Just about two-thirds of students enrolling in degree courses at universities complete them. On average, 34% of young people enrol in university-level studies; 22% leave with a degree. Completion rates range from above 80% in the Hungary, Japan, and the United Kingdom, to below 40% in Italy.

• If a child has a well-educated parent, the chances of being well-educated are at least doubled. A new indicator of "intergenerational educational mobility" compares how many adults have graduated from tertiary education according to the highest educational level of their parents. Typically, people whose parents never completed upper secondary education have a less than one-in-five chance of becoming tertiary graduates, whereas students whose parents were graduates have a two- to three-in-five chance.

101

Table B1.1a. **Educational Expenditure as a Percentage of GDP for all Levels of Education Combined, by Source of Funds (1995)**

	1995							1990	
	Direct public expenditure for educational institutions	Total public subsidies to households and other private entities excluding public subsidies for student living costs	Private payments to educational institutions excluding public subsidies to households and other private entities	Total expenditure from both public and private sources for educational institutions	Total expenditure from public, private and international sources for educational institutions plus public subsidies to households	Private payments other than to educational institutions	Financial aid to students not attributable to household payments to educational institutions for educational services	Direct public expenditure for educational institutions	Total expenditure from both public and private sources for educational institutions
Australia	4.5	0.18	1.00	5.6	6.1	0.48	0.48	4.3	4.9
Austria	5.3	0.21	n	5.5	5.6	a	0.12	5.2	m
Belgium (Flemish Community)	5.0	m	m	m	m	m	0.04	4.8	m
Canada	5.8	0.51	0.73	7.0	7.3	m	0.33	5.4	5.7
Czech Republic	4.8	n	0.84	5.7	6.0	m	0.34	m	m
Denmark	6.5	0.11	0.47	7.1	8.5	m	1.39	6.2	6.4
Finland	6.6	m	x	6.6	7.3	0.63	0.63	6.4	6.4
France	5.8	x	0.54	6.3	6.6	0.26	0.26	5.1	5.6
Germany	4.5	0.01	1.29	5.8	6.0	m	0.21	m	m
Greece	3.7	n	m	3.7	3.7	m	n	m	m
Hungary	4.9	n	0.61	5.5	5.7	m	0.16	5.0	5.3
Iceland	4.5	x	0.62	5.2	5.5	0.22	0.34	4.3	4.8
Ireland	4.7	0.12	0.42	5.3	5.7	m	0.37	4.7	5.2
Italy	4.5	0.12	0.01	4.7	4.7	m	0.03	5.8	m
Japan	3.6	m	1.16	4.7	4.7	m	m	3.6	4.7
Korea	3.6	m	2.58	6.2	6.2	m	n	m	m
Luxembourg	4.3	0.04	m	m	m	m	0.11	m	m
Mexico	4.6	x	0.97	5.6	5.6	0.32	x	3.2	m
Netherlands	4.6	0.24	0.12	4.9	5.4	0.60	0.47	m	m
New Zealand	5.3	0.28	m	m	m	m	0.59	5.5	m
Norway	6.8	n	m	m	m	m	x	6.2	m

	1995					1990			
	Direct public expenditure for educational institutions	Total public subsidies to households and other private entities excluding public subsidies for student living costs	Private payments to educational institutions excluding public subsidies to households and other private entities	Total expenditure from both public and private sources for educational institutions	Total expenditure from public, private and international sources for educational institutions plus public subsidies to households	Private payments other than to educational institutions	Financial aid to students not attributable to household payments to educational institutions for educational services	Direct public expenditure for educational institutions	Total expenditure from both public and private sources for educational institutions
Sweden	6.6	n	0.11	6.7	7.9	1.20	1.20	m	m
Switzerland	5.5	0.06	m	m	m	m	5.0	m	
Turkey	2.2	x	0.21	2.4	2.5	m	3.2	3.2	
United Kingdom	4.6	0.22	m	m	m	0.31	4.3	m	
United States	5.0	x	1.67	6.7	6.7	0.15	m	m	
Country Mean	**4.9**	**0.12**	**0.75**	**5.6**	**5.9**	**0.43**			
OECD Total	**4.7**	**0.13**	**1.20**	**5.9**	**6.0**	**0.24**			
WEI Participants									
Argentina [1]	3.4	n	0.75	4.1	4.2	n	m	m	
Brazil	5.0	0.11	m	m	m	m	m	m	
Chile [1]	3.0	0.10	2.51	5.6	5.6	m	m	m	
India [1]	2.4	x	0.21	2.6	3.8	m	m	m	
Israel [2]	7.0	0.10	1.20	8.3	8.3	0.50	m	m	
Malaysia [1]	4.9	0.07	0.11	5.1	5.1	m	m	m	
Paraguay [1]	3.1	m	m	m	m	m	m	m	
Philippines	3.0	m	m	m	m	m	m	m	
Russian Federation	3.4	n	m	m	m	n	m	m	
Thailand [1]	3.6	m	m	m	m	m	m	m	
Uruguay [1]	2.7	n	m	m	m	m	m	m	

[1] 1996 data.
[2] 1994 data.

Source: OECD Education Database.

Table B1.1c **Educational Expenditure as a Percentage of GDP for Tertiary Education, by Source of Funds (1995)**

	1995					1990			
	Direct public expenditure for educational institutions	Total public subsidies to households and other private entities excluding public subsidies for student living costs	Private payments to educational institutions excluding public subsidies to households and other private entities	Total expenditure from both public and private sources for educational institutions	Total expenditure from public, private and international sources for educational institutions plus public subsidies to households	Private payments other than to educational institutions	Financial aid to students not attributable to household payments to educational institutions for educational services	Direct public expenditure for educational institutions	Total expenditure from both public and private sources for educational institutions
Australia	1.2	0.15	0.49	1.8	2.0	0.20	0.20	1.0	1.2
Austria	0.9	0.20	n	1.0	1.0	a	a	1.0	m
Belgium (Flemish Community)	0.9	m	m	m	m	0.03	0.03	0.8	m
Canada	1.5	0.51	0.45	2.5	2.8	0.46	0.30	1.5	1.8
Czech Republic	0.7	n	0.31	1.0	1.1	m	0.08	m	m
Denmark	1.3	x	0.01	1.3	1.9	0.63	0.63	1.3	1.3
Finland	1.7	m	x	1.7	2.1	0.40	0.40	1.2	1.2
France	1.0	x	0.18	1.1	1.2	0.09	0.10	0.8	0.9
Germany	1.0	0.01	0.07	1.1	1.2	m	0.10	m	m
Greece	0.8	n	m	0.8	0.8	m	0.01	0.8	0.8
Hungary	0.8	n	0.20	1.0	1.2	m	0.13	0.8	0.8
Iceland	0.7	m	0.05	0.7	1.0	m	m	0.6	0.7
Ireland	0.9	0.12	0.28	1.3	1.5	m	0.17	0.9	1.2
Italy	0.7	0.06	0.07	0.8	0.8	0.06	x	1.0	m
Japan	0.4	m	0.58	1.0	1.0	m	m	0.4	0.9
Korea	0.3	m	1.58	1.9	1.9	m	n	m	m
Luxembourg	0.1	x	m	m	m	m	m	m	m
Mexico	0.8	n	0.24	1.1	1.1	0.03	x	0.7	0.7
Netherlands	1.1	0.13	0.02	1.3	1.6	0.34	0.28	m	m
New Zealand	1.1	0.23	m	m	m	m	0.39	1.2	1.2
Norway	1.5	n	m	m	m	m	m	1.1	m
Poland	0.8	m	m	m	m	m	m	m	m
Portugal	1.0	a	m	1.0	1.0	m	0.04	m	m

	1995					1990			
	Direct public expenditure for educational institutions	Total public subsidies to households and other private entities excluding public subsidies for student living costs	Private payments to educational institutions excluding public subsidies to households and other private entities	Total expenditure from both public and private sources for educational institutions	Total expenditure from public, private and international sources for educational institutions plus public subsidies to households	Private payments other than to educational institutions	Financial aid to students not attributable to household payments to educational institutions for educational services	Direct public expenditure for educational institutions	Total expenditure from both public and private sources for educational institutions
Spain	0.8	n	0.25	1.1	1.1	0.09	0.06	0.7	0.8
Sweden	1.6	n	0.11	1.7	2.3	0.59	0.59	m	m
Switzerland	1.1	0.01	m	m	m	m	0.04	1.0	m
Turkey	0.8	m	m	m	m	m	m	0.9	m
United Kingdom	0.7	0.19	0.11	1.0	1.3	0.28	m	0.7	0.7
United States	1.1	x	1.24	2.4	2.4	0.11	m	m	m
Country Mean	**0.9**	**0.10**	**0.33**	**1.3**	**1.5**	**0.24**	**0.19**		
OECD Total	**0.9**	**0.11**	**0.67**	**1.6**	**1.7**	**0.15**	**0.16**		
WEI Participants									
Argentina [1]	0.7	n	0.28	1.0	1.0	n	n	m	m
Brazil	1.2	0.11	m	m	m	m	m	m	m
Chile [1]	0.4	0.10	1.33	1.8	1.8	m	n	m	m
India [1]	0.6	x	0.13	0.7	0.7	m	n	m	m
Israel [2]	1.2	0.05	0.53	1.8	1.8	m	n	m	m
Malaysia [1]	1.1	0.06	0.05	1.2	1.2	m	m	m	m
Paraguay [1]	0.8	m	m	m	m	m	m	m	m
Philippines	0.5	m	m	m	m	m	m	m	m
Russian Federation	0.7	n	m	m	m	n	n	m	m
Thailand [1]	0.7	m	m	m	m	m	m	m	m
Uruguay [1]	0.7	n	m	m	m	m	n	m	m

[1] 1996 data.
[2] 1994 data.

Source: OECD Education Database.

105

Table B3.1. **Distribution of Public and Private Sources of Funds for Educational Institutions Before (initial funds) and After (final funds) Transfers from Public Sources, by Level of Education (1995)**

	Initial funds (original source of funds spent on education)						Final funds (after public-to-private or private-to-public transfers have occurred)					
	Primary and secondary education		Tertiary education		All levels of education combined		Primary and secondary education		Tertiary education		All levels of education combined	
	Public sources	Private sources	Public sources	Private sources	Public sources	Private sources	Public sources	Private sources	Public sources	Private sources	Public sources	Private sources
Australia	87	13	73	27	82	18	87	13	65	35	79	21
Austria	98	2	m	m	m	m	98	2	98	2	97	3
Belgium (Flemish Community)	100	n	m	m	m	m	100	n	m	m	m	m
Canada	94	6	82	18	90	10	94	6	61	39	82	18
Czech Republic	88	12	70	30	85	15	88	12	70	30	85	15
Denmark	98	2	99	1	93	7	98	2	99	1	92	8
Finland	m	m	m	m	m	m	m	m	m	m	m	m
France	93	7	84	16	91	9	93	7	84	16	91	9
Germany	76	24	93	7	78	22	76	24	92	8	78	22
Greece	m	m	m	m	m	m	m	m	m	m	m	m
Hungary	92	8	80	20	89	11	92	8	80	20	89	11
Iceland	m	m	m	m	m	m	m	m	93	7	88	12
Ireland	96	4	79	21	92	8	96	4	70	30	90	10
Italy	100	n	91	9	100	n	100	n	84	16	97	3
Japan	m	m	m	m	m	m	92	8	43	57	75	25
Korea	77	23	m	m	m	m	77	23	16	84	59	41
Luxembourg	m	m	m	m	m	m	m	m	m	m	m	m
Mexico	m	m	m	m	m	m	84	16	77	23	83	17
Netherlands	97	3	99	1	97	3	94	6	88	12	93	7
New Zealand	m	m	m	m	m	m	m	m	m	m	m	m
Norway	m	m	m	m	m	m	m	m	m	m	m	m
Poland	m	m	m	m	m	m	m	m	m	m	m	m
Portugal	m	m	m	m	m	m	m	m	m	m	m	m
Spain	87	13	76	24	84	16	87	13	76	24	84	16
Sweden	100	n	94	6	98	2	100	n	94	6	98	2

	Initial funds (original source of funds spent on education)						Final funds (after public-to-private or private-to-public transfers have occurred)					
	Primary and secondary education		Tertiary education		All levels of education combined		Primary and secondary education		Tertiary education		All levels of education combined	
	Public sources	Private sources	Public sources	Private sources	Public sources	Private sources	Public sources	Private sources	Public sources	Private sources	Public sources	Private sources
Switzerland	m	m	m	m	m	m	m	m	m	m	m	m
Turkey	m	m	m	m	m	m	88	12	m	m	91	9
United Kingdom	m	m	90	10	m	m	m	m	72	28	m	m
United States	m	m	m	m	m	m	90	10	48	52	75	25
Country Mean	**93**	**7**	**86**	**13**	**91**	**9**	**91**	**9**	**75**	**25**	**86**	**14**
WEI Participants												
Argentina [1]	87	13	66	34	83	17	87	13	66	34	83	17
Chile [1]	67	33	27	73	55	45	67	33	22	78	53	47
India [1]	96	4	m	m	m	m	95	5	82	18	93	7
Israel [2]	97	3	70	30	86	14	96	4	67	33	84	16
Malaysia [1]	98	2	96	4	98	2	98	2	91	9	96	4
Uruguay [1]	96	4	m	m	m	m	m	m	m	m	m	m

[1] 1996 data.
[2] 1994 data.

Source: OECD Education Database.

Table B4.1. **Expenditure per Student (US dollars converted using PPPs) on Public and Private Institutions by Level of Education (based on full-time equivalents) (1995)**

	Early childhood	Primary	Secondary	All	Tertiary Non-university	University-level	All levels of education combined
Australia	m	3 121	4 899	10 590	7 699	11 572	m
Austria *	4 907	5 572	7 118	7 943	12 834	7 687	6 763
Belgium (Flemish Community) **	2 391	3 270	5 770	6 043	x	x	4 694
Canada	5 378	x	x	11 471	10 434	12 217	6 717
Czech Republic	2 052	1 999	2 820	6 795	2 502	7 656	2 885
Denmark	4 964	5 713	6 247	8 157	x	x	5 968
Finland	5 901	4 253	4 946	7 315	6 933	7 412	5 323
France	3 242	3 379	6 182	6 569	x	x	5 001
Germany *	5 277	3 361	6 254	8 897	6 817	9 001	5 972
Greece **	x	x	1 950	2 716	1 750	3 169	1 991
Hungary *	1 365	1 532	1 591	4 792	a	4 792	1 782
Iceland	m	m	m	m	m	m	m
Ireland	2 108	2 144	3 395	7 249	x	x	3 272
Italy *	3 316	4 673	5 348	5 013	6 705	4 932	5 157
Japan	2 476	4 065	4 465	8 768	6 409	9 337	4 991
Korea	1 450	2 135	2 332	5 203	3 980	5 733	2 829
Luxembourg	m	m	m	m	m	m	m
Mexico	1 088	1 015	1 798	5 071	x	5 071	1 464
Netherlands	3 021	3 191	4 351	9 026	a	9 026	4 397
New Zealand	2 262	2 638	4 120	8 737	10 018	8 380	4 099
Norway *	m	m	m	9 647	x	x	6 360
Poland	m	m	m	m	m	m	m
Portugal *	m	m	m	6 073	m	m	m
Spain	2 516	2 628	3 455	4 944	3 973	4 966	3 374
Sweden	3 287	5 189	5 643	13 168	x	x	5 993
Switzerland *	2 436	5 893	7 601	15 685	8 226	18 365	7 241
Turkey *	m	m	m	m	m	m	m
United Kingdom **	5 049	3 328	4 246	7 225	x	x	4 222
United States	m	5 371	6 812	16 262	7 973	19 965	7 905

	Early childhood	Primary	Secondary	All	Tertiary Non-university	University-level	All levels of education combined
Country Mean	**3 224**	**3 546**	**4 606**	**8 134**	**6 016**	**8 781**	**4 717**
OECD Total	**2 685**	**3 595**	**4 971**	**10 444**	**7 447**	**12 018**	**5 212**
WEI Participants							
Argentina*[1]	1 075	1 158	1 575	m	m	m	m
Brazil*	562	870	1 018	m	m	m	1 121
Chile[1]	1 346	1 807	2 059	8 436	4 086	10 385	2 481
Indonesia*[1]	m	m	740	m	m	m	m
Israel[2]	2 433	3 162	4 305	10 132	7 426	10 883	4 482
Jordan*[1]	m	710	710	m	m	m	m
Malaysia[1]	395	1 228	2 308	11 016	7 290	14 520	2 176
Paraguay*[1]	m	343	492	m	20 667	m	m
Philippines*	m	337	342	m	m	m	m
Uruguay*[1]	548	920	1 022	2 441	3 340	2 289	1 092

Source : OECD Education Database.

* Public institutions.
** Public and government-dependent private institutions
[1] 1996 data.
[2] 1994 data.

109

Table B4.2. **Expenditure per Student (US dollars converted using PPPs) on Public and Private Institutions by Level of Education (1990)**

	Early childhood	Primary	Secondary	All	Tertiary Non-university	University-level	All levels of education combined
Australia	m	2 737	4 359	9 288	8 024	9 887	4 257
Austria *	3 169	3 942	6 779	7 621	11 725	7 401	6 057
Belgium (Flemish Community) **	m	m	m	m	m	m	m
Canada	4 884	m	m	11 662	13 030	10 934	6 220
Czech Republic	m	m	m	m	m	m	m
Denmark	m	m	m	m	m	m	m
Finland	6 967	4 717	5 813	7 070	7 219	7 025	5 675
France	2 506	3 106	5 382	6 601	m	m	4 546
Germany (FTFR) *	m	3 491	6 866	m	m	8 459	m
Greece **	m	m	m	m	m	m	m
Hungary *	m	m	m	m	m	m	m
Iceland	m	m	m	m	m	m	m
Ireland	1 567	1 596	2 785	8 032	m	m	6 004
Italy *	m	m	6 315	7 300	m	m	m
Japan	m	m	m	m	m	m	m
Korea	m	m	m	m	m	m	m
Luxembourg	m	m	m	m	m	m	m
Mexico *	601	484	1 233	4 463	x	4 463	862
Netherlands	2 650	2 867	4 064	10 036	a	10 036	4 164
New Zealand	m	m	m	m	m	m	m
Norway *	m	m	m	m	m	m	m
Poland	m	m	m	m	m	m	m
Portugal *	2 056	1 961	2 865	3 696	m	m	2 667
Spain	m	m	m	m	m	m	m
Sweden	m	6 287	6 937	16 022	7 091	19 663	m
Switzerland *	m	m	m	m	m	m	m
Turkey *	4 566	3 015	4 456	9 805	m	m	4 344
United Kingdom **	m	m	m	m	m	m	m
United States	m	m	m	m	m	m	m
Country Mean	3 218	3 109	4 821	8 466	m	m	4 480

Source: OECD Education Database.

*   Public institutions. ** Public and government-dependent private institutions.

B 5.1a. Educational Expenditure on Primary and Secondary Education by Resource Category for Public and Private Institutions (1995)

	Percentage of total expenditure		Percentage of current expenditure				Average compensation per student (in equivalent US dollars)				
	Current	Capital	Compensation of teachers	Compensation of other staff	Compensation of all staff	Other current expenditure	Teachers	All staff	Other current expenditure	Current	Capital
Australia	92	8	64	15	79	21	2 313	2 849	741	3 589	333
Austria	91	9	67	9	76	24	m	m	m	m	m
Belgium (Flemish Community)**	m	m	84	2	86	14	3 899	3 988	673	4 661	10
Canada	96	4	65	16	81	19	3 455	4 277	1 012	5 289	196
Czech Republic*	87	13	44	16	60	40	968	1 330	877	2 207	327
Denmark	95	5	53	27	80	20	3 044	4 566	1 168	5 733	295
Finland**	93	7	60	12	72	28	2 589	3 085	1 228	4 313	310
France	91	9	x	x	79	21	x	3 617	975	4 592	449
Germany*	92	8	x	x	76	24	x	3 262	1 057	4 319	371
Greece*	86	14	x	x	97	3	x	1 658	57	1 715	280
Hungary*	93	7	x	x	75	25	x	1 096	374	1 470	102
Iceland	88	12	x	x	71	29	m	m	m	m	m
Ireland*	96	4	84	6	89	11	2 243	2 391	288	2 679	123
Italy*	96	4	71	18	89	11	3 501	4 380	532	4 912	187
Japan	85	15	x	x	87	13	x	3 182	479	3 661	621
Korea*	80	20	90	10	100	x	1 636	1 810	x	1 810	439
Luxembourg	92	8	93	4	97	3	m	m	m	m	m
Mexico*	96	4	x	x	91	9	x	1 023	101	1 124	52
Netherlands	96	4	x	x	78	22	x	2 869	792	3 661	153
New Zealand	m	m	m	m	m	m	m	m	m	m	m
Norway*	88	12	x	x	82	18	x	4 220	900	5 120	690
Poland	m	m	m	m	m	m	m	m	m	m	m
Portugal*	93	7	x	x	96	4	x	m	m	m	m
Spain	95	5	x	x	84	16	x	2 502	486	2 988	160
Sweden	m	m	44	12	56	44	2 410	3 035	2 394	5 430	x
Switzerland*	89	11	74	12	86	14	4 452	5 174	858	6 032	771
Turkey	92	8	93	m	94	6	m	m	m	m	m
United Kingdom**	95	5	54	16	70	30	1 940	2 522	1 092	3 614	196

	Percentage of total expenditure		Percentage of current expenditure				Average compensation per student (in equivalent US dollars)				
	Current	Capital	Compensation of teachers	Compensation of other staff	Compensation of all staff	Other current expenditure	Teachers	All staff	Other current expenditure	Current	Capital
United States*	91	9	57	23	80	20	3 241	4 554	1 168	5 722	559
Country Mean	**92**	**8**	**69**	**13**	**82**	**19**	**2 745**	**3 063**	**822**	**3 847**	**315**
WEI Participants											
Argentina*[1]	93	7	66	31	97	3	617	1 190	34	1 225	93
Brazil*	92	8	x	x	84	16	x	708	133	840	69
Chile*[1]	92	8	x	x	69	31	x	943	431	1 373	127
India*[1]	97	3	85	7	91	9	m	m	m	m	m
Israel[2]	89	11	x	x	76	24	x	2 453	698	3 151	393
Jordan*[1]	87	13	83	11	94	6	512	580	39	619	91
Malaysia[1]	87	13	67	16	82	18	949	1 173	252	1 425	214
Paraguay[1]	93	7	82	12	93	7	282	324	23	346	27
Philippines*	87	13	x	x	90	10	x	264	30	294	44
Uruguay[1]	93	7	78	14	92	8	696	824	69.3	893	72

Source: OECD Education Database.

* Public institutions.
** Public and government-dependent private institutions
[1] 1996 data.
[2] 1994 data.

WHAT DO DEVELOPED COUNTRIES TODAY DEMAND FROM THEIR EDUCATIONAL SYSTEMS?

Torsten **Husén**
The Royal Swedish Academy of Sciences

Dynamic change dominates modern life and requires an individual to play several roles, including that of worker, parent, and citizen, and to constantly reorient. This has profound consequences for education from the outset. Until the 20th century, education, including formal schooling, was modelled to prepare the individual for a largely static society in two main stages and in two school systems. The child was educated in the family and then in school, either as part of a social élite planning to go to university and to take up élite positions, or as part of the majority, to prepare for civic life and unqualified jobs. At the end of the 20th century, these two systems are beginning to be integrated.

As we enter the 21st century, the school as we know it today will have to change. It will continue to prepare young people but now must equip individuals to meet change and mobilise resources to do so. This will affect pedagogical strategies. Specific substantial knowledge, which until recently has been the core of school learning, must be replaced by skills that will enable the pupils to acquire the specific competencies which will emerge from an as yet undefined repertory of tasks as working individuals and citizens.

This paper addresses the institutional, structural, and didactic changes of teaching and learning required to meet the needs of a changing society. And because socialisation by parents and the community is an important aspect of education, the role of parents and teachers and their potential replacement by technology in learning must be examined.

Characteristics of Institutional Schooling

Universal, full-time schooling is a 20th century product that developed concomitantly with the industrial society as a powerful instrument for establishing modern national states in both Europe and America. It also helped considerably in establishing a common national language by making populations within national borders literate in a standardised language. Pupils learned the history of their respective countries, often with a nationalistic bias. Universal primary school also served as a care taking or baby-sitting institution, particularly in urban industrialised areas where parents worked long hours outside the home. In rural areas, pupils often went to school part-time in order to continue helping their parents. In some countries, children were expected to learn the basics of reading (learning the alphabet) before entering school.

A 20th century school in developed countries can be broadly characterised in several ways.

- Primary school attendance is universal and compulsory. Literacy and certain concepts of society and nature must be acquired to establish a common frame of reference among citizens.

- Age specifications for school attendance have become increasingly uniform and stable, although a century ago the ages of school entry and school leaving were rather flexible, as they are today in developing countries. The schooling age crystallised at 5-6 through 12-14 years old.

- The model of "frontal" classroom instruction has become increasingly dominant as classes have become more homogeneous in age and ability. At the early stage, more advanced pupils, monitors, taught their less advanced classmates. The so-called Lancaster system was a widespread practice in Western and Northern Europe by mid-19th century.

- The graded curriculum with subject matter split into ordered, sequential pieces is also a rather late development. The more elaborate and textbook-guided curriculum was established and concrete learning material became structured into a syllabus for each grade.

- The local school house or compound of houses has grown in size, concomitantly with urbanisation and the consolidation of school districts and catchment areas. In industrialised countries in the early 20th century, the majority of primary school children went to a school with an enrolment of fewer than one hundred pupils; these schools are now exceptions. Secondary schools with their more diversified programmes, greater catchment areas, and higher percentage of enrolled age group, along with consolidation of districts, have grown enormously and are sometimes ironically called "pedagogical factories".

- The objectives the school is expected to pursue have widened considerably from imparting certain basic skills and knowledge to "educating" and contributing increas-

114

ingly to bringing up independent, critical and responsible citizens ready to exercise their duties in a democratic and pluralistic society. Custodial care has increased in a society where both parents work outside the home. Nutrition and health programmes have been introduced and new categories of professional personnel, such as social workers, psychologists, nurses, and medical doctors, have joined the school staff.

• Supervision by local and/or central authorities has gradually become tighter. The introduction of national assessments and standardised, central achievement tests contributes to the standardisation within countries of examinations, curricula, textbooks, etc.

• The size of the institutionalised system or sub-systems, the number of school units under the jurisdiction of the local, regional, and national school administration, and enrolment, particularly at the secondary level, have grown dramatically over the last few decades. Teaching and in particular the non-teaching staff have increased in relation to the number of students. On the whole, the system has become much more complex, calling for increased co-ordination which means more administrative staff.

Dilemmas Besetting the School as an Institution

By the 1930s in the typical developed industrial country, almost 90% of 13 to 14 year olds left the six- or seven-year elementary school, usually to go straight to work. Teenagers entered adult society early and had to assume adult roles, mainly in the working world. A few decades later, the legislated school leaving age had been raised to 15 or 16. But the majority of students goes on to upper secondary education which means that instead of only some 5-10%, as was still the case in the 1950s, now more than 50% qualify for entry into tertiary education.

A revolution has taken place as regards the status of youth in our society within a rather short time. Instead of learning about adult roles at the beginning of their teens, young people now find themselves in institutions where they have little if any contact with the adult world. This segregation has been reinforced by the rapid pace of urbanisation: more and more children grow up in cities and towns where parents spend the better part of the working day away from home, giving them little contact with working world.

Until recently, school responsibilities in taking care of the young were very limited in both substance and time. The overriding task of socialisation has fallen outside the school. Learning to shoulder personal responsibility and to be independent took

115

place in the family and/or the small community, where youngsters learned adult roles in the course of interpersonal relationships with parents, relatives, neighbours, and co-workers.

Today, a young teenager stays on in school. Some claim that the school now has a broader mission with regard to imparting knowledge. Working life has become more demanding and complicated. The information explosion makes it increasingly difficult for an individual to orient inside or outside the working world. There are fewer and fewer unqualified jobs available to youngsters tired of school, many of whom come from homes which have not been particularly conducive to their socialisation. Big cities in Western industrial countries have considerable depressing experience with this. This has led to the conclusion that schools should keep unmotivated youngsters as long as possible, even if by legal coercion, and keep them off the streets.

The real revolution has been the enrolment explosion, but very little has happened with regard to the modes of operation. The overriding problem is that schools are information-rich but action-poor. Given the lack of self-initiated activity, young people are not well prepared to shoulder adult responsibilities after many years of uninterrupted schooling. They have become used to having their work planned in minute detail by the teachers hour after hour, day after day. As the school performs its mission as an institution to impart increasing subject matter to increasing numbers of students for more and more school years, other institutions, the media, and technology - newspapers, magazines, broadcasting, and computers - are beginning to take over many of the school's time-honoured tasks. Thus, as traditional teaching strategies are reinforced, the conflict between theory and practice is exacerbated.

The situation is paradoxical indeed. When the school's tasks of developing basic skills and imparting certain basic elements of knowledge can be taken over by agencies outside the school that have been responsible for upbringing, the family, the neighbourhood group, and the working-at-home group are no longer as capable of performing their task. As society becomes information-rich, it also becomes action-poor. Central to the problem of socialising young people is the unrealistic expectation that they become more independent, take more initiative, and develop a sense of responsibility greater than what we enable them to acquire.

New Modes of Pedagogical Production

Since the mid-19th century when primary schooling in the leading industrial countries became legally universal, the competencies needed for adult life have been imparted according to a standard model of school instruction. Schools divided students into approximately equal-sized classes of some 20-40 students, generally by age cohorts, regardless of the kind of work that goes on in the classrooms, typically taught by a teacher sitting behind a desk lecturing to the students. The teacher conveys proper "chunks" of knowledge which students are expected to master, and which can then be checked by proper examinations. In addition to the "flow" of subject matter, the teacher instructs students on what they are expected to do in school or at home.

To what extent can frontal instruction be used by groups of students as large as say one hundred, instead of only 30? This was done in the early 19th century in the Lancaster schools with one teacher responsible for one hundred or more students who could be divided up into small groups under the supervision of more advanced monitors acting as a kind of drill corporal under the teacher. To what extent can this model of pedagogical "production" be used in the school today? Why has this model become so ingrained that it has been able to withstand all kinds of reform movements?

Half a century ago, the American Association of School Administrators launched a pilot programme supported by the Ford Foundation on flexible classroom group size that attracted much interest on both sides of the Atlantic. The core idea was that the size of the instructional groups should be geared to the kind of work or instruction taking place. The experiment, led by Dr. Lloyd Trump, created three different work modes. To convey large chunks of information, the teacher could appear before a class of about some hundred students, as limited by classroom size and disciplinary problems that easily occur in the anonymity of a crowd. Second, when students worked on their own with individualised teaching material, they were divided into smaller groups of some 15 to 20; even smaller groups of two to five were set up for a typical group work. Team-teaching was a key feature of this strategy, usually with three teachers working closely together responsible for about one hundred students.

Teachers and Teacher Training

Formal schooling, like the health service, is a highly labour-intensive "industry". In manufacturing machinery, automation and rationalisation have radically reduced the need for physical and intellectual human effort. The learning that goes on in upbringing and imparting of skills and knowledge presupposes an interaction between an adult and the child or adolescent for two obvious reasons. First, the emotion and motivation that go into the learning process can only be instigated by a competent adult. Second, young people need role models both at home and in school.

Given the high cost of the teacher's time and the demand for more teachers for the increasing proportion of young people who are staying in school for an increasing

117

number of years, the issue of pedagogical responsibilities needs to be addressed. The key problem is the degree of individualised teaching that is called for. Lecturing is a productive pedagogy in classes of from one hundred to one hundred and twenty-five students but once feedback is expected, class size becomes critical.

The rigid tradition of classes with regulated numbers of students more or less independent of the mode of teaching would have to be abolished as some kind of team teaching, which is part and parcel of a system of flexible class size, is introduced. This system attracted attention at a time when rapidly increasing enrolment due to the high birth rate and the expansion of secondary education could not be met by recruiting competent teachers. It had to contend with a deeply ingrained tradition of teaching classes of standardised size and also implied extra work for teachers.

Teacher training traditionally consists of subject matter preparation, pedagogical course work, and classroom practice. A major issue has been how to achieve a proper balance between subject matter and pedagogical competence. In most countries, primary school teachers in charge of children during the first four to seven years of schooling have been deemed competent to teach all subjects in the curriculum. Subject matter preparation has been considered to be the main field of competence for secondary school teachers and conversely pedagogical preparation was less important. The proper balance between the two fields of competence, however, is affected by ongoing specialisation in various academic disciplines as well as the flow of new information made available. The difficulty of recruiting sufficient numbers of teachers has been compounded by a tendency to reduce the quality of subject matter preparation at the primary and especially at secondary levels.

The overwhelming flow of new information and the need to connect it with the student's everyday experience, however, has created a need for lifelong upgrading of teacher subject matter orientation through regular, in-service training. In some instances, this has become an important task for universities.

It is difficult to recruit enough competent teachers, particularly at the secondary level. It has been suggested that the teaching career should be redefined so that a good teacher could stay on as a teacher trainer and pursue a career in that role. In most countries outstanding pedagogical performance is rewarded by promotion to administrative positions. It has been suggested that one should have at least two categories of active classroom pedagogues: "master" teachers and teaching assistants. The fully trained teacher has to perform many chores inside and outside the classroom which do not require special pedagogical competence. If, for instance, housewives were coming in on a part-time basis, the trained teacher could spend all or almost all of his or her time on tasks requiring particular pedagogical competence.

A Core Curriculum in a System of Lifelong Education

The structure and content of the school curriculum in a changing society must be considered differently in the perspective of lifelong education. This means that the school from an early stage onwards would have to concentrate on skills that constitute an ability to learn new things. Such skills should have a wide repertory of applications in a broad range of future situations that can be barely foreseen. The content of the curriculum would have to evolve from providing encyclopaedic knowledge of more or less disconnected items to providing intellectual instruments helpful in orienting in an expanding knowledge society. But the school's role in socialising students should not be underestimated, particularly since the role of the family (Husén, Tuijnman, Halls, 1992) has been reduced.

A Common Frame of Reference

In order to educate a participating citizen in a democratic society, the school should provide the cognitive skills and core values that are central to its society. It is easier to specify cognitive skills than core values.

• Skills epitomised in the expression "learn to learn" are not particularly emphasised in a school where the encyclopaedic goal is central. They consist of the ability to find information and discern the most from the least relevant, to relate it to previously acquired knowledge, and to put it into context. On the whole, what is required here is familiarity with the potential, available sources of information.

• Critical reading skills constitute the core of reading comprehension and ability to catch the main points in glancing through reading material all the way from newspapers to a technical report.

• Analytic skills consist of the ability to weigh pros and cons in an argument and to structure the consistency and logical coherence in a text under scrutiny.

Few studies have been conducted with the aim of more empirically identifying skills which constitute a common core of competence in a modern, information society. A massive attempt was made by the Swedish Industrial Council for Social and Economic Studies (SNS) some 35 years ago (Husén and Dahllöf, 1960). It is striking that employers criticism of the competence of school leavers much more frequently designates the basics of communication and computational skills rather than the lack of knowledge that constitutes orientation in history, literature, and science. These form part of the backbone of the common frame of reference of values. As a perspective on the social and cultural problems of today, one needs some historical background, including a rough chronology; in order to be able to form an opinion for instance on ecological issues, a certain minimum of scientific knowledge is required.

Policy Conclusions Concerning the Structure and Curricula of the Formal Educational System

A different temporal balance in the various stages of basic formal schooling is provided to all citizens. Lifelong learning calls into question the traditional tenet that most of the competencies "needed" in adult life should be squeezed into schooling during the early years.

In a society of lifelong learning, a bond-guaranteed system could provide every citizen a free, publicly provided, education for a specified length of time with a certain minimum of basic school attendance - nine to ten years. Many mid-teens who weary of school could leave for a certain time to work, for example, and then return. The individual pupil and/or the parents would decide whether to use up all the "bonds" at a stretch or spread them over time. Fed up 15- or 16-year-olds could leave school despite their parents desire to have them continue and go out and try one or several jobs. Knowing that further formal education is guaranteed they could gain experience and maturity and return to schooling that would become more meaningful.

School entry could begin earlier than at six years of age, the norm in most countries. Certain basic skills, such as reading, could be introduced at the age of four or five.

The "enrolment explosion" at the secondary level in all OECD Member countries that has increased the percentage of young people qualifying for tertiary education has radically changed the issue of the proper school structure. The core issue was long the stage or age at which academic and vocational programmes should branch. As late as the mid-1960s in most European countries, only some 10-15% of the age cohorts completed upper secondary schooling. The percentage has since risen to 70-90% which means that at least lower secondary education has become comprehensive in the sense that by and large all pupils take the same curriculum. It also postpones the selection of programmes (some with prevocational elements) and students from age 10-11 to age 15-16.

The difficulties of predicting what kind of substantive competencies an individual will need in the future have increased the relative importance of basic skills, such as critical reading comprehension, ability to communicate, analytical ability, and ability to find information and acquire new information. This means that such skills take the upper hand over pre-vocational, substantive competencies.

Reform Strategy

When undertaking educational reforms, some strategic principles related to formal education must be considered. First and foremost, building and changing institutions take a long time. We only need to look at how many decades it took to implement universal primary schooling everywhere in European countries during the 19th century. Similarly, educational reforms take time. Swedish school reform making comprehensive nine-year schooling universal in Sweden took three decades to plan, try out, and implement, and this was during a period of remarkable political stability with the same prime minister for a period of 23 years! To improve quality, for instance, we would have to consider both institutional inertia and the decades-long lag time before political decisions become effective. For example: downgrading of subject matter competence among teacher candidates for the middle grades legislated by the Swedish parliament in 1967 was reflected some 10-15 years later in mathematics competence assessed by the second international mathematics survey.

Educational provisions, reforms, and outcomes have to be seen in a socio-economic context. When families no longer needed to keep the children at home to fulfil their part of the work, and when legislation prohibiting child labour up to a certain age was introduced in Britain in the last century, some kind of institutional care became important. Nursery school for five to seven year olds was established and the school had to serve as a baby-sitting institution as well. In agricultural areas in Western and Northern Europe well into this century, there was no full-time attendance: 7- to 13-year-olds went to school half-time or even less and spent the rest of their time working in the family. The dropout problem which causes such concern among experts familiar with the urban school problems has to be seen in this context: children cannot be away from home full-time. School resources do not suffice to provide full-time instruction anyhow.

Educational planning faces different challenges in developing and developed parts of the world. As *Learning: The Treasure Within* emphasises, about a billion adults in the developing world are illiterate and several hundred million cannot avail themselves of basic formal schooling. The difference between the developed and developing countries is highlighted by the fact that in practically all industrialised countries, 100% of school age children are in school for six to eight years. In countries like the United States, Britain, and France, the majority of children attend school up to the age of 17-18.

In developing countries, the problem is to build a basis of formal schooling for all, whereas in developed countries, the main problem is how to organise a post-primary or even post-secondary lifelong education that builds upon the basic schooling for all. This difference must be squarely faced. We tend to forget that discussion about permanent and lifelong education is a very new phenomenon in the developed world. It was not until the 1960s that organisations like UNESCO and the OECD began to raise the problem of lifelong education under the impact of rapid socio-economic changes. This issue does have the same urgency in most developing countries, where the establishment of universal basic formal education and institutions providing it has to be the central problem.

Thought Provoking Lessons

The role of formal education needs to be rethought and attention needs to be paid to enhance the quality of formal schooling within the framework of the learning society. The 1996 Delors Report pointed out that formal education is the irreplaceable basis for lifelong education that, ideally, is offered to all young people world-wide.

When considering formal schooling from a global point of view, the "education gap" between developed and developing countries and the adequacy of the Western model of formal schooling are the two principal issues.

In a recent study (Lockheed and Verspoor, 1994) sponsored by the World Bank, the threefold "education gap" between developed and developing countries is statistically documented. The gap refers, first, to access to formal education. In the developing countries several hundred million children have no opportunity to enter regular schooling at all at the primary level. Secondly, it relates to the quality of available formal education. Material resources, such as classrooms and teaching materials, impair the outcomes of teaching, which also affects the very high dropout rate in developing countries.

We need to rethink the very nature of formal schooling and its role in different types of society. Simply put, the model of schooling that was being developed in Europe at the pre-university level already in the Middle Ages, and then was given universal application in Western countries when primary schooling became mandatory, is not adequate in societies with mainly subsistence and agricultural economies. The history of education in industrialising Europe offers illuminating lessons. Universal primary education became a political priority in Western and Northern Europe in conjunction with industrialisation and democratisation. Even at the beginning of the 20th century in most rural areas, children began working at an early age in their family working teams on the farms.

Full-time attendance occurred only in the urban areas and cities, where the majority of the parents were employed in industrial enterprises and the schools therefore served as something resembling baby-sitting institutions. The impact of early industrialisation in Britain, even after child labour before a given age was prohibited, gave rise to the establishment of so-called nursery schools which took care of children before the age of seven to eight, a system studied with keen interest by visitors from other European countries. In rural Europe, therefore, full-time school attendance was exceptional, something we might usefully recall when we note the high dropout rate in most of the developing countries with their subsistence economies.

In his introductory essay to *Education: The Necessary Utopia*, Jacques Delors indicates six "tensions" which can be expected to constitute central problems in education during the twenty-first century: the tension between the universal and the individual, and between tradition and modernity. Another tension which seems central, particularly in the Third World in an era of massification of formal education, is that between quality and equality or rather between quality and opportunity which can be much more painlessly resolved in affluent societies with growing economies and declining birth rates. In developing countries with half the population below the age of 15 and scarce material resources, equality and the massification that goes with it has to be bought at the price of lower quality both in terms of educational facilities and outcomes.

Finally, certain questions have particular bearing on developing countries:

• How do we make extended basic schooling covering eight to ten years meaningful to teenagers who have become "school-tired", particularly to children with underprivileged background who have failed to reach the goals of instruction during the first five to six years of schooling?

• How do we build a curriculum that more strongly emphasises the basic skills so that we can reduce the percentage of those who leave school at the age of 15-16 as functional illiterates?

• How do we build preparatory elements of vocational competence into the curriculum without making a definitive vocational commitment?

123

REFERENCES

BURGEN, A., ed. (1996),
  Goals and Purposes of Higher Education in the 21ˢᵗ Century, London: Jessica Kingsley
  Publishers.

COLEMAN, J. S. (1961),
  The Adolescent Society, New York: Free Press.

COLEMAN, J. S. (1990),
  Foundations of Social Theory, Cambridge, Massachusetts, Harvard University Press.

CREMIN, L. (1976),
  Public Education, New York, Basic Books.

DELORS, J. *et al.* (1996),
  Learning: The Treasure Within, Report to UNESCO of the International Commission
  on Education for the Twenty-first Century, Paris, UNESCO.

HUSÉN, T. (1968),
  "Lifelong Learning in the 'Educative Society'", *International Review of Applied Psychology*, Vol. 17:2, 87-99.

HUSÉN, T. (1968),
  "School in a Changing and Industrialised Society", *Educational Leadership*, Vol. 25:6,
  524-530.

HUSÉN, T. (1974),
  The Learning Society, London, Methuen.

HUSÉN, T. (1979),
  The School in Question. A Comparative Study of the School and Its Future in Western Societies,
  London & New York, Oxford University Press.

HUSÉN, T. (1982),
"Present Trend in Education", Prospects, Vol. XII, No. 1,45-56.

HUSÉN, T. (1990),
Education and the Global Concern, Oxford, Pergamon Press.

HUSÉN, T., A. TUIJNMAN and W.D. HALLS (editors) (1992),
Schooling in Modern European Society: A Report of the Academia Europaea, Oxford, Pergamon Press.

LOCKHEED, M. E. and A. VERSPOOR et al. (1991),
Improving Primary Education in Developing Countries, Washington, D.C., Oxford University Press.

OECD (1995),
Education at a Glance: OECD Indicators, Paris, OECD.

OECD (1996),
Lifelong Learning for All: Meeting of the Education Committee at Ministerial Level 16-17 January 1996, Paris, OECD.

TRUMP, J. L. (1959),
Images of the Future: A New Approach to the Secondary School, New York, The Ford Foundation.

TRUMP, J. L. (1961),
Guide to Better Schools, Chicago, Rand McNally Co.

UNESCO (1972),
Learning to Be: The World of Education Today and Tomorrow, Paris, UNESCO and London, Harraps.

OECD 2000

WHAT DO DEVELOPED COUNTRIES EXPECT OF THEIR EDUCATION SYSTEMS?
Reflections on the French Experience

François **Louis**
French Ministry of Education, Research and Technology

In an environment that is broadly conducive to evaluation and change in the public services, the education system tends to be less frequently cited, in France at least, as an area with scope for modernisation and change than, for example, the postal service, telecommunications, transport, social welfare, local government, or running legal institutions. Positive initiatives such as "community schools", or schools that play a role in local development, are occasionally quoted precisely because they are examples of how public services can adapt to the genuine expectations of their users. In both cases, however, school standing may be enhanced primarily because of achievement in terms of urban policy or territorial development, rather than to its mission to educate.

Why do schools give the impression of being less involved than other institutions in the debate on public policy renewal and evaluation? On what grounds, explicit or implicit, are they outside the drive to improve the measurement of public service performance and quality? What obstacles are so specific as to stand in the way? Public service values are sometimes given as an argument against looking into the cost-effectiveness of education systems, but these values should be viewed rather as a requirement that lends impetus to action by all those who work in education.

Analysing the Cost Effectiveness of Education: From Underachievement to Cost-effective Education

During the 1960s, for the first time in France, Guy Avanzani presented research into the functioning of schools formalising the notion of underachievement viewed in its own right as distinct from the weaknesses of individual pupils. This new notion subsequently led schools to question how they functioned and whether they themselves had any inadequacies or weaknesses. In 1985, Roger Establet actually asked "Are schools

127

cost-effective?", a question which has since become a recurrent, and even persistent theme not only in France but in most of the developed world where research institutions are discovering how high public expectations are regarding effective education systems. As the French Institute for Research into the Economics of Education (IREDU) put it, "The quality of education was long measured in terms of the quality of its inputs. It was naturally felt that better trained teachers, smaller classes, more and better designed teaching-aids, more suitable remediation techniques for low achievers, in short, more resources, necessarily generated a corresponding improvement in the cognitive performance of learners". Without challenging any of these ideas, modern research is endeavouring to grasp the laws that link inputs and outputs; these laws are rarely linear. There are threshold effects, combined increasing/diminishing effects, interactions between inputs, and the laws vary depending on the context, level of education, and pupil or family profiles.

Effective Schools and High Public Expectations: A Common Debate

Public concern about the rise in long-lasting, extensive, structural unemployment since the late 1970s, together with the widespread feeling that France is making a substantial and costly effort to develop education, are probably the two main reasons for such high public expectations of the education system. The debate as to whether schools are effective has been growing more heated and more pressing year the year. Are schools equal to their own ambitions and to the resources allocated to them nationally? What impact is such an investment in education having in terms of results and overall cost-effectiveness? Pierre Dasté, then responsible for secondary education teaching staff, acknowledged, a few months before the adoption of the Education Act, that this was "a real problem" because "the nation allocates considerable resources to the education system and is about to increase them significantly: we are, and will become increasingly accountable". He stressed the need for "a drive for coherence and transparency, but at the same time individual awareness: the education system will have to be effective, but also subject to evaluation".

Alain Mingat points out, in analysing the cost-effectiveness of education, that it is not only desirable but feasible because for each factor in school organisation there is a corresponding ratio in terms of cost-effectiveness, with the median characterising the average situation in the education system. A comparison of these ratios gives an overall picture of how effective a combination of actors is in the initial situation. If the various factors that are or could be mobilised vary a great deal in their cost-effectiveness ratios, it indicates that changes are required in the way schools are run. This will mean allocating more resources to factors with the highest impact on the "performance per monetary unit" variable, and fewer resources to factors with the lowest impact. The organisation of the system will be deemed largely cost-effective when each factor has been allocated enough resources to equal out the different cost-effectiveness ratios.

As a principle and a general approach, cost-effectiveness analysis offers considerable scope for evaluating education systems. It can be useful in tackling problems as wide-ranging as teacher training, technical curricula, the usefulness of pre-school education, the use of teaching methods and educational technology, the role of inspection, repeating years, setting, or justifying re-education activities in primary school. It is probably the most powerful and appropriate tool for learning from the experience acquired by the education system and the way it functions on a daily basis, since a rigorous and organised evaluation of the current situation often provides the rationales for change when resources are scarce.

Similar Issues in Other Countries

Since the early 1970s, several research programmes have been developed to address the economics of education. The main topics include the cost and financing of education, factors affecting the operational effectiveness of schools, the evaluation of broad education policies, and studies on the linkages between education and training, on the one hand, and employment and income on the other. This work, in France and abroad, particularly in the developed world, is now widely published and the findings are of concern to the major education policy stakeholders.

In North America for instance, over the past twenty years, a school of thought has been developing on "effective school". It maintains that every student can succeed, provided that the school optimises its internal organisation. Anne Lewis reports on a four-year survey by the Department of Education covering a sample of 1 700 schools that holds that the best schools are those which combine clearly-defined educational goals with high expectations of the skills and behaviour of each student. These high standards must be shared, in this particular case, by highly-motivated teachers with a desire to prove their professionalism and meet pupils' needs with high-quality teaching. Describing an "effective school" a few years earlier, Edmonds Ronal listed two further factors that make for effective schools: efficient school management and the regular monitoring of educational achievement. In Quebec, the evaluation approach to the education system began to develop from around the mid-1970s, as Edmonds Ronal reports. In 1989, Paul-Emile Gingras noted that during the 1980s, "growing awareness among stakeholders managed to counter the reluctance shown by administrators and staff and led to a basic agreement on the validity of evaluation and the need for schools to have evaluation policies. Other positive factors include the development, by the Ministry of Education, universities, and a few specialised research and development centres like the CADRE, of some initial tools such as evaluation guides, techniques, data collection/measurement tools, indicators, and centres for documentary resources on evaluation".

In the European Community, the Eurydice education information network published a report giving details of the measures taken in 18 countries (the 15 EU Member States, Iceland, Lichtenstein and Norway) from 1984 to 1994. It points out that these countries were facing similar challenges and needed to make quality teaching accessible to broader sections of the population. These countries faced the same issues such as the evaluation of pupil attainment and the outcome of reforms in relation to financial effort over the ten-year period. When Tony Blair's Labour Government came to power in the United Kingdom in May 1997, it immediately focused on education issues. David Blunkett, UK Secretary of State for Education and Employment, in Le Monde of December 1997, was reported as saying that social cohesion and economic prosperity were based on acquiring basic skills and the ability to adapt knowledge on an ongoing basis. Lifelong learning was vital to the economy and to survival. The British government believed that most young people had inadequate skill levels. For the past thirty or forty years, excellence had been confined to a small number of people and the economy was still able to function with a small, well-educated elite, whereas the majority had a far more varied standard of education. While the economy could, at one point, survive on that basis, this was no longer feasible today.

Impetus and Input from the OECD

The issue of effective education systems has also been addressed by some intergovernmental organisations, in particular in an OECD assessment of thirty years of educational policy. Global economic competition, the development of trade, and the resources invested by each country in education and training have raised awareness, mainly since the 1960s, that education systems and education polices have indeed become a major, even strategic, economic challenge in a context of global competition. "The performances of these systems are accordingly subject to scrutiny and comparison". Norberto Bottani, responsible for the OECD Education Indicators project, points out in an article in Administration and Education, that "there is less and less reluctance to draw real or notional correlation between educational outcomes and economic performance, or between the quality of a country's schools and its well-being or wealth".

The OECD has long been known for its statistics in economy, international trade, employment, industry and technology, among others. Bottani remarks that "These data are widely quoted and used, by both governments and the media, to analyse policy outcomes and guide government policy. Unfortunately, this is not the case for education. For a long time there was a reluctance to produce a coherent set of statistics and indicators on education. The situation has changed since the launch of the INES project, aimed at defining and producing a set of international indicators on education". There are several reasons for this change of attitude over the past few years among OECD Member countries: "First, there has been a shift over the past decade, as concerns about the quality of education have begun to override traditional concerns focusing more on planning to cope with ever-expanding systems. Norberto Bottani adds, "the jobs crisis and serious unemployment have drawn attention to the importance of developing human resources and education. Owing to the role that education plays in largely knowledge-based economies, enhancing the quality, equity and effectiveness of education systems has become a priority in modern society".

While there now appears to be a broad consensus in favour of evaluating the performance of education systems, the production of comparable indicators is nevertheless a difficult exercise with many obstacles. Norberto Bottani points out, first, that the International Standard Classification of Education (ISCED) indicators drawn up by UNESCO in the late 1970s to facilitate the production of comparable data have not really proven satisfactory. Furthermore, how can a single definition of the "education system" win unanimous approval and encompass all the information required to paint a true picture of a country's efforts? The issue is all the more complex in countries with federal government structures (such as Australia, Germany, the United Kingdom or the United States). Here, some rather tricky aggregates have to be made since the data refer to separate education systems (e.g. in Scotland, Wales) rather than national ones. The very issue of comparative evaluation probably explains why the two sets of international indicators on education published by the OECD in *Education at a Glance* and by the CERI since 1992 have been such a success, besides the fact that they clearly meet a need in this area.

What Share of Resources for Education?

The inevitably constrained nature of the public resources that any society can allocate to education generally acts as a strong incentive for the rationalisation and refined costing of educational goods and services. So the budgetary constraints that determine educational policy options in any country and crucially in developing countries, together with work on the basic factors governing economic growth and productivity have lent particular relevance and topicality to research into the economics of education. Alain Mingat points out that "when there are constraints on resource availability…choices have to be made for there are, a priori, all kinds of possible trade-offs regarding the organisation and running of an education system (from the state-controlled macro-organisation right down to the micro-organisation at individual class and student level), and the alternatives are not all equal in terms of how far they will help the education system achieve the goals it has been set".

131

What conclusions can be drawn in this regard from the indicators produced by the OECD? Most striking are the wide disparities between the Organisation's own Member countries. Educational expenditure relative to GDP, for example, varies from 5 to 7.4% across countries. Another is the considerable difference in private sources of funding for education and training: the OECD average is around 12% but the figures range from 0% in Sweden and 0.6% in Denmark to 26.1% in Japan and 27.1% in Germany. In France, the private sector accounts for 10% of educational expenditure. Wide variations exist in annual public expenditure per pupil (or student) across Member countries: the OECD average is around USD 4 200, but the figures range from USD 3 000 in Spain and Turkey to USD 3 800 in France and USD 6 500 in the United States and Germany. There are also noticeable disparities in participation beyond compulsory schooling; similarly, opportunities for tertiary education vary considerably according to country and gender, since the university graduation rate for women in Norway is seven times that of Switzerland. However, the OECD stresses how difficult it is to interpret all of these indicators and the disparities they reveal. They should not be viewed as the manifestation of a desire for uniformity, for no one can set universal or ideal standards for every education system. On the contrary, comparisons should be an incentive to further refine the analysis of educational situations in OECD Member countries.

Three Important Performance Issues

In public debate, an education system may be challenged about its performance on several counts, but there are three particularly burning issues: educational achievement, preparing pupils for the job market, and equal opportunities. This is the case, at least in France, where public opinion most certainly wants transparency on how the education system is actually performing.

The 1991 L'état de l'école (The State of our Schools) can be said to have been a significant step forward. It presented, for the first time, 30 indicators on important functional aspects of the education system. Intended as an annual publication, it has since been regularly updated. In every edition since 1991, the Directorate for Evaluation and Prospective Analysis (DEP), which became the Directorate for Planning and Development (DPD) when the Ministry of Education was restructured in December 1997, has emphasised that this publication is to paint a broad picture of the situation and trends in the French education system from nursery schools to higher education, including continuing education. By adding a number of new indicators, the DEP has also sought to improve the measurement of the system's performance. The 1997 edition of L'état de l'école for instance, presents data on trends over the past few years in the attainment of pupils completing their fourth year of general lower-secondary education (i.e. completing ISCED 2), to supplement the data on their skills on entering lower-secondary school (*i.e.* entering ISCED 2). The same edition also looks at access to the *baccalauréat* (secondary-school leaving examination) and higher education depending on social origin, in relation to equity, one of the basic stated aims of the French education system. Wherever possible, it presents its indicators along with international comparisons to give a better picture of how France fares in relation to the leading European countries, the United States and Japan. This was already the case in earlier editions, most of the international comparisons being based on work co-ordinated by the OECD and published in 1992.

Attainment

The first question concerns pupil attainment and skills: are standards declining or improving? Do today's pupils really know how to read, write, and count? Is the *baccalauréat* being "given away", as some would have it? Stressing that this has been a recurrent theme ("an unquashable rumour" as Bernard Toulemonde calls it) does nothing to calm the controversy. In Le *niveau monte* (Improving Standards) Christian Baudelot and Roger Establet seek to "refute an old idea about the so-called decline in our schools" by highlighting the considerable effort made in France to increase enrolment over the past few decades. At the end of the century, 60% of all young people used to leave school with no qualifications, before the Second World War 40% and at the end of the 1980s 20%. The authors add that the average marks out of 20 obtained by conscripts in army tests rose from 10 to 13.5 between 1967 and 1982; they also believe that the *baccalauréat* examination is becoming harder owing to an increasingly demanding curriculum. However, they clearly call attention to the crucial situation of young underachievers, and take on board the idea launched by René Haby, Minister for Education in the 1970s, that anyone leaving school should have received a "minimum standard of education" enabling them to find work and a place in society.

In 1992, when more than half a generation passed the *baccalauréat* for the first time, results that some attributed to falling standards, the Minister for Education asked the Director for Evaluation and Prospective Analysis to look at all known comparative work on trends in educational standards and skills, going back as far as 100 years. Claude Thélot presented a report in October 1992 as sixteen fact-sheets on specific themes, including spelling, mathematics, reading standards and geography. Tracing the rise in enrolment and qualifications, it conceded that in 1992, when 20% of the labour force had no qualifications (compared with 50% 30 years earlier), France still lagged behind other countries, but less so than before. It noted that enrolment was on the rise along with the number of "top" pupils; at the other end of the scale, illiteracy was declining. "The popular idea that illiteracy was on the rise was not backed up by evidence and was in fact inaccurate", wrote Thélot. Overall, and judging by the conscript tests, it would seem that standards have actually risen. While the mathe-

133

matical skills of primary-school leavers from 1958 to 1991, and lower-secondary school leavers in the 1980s have improved, the standard of English and German language skills among lower-secondary school leavers is the same as in the mid-1980s; in geography, young people's skills match those of their grandparents. Internationally, the report ranks France 5th among 31 countries for reading skills among 9-10 year olds. France is ranked 2nd for reading among 14-15 year olds, 6th among 20 countries in mathematics tests of 13-year olds whose science skills are somewhat average; in languages, the comparison with young Germans, Italians and North Europeans is not particularly flattering.

With regard to standards, attention has, understandably, focused mainly on two sets of data:

- Data that still create concerns about illiteracy and reading skills among primary-school leavers.

- An equally disturbing share of young people leaving the education system with not qualifications other than the primary-school leaving certification. Far more young people used to be in this situation - 220 000 in 1973 - while twenty years later, the 1993 figures were 105 000; over that period, however, unemployment became fundamentally structural, affecting a major share of the labour force and, more specifically, young people with no qualifications at all.

Diagnostic Evaluations and Evaluation Tools

The recommendations of a report on reading skills by Chief Education Officer Migeon, led to the introduction of evaluation test at the beginning of the 1989-90 academic year, for all pupils in the third year of primary school (age 8), and the first year of secondary school (age 11), in French and mathematics, two basic subjects. The tests were to help teachers diagnose their pupils' strengths and weaknesses using an objective means to analyse the obstacles that pupils were encountering; teaching staff could then, in principle, introduce appropriate and differentiated teaching methods. At the start of school year 1992-93, a similar evaluation scheme was organised as part of "pedagogical renewal in upper secondary schools" for all pupils in the fifth year of general or technical secondary education (age 15). The scheme was launched to coincide with the introduction of modules; by testing their pupils in four subjects, teachers would discover their individual strengths, weaknesses, and needs. They could then improve the module approach and divide their pupils into uniform groups for module teaching. Every year since 1989, the DEP/DPD has drawn up evaluation protocols and collected representative test samples to provide schools and teachers with performance benchmarks. Besides measuring pupil skills at two key stages in their schooling, the tests at ages 8 and 11 are a means of drawing up national benchmarks on a regular basis for comparison purposes. Tests at age 15 are more an evaluation of skills than of knowledge.

But do these national evaluation schemes genuinely encourage teachers to question their own teaching practices and, where necessary, change them? It is hard to be optimistic: the conclusions drawn from all these widespread evaluation schemes have, for several reasons, only been partially capitalised upon in schools largely because the French education system does not have a very widespread "evaluation culture", although it is gaining ground. The DEP has actually sought to rectify this cultural factor. Some consider that putting pupils through tests at the start of every school year is an obligation and, as such, may foster or reinforce the idea that the Ministry is making an unwarranted imposition, solely for statistical purposes. This impression may also stem from the technical constraints imposed by the computerisation of test results. This practical problem should not mask another, more fundamental and pronounced problem, however, which is individualised teaching. How, on the basis of test results, can differentiated teaching be introduced to meet the needs of individual pupils as revealed in the tests? What should be done, and what approach adopted? Apparently, many teachers consider that "the conventional means of evaluating skills are quite adequate". While they are not necessarily hostile to the more overarching view of their pupils' skills gained through nation-wide evaluation schemes, many of them still find it hard to differentiate and adapt their own teaching practices. Some French education inspectors maintain that younger teachers are, on the whole, more receptive to such issues than colleagues with longer service. This is precisely why the focus should really be on newly trained teachers; after a few years' experience, even the more dynamic young teachers may begin to be just as pessimistic as their longer-serving colleagues towards any challenge to the prevailing, more conventional teaching practices. In reality, evaluation has not become a more integral part of teaching strategies largely because it may represent a challenge. Is underachievement solely due to a pupil's inability to understand or master a particular skill, or could it be to some extent put down to unsuitable teaching methods? Do teachers use the same methods, for instance, in a teaching priority education zone as in other areas? Does a school sufficiently encourage its staff to adapt their methods? Does it provide them with the resources and support they definitely need in cases like this?

In addition to the three national schemes to evaluate attainment, the DEP also prepared and distributed to primary teachers a "toolkit" or "exercise kit" for French and mathematics in Spring 1992. Since 1994, these evaluation exercises have targeted all three cycles of primary education and can be used by teachers quite freely during the school year. Similar tools were developed to cover science subjects (life sciences, physics/chemistry, technology), and were provided for lower-secondary

135

schools in 1994 and 1996, and for the fifth year of secondary schooling in 1995, 1996 and 1997. They all offer teachers an opportunity to monitor their pupils' progress on an educational continuum from primary school to upper-secondary entrance, and they have been regularly extended to cover changes in teaching structures and programmes. Until now the toolkits have been sent out in hardcopy form, but there are plans to put them onto computer disks, CD-ROMs and the Internet for easier access and use.

Preparing Young People for the Job Market

Underachievement is another issue. In a difficult social context, it is viewed as leading inevitably to unemployment and social exclusion. Youth employment has been a major issue in France's electoral 1995 presidential elections and the general elections in 1993 and 1997. Taking the 15-25 age group as a whole, one young person in four was said to be unemployed, as if two-thirds of them were not now at school or in higher education. The 1960s method of calculating the unemployment rate was indeed out of date. Nevertheless, youth employment problems are real enough. In a society with over three million unemployed, the public is justifiably concerned about adapting education to the job market, as the IGAEN report made clear. People ask whether schools might be responsible for youth unemployment, whether skills are relevant to jobs, and whether schools are meeting one of their main objectives of preparing young people for the job market.

The available data shows that 97 000 young people left the education system in 1995 without any qualifications (or with the primary school-leaving certificate), while the proportion of unqualified school-leavers that year was half the 1977 figure. Six years after the Education Act was adopted in July 1989, declaring that "each person has a guaranteed right to education ... to find a place on the job market", the 1995 figure was still 14% of all those leaving the education system. A crucial point is that those with no qualifications are the most vulnerable to unemployment, which rose sharply in this category from 1974 to 1985, when it stood at 37%; in 1996, it hit the 40% mark, as the 1997 DEP report points out. An INSEE study (National Institute of Economic and Statistical Information), referred to in L'état de l'école, addressed the importance of education in the debate on unemployment, and more specifically youth unemployment. It stresses that there is a "widely held belief that the fact that training fails to meet the demands of the productive system is not a complete explanation, since there is no strict correlation between education and employment". However, the growing strain on the job market makes the situation of young people without qualifications worse, partly because of de-skilling, as some young people with qualifications are obliged to accept jobs that do not match their standard of education, those with fewer qualifications are crowded out of the job market.

**Unemployment Trends in the Under-25 Labour Force,
by educational attainment (1971-1996)***

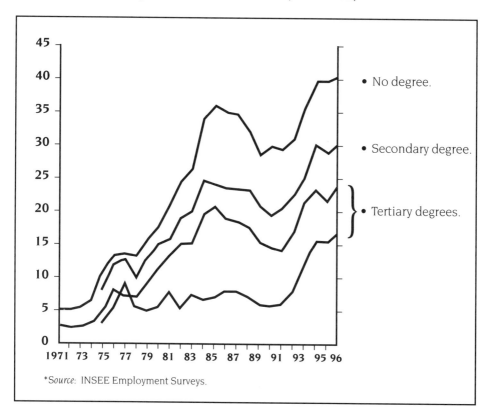

*Source: INSEE Employment Surveys.

At the European Jobs Summit in Luxembourg in November 1997, the Heads of State or Government of the 15 EU Member States defined four priorities to combat unemployment. They also included a determined effort to cut by 50% the number of young people leaving the education system with no skills or qualifications within five years. Besides the emphasis on developing apprenticeships, the European Commission promoted the example of Denmark, where any young person under the age of 25 who has not completed a cycle of education cannot remain unemployed for more than six months without being offered a training course.

That a majority of students fail the first two-years of French university education because they have been poorly advised or have inadequate study methods may also reinforce this adverse impression and fuel scepticism about how initial education is really performing and how well it is preparing young people for the world of work.

137

Equal Opportunities

This is the third issue is school capacity. It is based on the principle of equality; everyone is ostensibly given a fair chance of succeeding in school and subsequently on the job market and in society. Here, the work of Pierre Bourdieu or Christian Baudelot and Roger Establet for instance, together with work assessing the outcomes of specific policies to reduce inequities, more specifically priority education zones, reported on by Elisabeth Bautier, tend to show that schools have and are still failing to live up to expectations or meet their goals. Today, the children of professional staff still have three times more chance of obtaining the *baccalauréat* than the children of manual workers. In a 1997 article on the democratisation of education, Dominique Goux and Eric Maurin show that the contemporary development of education has not really generated a marked improvement in equal opportunities; inequities persist and are increasingly attributable to cultural factors. "As the education system has expanded, it has opened up to social groups that were once virtually excluded", they write. However, "although of benefit to everyone, it is not clear that this trend has modified the educational hierarchy among children according to their social origin. General standards are improving, but is there any change in the way children are ranked? In France, as in almost every other country, the expansion of the education system is generating the very mechanisms that allow inequities to thrive. While it is less important than it used to be to come from an affluent family in order to perform well at school, when it comes to choosing the right schools and options, it is increasingly advantageous to have parents who have themselves successfully negotiated the system. As they evolve from one generation to another, educational inequities seem to be growing more and more cultural, and less and less social or economic".

In addition to persistent inequities in outcomes, and more specifically in educational pathways, other work has highlighted very marked variations in resource allocation and effective practice. In their comparison of geographical disparities from one French *département* to another, Alain Mingat and Marc Richard show how the chances of young people entering upper secondary education with similar social profiles (same socio-professional category, nationality, living conditions and family size) vary a great deal depending on where they live. The difference may be substantial and due more specifically to educational provision in the broadest sense: "The effects may be qualitative but far more commonly quantitative in terms of the availability of places in schools. The role this plays has been illustrated in a relatively large number of studies and we now know that the availability of places can channel applications from families and ultimately determine the volume and structure of actual enrolment. The education system, argued Mingat in 1997, is better at defending principles and formal ideals, which it probably does in all sincerity, than at actually allocating on an equitable basis the resources it has at its disposal".

The issues raised by the public debate on equal opportunities in the French education system were certainly behind the special measures introducing positive discrimination and, more specifically, the creation of priority education zones in 1982; but do the outcomes meet the goals? Should we consider, like Patrick Bouveau and Jean-Yves Rochex, that an educational divide may well be threatening to isolate schools, and the educational values they defend, from those sections of the public they are supposed to serve?

The 1992 *Géographie de l'école* (*The Geography of Our Schools*) was a kind of litmus test of equal opportunities in that comparisons between the various education authorities (*académies*) and regions clearly showed a pattern of national inequity with figures and maps depicting these geographic disparities. The book was a revelation and contradicted a myth firmly rooted in educational goals, but less convincing in real life, whereby the Republic's schools offered equal educational opportunities to children wherever they lived. In their introduction, the authors stressed that the publication "was part of a general drive to inform and evaluate, through its intention to describe, collate and compare the main features of our education system, by region and by *académie* (that there was a need to) reconcile the principle of equity with the need for diversity while our education remains a nation-wide system, it is no longer - and can no longer be - a uniform, centralised system. Comprehensive education, open to all, serving republican values, the first of which is that citizens are equally entitled to education, is based on generous intentions. Government policy on education has long been centralised and predominant in allocating resources on the basis of fair access to education for all…. (it should nevertheless be acknowledged that) such a policy has not removed major disparities between northern and southern France in the field of education…. Today, at the centre of far-reaching social and economic change, in an education system that is shifting towards decentralisation and deconcentration, education can no longer be designed to fit everyone into the same mould. If performance is to be equitable, will resource policies not have to become, to some extent, inequitable ('positive discrimination')?"

The 1997 edition of *Géographie de l'école* presents 34 indicators comparing educational authorities:

- Four indicators on the social and cultural environment: demography and enrolment, household and regional wealth, unemployment and job insecurity, qualifications, social structure and sector.

- Seven indicators on resource availability and use, including educational expenditure by the Ministry of Education and local authorities, teaching staff mix, the spread and size of secondary-school classes in 1995-1996, and places in public secondary schools in priority education zones.

139

- Seventeen indicators on aspects of how the education system functions, including enrolment from age 2 to 5, educational underachievement in primary school, access to the *baccalauréat*, female enrolment, disparities between schools, foreign enrolment, private schools, and university entrance flows.

- Six indicators on attainment in each *académie*, and entry onto the job market: educational skills at ages 8 and 11, general educational standards among conscripts, proportion of pupils passing the *baccalauréat*, secondary-school leavers by attainment and their situation seven months after leaving the education system, and finally access to *employment in relation to attainment*.

Optimising Resources: Better Understanding Teaching Practices, How schools Function

Emile Durkheim, one of the founders of the French school of sociology, remarked that it is impossible to change an education system effectively unless one first knows what this system is, what its components are, on what concepts it is based, what needs it meets, and why it has been organised in a certain way. It is therefore indispensable to undertake a comprehensive study that is scientific and objective, but which produces results that can be readily applied in practice.

How exactly should one go about learning more about the school system? There can be a challenging, external approach based on the observation of the effects actually produced.

Marie Duru-Bellat and Agnès Henriot-van-Zanten, in their 1992 book on the sociology of schools, remark that "since the 1970s, the sociology of education has been focusing more closely on what the sociologists of the 1960s tended to take for granted, *i.e.* curricula, classroom relations, the rules for reaching a consensus within schools and the integration of schools into their local environment. This has led to a growing interest in studying units such as the community, the school or classroom, and to the development of qualitative methodologies". The goal of this kind of sociological analysis of how the education system functions is to open up the education system's "black box". Some researchers use the "external approach" based on the observation of the effects actually produced by a given system or institution, which can lead to unexpected results that sometimes run counter to widely accepted ideas. Conversely, an internal approach is basically descriptive and does not go beyond the characteristic functioning of a system or institution. Over the past twenty years, this external approach has made it possible to reach some relevant conclusions and raise some valid questions. As Marie Duru-Bellat and Alain Mingat point out, "In analysing how schools function, an initial approach of an internal type consists of

140

describing their current functioning and examining how they can be approved, both from an institutional standpoint and in terms of the behaviour of actors, without questioning their actual impact on pupils' education. An external approach, however, based on the premise that schools are supposed to provide a favourable environment for the education of pupils, will seek to determine if the pupils attending a given school learn more effectively or perform better than comparable pupils enrolled elsewhere".

The Guidance System: a Characteristic Area of the "School Effect"

For a number of years now, the pupil guidance system in French lower secondary education has been considered problematic. Using data on guidance, some study and research bodies have used an external approach to try to identify the factors that explain social differentiation. One study suggests that it is necessary to broaden an overly narrow vision of a school pathway. Academic attainment is unquestionably the result of satisfactory pupil outcomes, but it is also largely due to the fact that families know how to choose successful educational strategies, in particular by choosing specific options. It also accrues to a "school effect" produced by schools' differing practices at different points of the counselling process. The fact is that schools appear to have well-defined characteristics as being more or less "strict", and marks may vary widely for the same tests; some schools appear to give good marks to average or even weak pupils, while others mark more strictly. Transition and repeat rates also show that the practices of class councils vary across schools. This is all the more likely to generate inequalities of academic "attainment" inasmuch as class councils generally do little to encourage pupils and especially their families to have higher academic aspirations. However, well-to-do families tend to be sure of themselves and encourage their children's aspirations, while poorer families are more reserved and rarely call into question the verdict of class councils.

Contextual or environmental effects thus cause or increase the social inequalities of pupils' school pathways that do not reflect their real academic merit. Marie Duru-Bellat and Agnès Henriot-van-Zanten call these an "academic destiny that varies with the school attended". The guidance process is not the only element of the "school effect", but research has shown that it has a significant impact on pupils' school pathways. Moreover, to go beyond merely identifying this environment effect, research teams have tried to classify the possible factors that explain the school effect. Is it due to the sociological characteristics of schools and to the population enrolled? Is it due to the nature of the teaching staff and their qualifications? To teachers' teaching practices in their classes and to collegial co-operation? Or is it due to the role and personal involvement of headteachers? Or, finally, is it due to the more or less close relations the school establishes with families?

141

Another closely related issue regarding this school effect touches upon the theme of this Luxembourg conference and more generally to the useful work carried out by the OECD in the PEB: school setting. In the quality of the education provided in a given school, how much of the school effect can be explained by the school's setting? Such factors as school size, surroundings, layout, attractiveness of classrooms and facilities, availability of sports and recreational facilities, and technological equipment are all factors that can have an impact on the practical teaching conditions and on schools' "atmosphere" and pupils' peace of mind: on the quality of education. A careful analysis of how schools function certainly cannot afford to overlook these factors.

Student Attainment and Progress: Identifying Class and Teacher Effects

Researchers in the 1980s and 1990s also used on an external approach to demonstrate the impact of a "teacher effect" on pupils' attainment and individual progress through the system, even though teaching practices are complex and difficult to know and analyse. Marc Bru has spoken of "the difficulty of opening the black box" emphasising that in the research on the factors that generate differences in pupils' learning and progress, "the studies initially carried out in the United States and more recently in France ...have shown the weight of various factors: some have to do with the characteristics of pupils (school pathway, initial performance, socio-economic background, etc.), while others are due to conditions of education, including general organisational variables and variables linked to their individual class. The latter constitute a class effect, the weight of which, estimated through an analysis of variance of attainment, ranges between 10 to 20%. The assessment of the relative importance of structural variables, such as the number of pupils or the make-up of the class group, and variables related to teaching makes it possible to identify what is known as the "teacher effect", which in itself accounts for most of the class effect.

Pascal Bressoux used three empirical research studies evaluating primary school pupils' attainment in reading and mathematics and using the methodology selected for other work of this kind to show a teacher effect "but first and foremost a class effect. There are, all things being equal, classes in which pupils progress more rapidly than in others. Since the differences observed are differences between classes, it is valid to speak of class effects. Does this reflect differences in the effectiveness of teachers? In this regard, it must be borne in mind that teachers are not necessarily responsible for everything that takes place in class, since there are characteristics of classes that are givens over which the teacher has no control. It is observed that, no doubt to the contrary of what is widely believed, these "given" factors play only a very minor role in explaining academic achievement. Since the effect of "givens" is slight, much of the class effect can probably be attributed to a teacher effect. Here again, this teacher effect can be analysed and broken down into the characteristics of the teacher and those of his/her teaching". However, as Marguerite Altet *et al.* point out, "research shows that the individual characteristics of teachers are far from being the only components of the teacher effect. For example, although length of service has a slight positive impact, the teacher's educational background and training do not, except at the very beginning of their career; as for headteachers, they are somewhat more effective than their deputies. Consequently, teacher-pupil relationship, teaching practices and the organisation of the class explain most of the differences in teacher-effectiveness".

Educational Professions

In France, the Ministry of Education's General Inspectorate (IGEN) makes a major contribution to better understanding the actors of the education system, especially teachers. Its statutes, adopted in 1989, give it a general mission to evaluate the functioning of the education system. Its programme of work, decided by the minister, comprises approximately ten specific topics of study annually, in addition to topics studied on an on-going basis, such as new education technologies, curricula, teacher training, the role of alternating in-school/enterprise-based training and initial training of young people through apprenticeship, etc. The annual report presents a number of in-depth analyses of pedagogical innovations and renewal introduced into primary and secondary schools at the initiative of the Ministry. The 1997 edition, the seventh in this series of public annual reports begun in 1991, also deals with the all-round competency of primary school teachers, the *baccalauréat*, graduate employment and communication technologies.

To learn more about the professions of the education system, the DEP-DPD has made several surveys of primary and secondary teachers, particularly regarding continuing education and training, professional practices, teachers' use of available pedagogical and educational resources or perception of the roles of other actors of the education system including senior masters, librarians and guidance counsellors. In addition, a qualitative study of the tasks and missions of regional education inspectors, published in April 1995 was carried out in November 1994, involving 32 inspectors from six different education authorities (Amiens, Bordeaux, Caen, Limoges, Orléans-Tours and Versailles) and over ten fields or specialisations. As regards the knowledge of teaching practices and their effectiveness, various studies on secondary education compare the practices actually observed with those described by teachers themselves, and which also take into account pupils' outcomes. In addition, a further survey on the teaching of reading was carried out in 1998 by extending the initial 1990 survey to teachers of reading practices from preparatory class through first year primary class. The survey was designed to take stock of the practices in the initial stages of teaching reading and to assess how they had changed over seven years in the light of the new measures introduced in primary education policy. In 1997, as a follow-up to a 1995-1996 sociological study on the evaluation and rating of education professionals, the DEP department for evaluating teachers, resources and educational innovations helped design a summer university on the theme of the rating and evaluation of secondary school teachers in co-operation with the directorate responsible for teaching staff in lower and upper secondary schools and the IGEN conference held in November 1997. The IGEN proceedings were published in the spring of 1998.

How do Schools Function? The Utility of Research and Indicators

Implementing a system of indicators for evaluating secondary schools can enable lower and upper secondary schools to assess this generally acknowledged school effect. School management and headteacher and teaching staff implementation of a "school plan" invariably effect performance and effectiveness.

The IPES System of Indicators for Secondary Schools: Assessing the "Value Added" of Lower and Upper Secondary Schools

The IPES project to create indicators to manage secondary schools was prompted by the desire to assess the overall educational effectiveness of upper and secondary schools. It is consonant with the initial work undertaken by the Directorate for Evaluation and Planning in 1988. Its two-fold objective was presented by Jean-Claude Emin. First, "to provide schools with data gathered in annual surveys in a form they can use to analyse and monitor their situation. Second, for general and technological *lycées* (upper secondary schools), to provide them with indicators for assessing their performance that are more relevant than their success rates on the *baccalauréat* alone". In 1988, this range of indicators was fairly limited. It did not encompass of school activity and organisation; but it did constitute an initial approach and showed headteachers that they could benefit from feedback from the surveys launched by the national education administration.

The IPES system was designed using several key methodological principles. First, a strong emphasis on providing assistance and services to schools "by providing them with a base of previously calculated indicators based on data gathered from nation-wide data and management systems. Next, by combining these indicators with national and education authority district (*académie*) benchmarks enabling them to compare their performance with other schools; lastly, by giving them the means to calculate, monitor and store the specific indicators they wish to develop to evaluate and adapt their school plan". The system was also designed to make a tool available to lower and upper secondary schools so that they could assess their functioning and be held accountable. In the fullest sense of the term, since an institution performing a public service mission must be accountable to its supervisory authority and also to the community at large. The third methodological principle was to design a tool that would make possible an evaluation based both on a relatively complete base of indicators common to all schools, and on indicators specific to each school and its plan. This meant a standard base and specific indicators able to describe and evaluate given aspects of the functioning or performance of each school. Lastly, it was decided rapidly to extend the IPES system to all secondary schools which naturally calls for an ambitious effort to train, or at the very least to inform headteachers so that they can adapt these indicators to their needs and use them as effectively as possible. The range of standard indicators developed especially for upper secondary schools comprises two main types of data.

Primary Characteristics of the School Population and Resources

The indicators on a given school population aim at defining the main characteristics of its pupils as a whole. They do not make it possible to assess their knowledge level directly, but make it possible to compare themselves with major benchmarks at the education authority district and national levels. With regard to the means and human resources available to schools, IPES provides three indicators that also include educational authority and national benchmarks so that schools can compare themselves with other schools. The first of these not only assesses teaching hours per pupil, but more broadly the available human resources in terms of staff per pupil, broken down into teaching, education, supervisory staff, etc. The second indicator describes the main socio-demographic characteristics of teaching staff, and the third assesses the range of options offered to pupils in the second and first grade and their distribution among these options.

Functioning and performance indicators

The first indicator assesses the situation of pupils at the end of the second grade. The second, one of the most important, seeks to determine the proportion of hours actually taught per pupil by subtracting the number of hours of teaching "lost" for various reasons from the number of hours in a normal schedule. Consequently, this indicator provides quantified data on a sensitive issue often subject to preconceived ideas. It also makes it possible to show that factors that were previously grasped intuitively, can now be measured. It "is therefore particularly useful for managing the school and

145

keeping the educational community's various partners informed, as well as for providing the education authorities and national authorities with homogeneous data that can ultimately be used to adjust the resources available for replacing teachers who are absent or undergoing training. Furthermore, this is no doubt one of the most sensitive indicators to present in training headteachers". Functioning and environment indicators also include an indicator showing the average size of divisions and another aimed at assessing more qualitative aspects of the functioning of schools, such as the relative importance of school services and student activities.

The main contribution of the IPES system is doubtless the fact that it develops indicators for assessing schools' performance. A major step forward towards assessing school effectiveness would be to go beyond the basic figures on student outcomes, especially on the *baccalauréat*, in order to try to evaluate the school's value added. Exam success rates give an incomplete and therefore biased vision of school performance. It would also make it possible to provide objective data refuting unfavourable rumours about the quality of education in a particular school. What is more, reliable performance indicators are necessary for lower and upper secondary schools to self-evaluate. "The 'mirror effect', as Jean-Claude Emin dubs it, of performance indicators is essential, for it is only by knowing one's successes and failures and trying to analyse them that one can make improvements". The first step towards this consisted of producing three indicators based on raw data public and private upper secondary school performance based on the results of the 1993 *baccalauréat* which will be presented together as they are complementary. The first was the success rate on the *baccalauréat*, which is not very meaningful. The second was the percentage of second-grade pupils who later took the *baccalauréat*, which measures the probability that a second-grade pupil in a given *lycée* will obtain the *baccalauréat* irrespective of the number of years required to do so. The third was the proportion of exiting pupils who had passed the *baccalauréat*, which determines the percentage of all school-leavers who obtained the *baccalauréat*; this indicator, like the previous one, encompassed the entire upper secondary school population.

In order to more accurately determine value added in designing these indicators, the DEP-DPD offset the impact of pupils' age and socio-professional origin, two important external factors that introduced a bias into the raw data on the *baccalauréat*. This made it possible to project an expected success rate on the *baccalauréat* for a given school corresponding to the success rate it would normally have if its pupils passed the *baccalauréat* at the same rate as all candidates of the same age and socio-professional origin in all schools. Comparing the probable and actual success rates in the final session of the *baccalauréat* makes it possible to estimate the value added. Is this a satisfactory method of calculation? Does it sufficiently offset the external factors that may distort the results? Some *lycées*, mainly in large cities, and especially in Paris, are in a position to select the best pupils from among pupils of comparable age and social backgrounds. The method used to assess the value added until now has not eliminated the real relative advantage of these *lycées*, however. The DEP-DPD therefore built models estimating the probability that pupils would pass the *baccalauréat*, depending on their age, social background, written test results of the certificate of lower secondary education, or two or all of these factors combined. Not surprisingly, age is by far the best predictor of a pupil's success on the *baccalauréat*, which is logical in the French education system where age norms appear to be particularly important regarding progress. If an index that more directly reflects pupils' academic levels (*e.g.* grades on their certificate of lower secondary education) were included, it would doubtless change somewhat the assessment of value added in *lycées* whose population is largely very privileged young pupil. However, the value added that can be calculated using the pupil's socio-professional category, and especially their age, appears to be satisfactory for the vast majority of *lycées*.

Another indicator follows up pupils after they leave the *lycée* (whether they continue in school, work, are looking for a job, are inactive or do their national service), regardless of when they left school and whether or not they obtained the *baccalauréat*. Jean-Claude Emin emphasises that the system attempts to give a relatively complete and comparative vision of a school's performance and effectiveness; but what is important for the management and teaching teams of *lycées* is ultimately that they do not limit themselves merely to assessing their school's performance, but that they have tools that can help them to analyse the causes of problems and take action to solve them, in short that they have additional means for developing, implementing and monitoring their school plan. This system will only be truly effective if it enables schools to achieve these objectives, and every effort has been made to ensure that it makes it possible to assess school's functioning as completely as possible.

In an initial phase, the IPES system was introduced into 600 schools on an experimental basis in the Spring of 1994. Headteachers who wanted management and accountability tools reacted positively to the implementation of this self-evaluation tool. However, the fact that this kind of x-ray of schools was possible and that all this information was made available, in particular to the education authorities, inevitably led some management staff to fear that "with the self-evaluation first of upper and then of lower secondary schools, will this not ultimately become a tool for evaluating principals?" Some headteachers are probably asking this question about a sensitive aspect of the management of administrative staff.

The InPEC System for Primary Education: Developing the Management Function

Just as it had developed indicators for the management of secondary schools, the DEP began work in 1997 to prepare a management tool for the primary level focused

OECD 2000

particularly on the articulation of primary and lower secondary schools. It tried to find performance indicators for individual schools that could be correlated with other indicators on the school population, school functioning, and the environment. This work resulted in the development of management indicators ranging from primary through lower secondary school (InPEC), a computer product with a national database and a small computer application designed to be used by school districts, all of which is on a diskette. The InPEC product comprises three types of indicators for developing the management function at the primary level.

- *Primary schools* contains statistics describing the distribution (the three quartiles) of indicators for the schools in the school area and the district, the *département* and the education authority district, and for metropolitan France as a whole. This includes the percentage of pupils who are behind in preparatory class, the percentage of pupils who are ahead or behind on entering and leaving cycle 3, the percentage of pupils twelve years old and older, the percentage of pupils monitored by RASED, a network of specialised aid to underachievers. These indicators cover all public primary schools and private primary schools under contract (except for specialised schools) but they are only calculated for a given school if at least one pupil with the required characteristics is enrolled. An indicator such as the percentage of pupils behind in preparatory class, for example, enables teachers to assess their teaching practices, their approach to differences among pupils, and their use of the RASED. The statistics on the percentage of pupils twelve years and older make it possible to compare the percentage of these pupils with the same rate in the lower secondary school area, in the school district, *the département* and the education authority district and in metropolitan France as a whole. This enrolment should normally be marginal.

- *Primary school district* contains indicators that provide many descriptive and comparative elements that can be interrelated. These include: the ratio of the number of two-year old pupils to the number of four-year old pupils; the percentage of schools with more than 10% of their pupils behind in preparatory class; the percentage of pupils in priority education zones (ZEP) among pupils in public schools; the percentage of schools with more than 25% of pupils behind at the end of cycle 3; and the percentage of pupils enrolled in CLIS, regular classes that integrate handicapped students. Several approaches are possible: consider all indicators for the school district in order to have an overview; study only the rate of students who are behind in second-year intermediate class in a given school; compare the indicators for the school district, the upper secondary and primary school areas. The third approach might consist of preparing school profiles.

- *Lower secondary school area* contains statistics describing the distribution (the three quartiles) of indicators on school areas (or lower secondary schools), on *département* and education authority districts, and on metropolitan France as a whole. These include the percentage of schools with more than 15% of pupils behind at the beginning of the third cycle, the percentage of schools with more than 25% of pupils behind, the percentage of repeaters in the sixth grade in public lower secondary schools, the percentage of pupils in sixth grade who take school lunches (in lower secondary schools and ZEPs), etc. These indicators cover all public lower secondary school areas except for those that have no public lower secondary school, for example if the area is being rezoned, and schools that are not attached to any lower secondary school sector have also been excluded. More than for the indicators on primary schools, these indicators on lower secondary school areas have been developed to promote primary-lower secondary school dialogue within a given lower secondary school area and even within a same *département* insofar as possible. All of these indicators on lower secondary school areas must naturally be compared with primary school indicators in order to give an idea of the network of primary schools. The percentage of schools with more than 25% of pupils behind at the end of cycle 3, for example, provides an index of the number of low achievers and information on teachers (practices regarding repeaters) and the functioning of schools (limiting the number of pupils in classes). This cannot be interpreted, however, as a performance indicator since pupils may be behind partly because of the teaching practices in other schools or sectors. Consequently, this kind of indicator must be combined with indicators on children who are behind in preparatory class and first-year primary class.

Conclusion

The term "management" used for the primary education indicators that have been recently developed in France emphasises what may seem to be an obvious point. This is that any evaluation of an education system, whether carried out through surveys, analysis, or indicators, must be organised around a key objective, namely improving the conditions for managing the educational system at the various levels - central, intermediate and school levels.

Evaluation is neither an end in itself nor a purely intellectual exercise; action gives it its purpose and meaning. It must therefore be thought of as a management tool and a sound investment, since the conclusions it produces should normally result in decision-making that can improve the conditions of academic achievement for all pupils in democratic societies.

OECD 2000

REFERENCES

ALTET, Marguerite, Pascal BRESSOUX, Marc BRU and Claire LECONTE-LAMBERT (1994),
Etude exploratoire des pratiques d'enseignement en classe de CE2, *Les Dossiers d'Education et Formations* n° 44.

AVANZINI, GUY (1965),
L'échec scolaire, 1961, Editions Universitaires; "L'échec scolaire", numéro 53, *Cahiers pédagogiques*.

BAUDELOT Christian and Roger ESTABLET (1979),
L'école primaire divise, La Découverte, Paris.

BAUDELOT Christian and Roger ESTABLET (1989),
Le niveau monte - Réfutation d'une vieille idée concernant la prétendue décadence de nos écoles, Le Seuil, Paris.

BAUTIER, Elisabeth, Bernard CHARLOT, Ruth KOHN, and Jean-Yves ROCHEX 1992),
Rapport au savoir et rapport à l'école dans les zones d'éducation prioritaires, Report to the French Ministry of Education; Part III, section 2.

BOTTANI, Norberto (1994),
Education at a Glance: OECD Indicators, n°4.

BOURDIEU, Pierre (1966),
Les Héritiers, Paris: Minuit; (1970),
La Reproduction, Paris: Minuit.

BOUVEAU Patrick and Jean-Yves ROCHEX (1997),
Les ZEP entre école et société, CNDP-Hachette, Paris.

BRESSOUX, Pascal (1995),
"Les effets du contexte scolaire sur les acquisitions des élèves: effet-école et effet-classe en lecture", *Revue Française de Sociologie*.

BRESSOUX, Pascal (1997)
"Le maître aussi fait son effet", Les Cahiers pédagogiques.

BRU, Marc (1997),
"Mieux connaître les pratiques enseignantes et chercher en quoi consiste l'effet-maître", DEP-IREDU Seminar, 1995-1996.

DASTE, Pierre (1989),
"L'exigence d'efficacité dans le système éducatif", Administration et Education n° 42, April.

DEP, French Ministry of Education, Repères et références statistiques sur les enseignements et la formation, L'état de l'Ecole, No. 7, October 1997; Géographie de l'Ecole, March 1997; Les dossiers d'Education et Formations : Profession: enseignant, les débuts d'un métier, n° 20, December 1992; Enseigner dans les collèges et les lycées: enquête sur le métier d'enseignant, n° 48, January 1995; Enseigner dans les écoles: enquête sur le métier d'enseignant, n° 51, January 1995; Les documentalistes des établissements scolaires, n° 57, September 1995; Etude sur la fonction de conseiller d'éducation et conseiller principal d'éducation, n° 72, July 1996 ; Etude sur les fonctions de conseiller d'orientation-psychologue, n° 94, 1997; Les inspecteurs pédagogiques régionaux, étude qualitative sur les tâches et missions, April 1995; Les dossiers d'Education et Formations n° 54; Etude sociologique sur l'évaluation et la notation des professionnels de l'éducation, August 1996; Les dossiers d'Education et Formations n°73; Trois indicateurs de performances des lycées, Résultats établissement par établissement (2 volumes), 1994; Les dossiers d'Education et Formations n° 98, March 1998.

DURU-BELLAT, Marie and Alain MINGAT (1993),
Pour une approche analytique du fonctionnement du système éducatif, L'éducateur, PUF, Paris.

DURU-BELLAT, Marie and Agnès HENRIOT-VAN-ZANTEN (1992),
Sociologie de l'école, Armand Colin, Paris.

EMIN, Jean-Claude
"Les indicateurs IPES et les mutations des fonctions d'encadrement", paper presented at the international colloquium of the Ecole supérieure des personnels d'encadrement on the theme "Piloter des systèmes éducatifs en évolution", November 1997, Poitiers, France.

EMIN, Jean-Claude and Claude SAUVAGEOT (1995),
"IPES, un dispositif d'indicateurs pour le pilotage des établissements scolaires" et "Trois indicateurs de performance des lycées", Administration et éducation n° 4, "Les nouveaux systèmes d'information du Ministère de l'Education", Paris.

|151|

ESTABLET, Roger (1987),
L'école est-elle rentable?, PUF, Paris.

EURYDICE (1997),
Dix années de réformes au niveau de l'enseignement obligatoire dans l'Union européenne (1984-1994), Brussels.

GINGRAS, Paul-Emile (1989),
"L'évaluation du système éducatif au Québec", Administration et Education, n° 42.

GODET, Michel (1994),
Le Grand Mensonge, Fixot, Paris.

GOUX, Dominique and Eric MAURIN (1997)
"Démocratisation de l'école et persistance des inégalités", Economie et statistique n° 6.

IGAEN (March 1993),
"Les actions entreprises en matière d'adaptation des formations aux perspectives d'emploi", Report to the French Ministry of Education and to the State Secretary for Vocational Education.

LEGRAND, Louis (1993),
"Pour un collège démocratique", report to the French Ministry of Education.

LEWIS, Anne (1986),
"The search continues for effective schools", Phi Delta Kappa, 64:4.

MINGAT, Alain (1989),
"Analyse coût-efficacité en éducation", Administration et Education n° 42, April.

MINGAT, Alain (1997),
"La complémentarité entre pilotage interne et externe des systèmes éducatifs", paper for the international ESPEMEN colloquium, Poitiers, France.

MINGAT, Alain and Marc RICHARD (1990),
Disparités géographiques de scolarisation en classes de 4ème et de 2nde, Analyses inter-départementales, IREDU, University of Dijon, France.

OCDE (1994),
Implementation of a System of Indicators for Guiding French Secondary Schools, Paris.

OECD (1992),
   The OECD *International Education Indicators*, OECD, Paris.

OECD (1996),
   Education at a Glance, OECD/Centre for Educational Research and Innovation (CERI).

PAPADOPOULOS, Georges (1994),
   Education 1960-1990, the OECD Perspective.

PROST, Antoine (1994),
   L'enseignement s'est-il démocratisé?, PUF, Paris.

RONAL, Edmonds (1979),
   "Effective schools for the urban pool", *Educational Leadership*, 37 - 1.

THÉLOT, Claude (1992),
   "Que sait-on des connaissances des élèves?", Les dossiers d'Education et Formations n°17.

TOULEMONDE, Bernard (1993),
   "Peut faire mieux encore", October-December, *Savoir- Education-Formation*, French Ministry of Education.

Chapter Three

MANAGEMENT OF PHYSICAL RESOURCES
FOR EDUCATION

MAKING BETTER USE OF SCHOOL BUILDINGS: SCHOOLS AS SOCIAL CAPITAL

Kenn **Fisher**
Woods Bagot Architects, Australia

The Educational Infrastructure and its Relationship to Society

In the last five years, there has been a major thrust in all education sectors towards the performance measurement of a range of educational activities including teaching, learning, management and research. There has been little focus, however, on the performance of educational facilities. The Higher Educational Funding Council (HEFC) in the United Kingdom and the Department of Education (DEETYA) in Australia have both implemented quality audit measures for these activities, but neither has attempted to specifically audit facilities from a quality or performance perspective.

With educational facilities consuming as much as 20% of recurrent educational budgets, this position is extremely surprising as we move to the mature stage of the "economic rationalist era". That educational facilities have escaped performance measurement virtually unscathed is remarkable. They have, of course, suffered from incrementally reduced funds as educational facilities seem to be able to best bear cost reductions in times of financial stringency. Cuts to staff positions clearly affect the quality of service delivery.

As developed world economies mature and stabilise, with many cathartic changes having been made over the past 10 to 15 years, there is now a trend towards exploring the social health and wealth of these countries. This is the result of a number of pressures, not least being the impact of technology on employment, with a resultant level of unemployment, which is unlikely to fall below current levels in the foreseeable future.

As a result, as J. Coleman points out, many countries are exploring the impact of social factors on the development of human capital. In this context, the European Union (EU), in its Amsterdam Statement of 1996, available on the Web, decreed that

157

it would focus investments and activities on the social fabric of the Union. To that end, it would seek investment in health, education and housing that would be sharply focused on improving the social health and wealth of the respective countries in the Union. In this context, the EU also wished to ensure that these investments were made to the best effect by measuring social performance outcomes of the projects funded and educational facilities in particular.

Schools in the Environment - PEB studies

The relationship of schools to the community and to the social environment has long been recognised and studied by the OECD Programme on Educational Building (PEB) and the UNESCO Programme on Educational and Cultural Buildings. Over the past few years, PEB has organised a sequence of conferences around the theme of educational facilities and the community. PEB is also increasing its collaborative efforts with the OECD Centre for Educational Research and Innovation (CERI) and other activities in the OECD Directorate for Employment, Education, Labour and Social Affairs (DEELSA). Seminars have addressed the following themes:

- Educational buildings and the environment.

- Broadening the uses of educational buildings.

- Under one roof – sharing community facilities.

- Producing a secure environment for learning.

- Grounds for celebration – using school grounds for learning.

- The ecologisation of schools.

Each of these seminars followed a well-tested formula of plenary papers, site visits, case studies and workshop groups to develop ideas on "best practice" in the study of the school and its relations to society and the environment. The following section briefly analyses the various seminar outcomes in this context.

Educational Buildings and the Environment - Vienna

In Austria, the environment has featured strongly in education for more than a decade. Thirty-three conclusions were drawn from this seminar; the following are particularly relevant:

- The human factor is important and centralised management may be disadvantageous.

- It is better to give the school decentralised budgetary responsibility.

- It is difficult to define a healthy school and in this context mental and physical health must be distinguished.

- Architects need to show more understanding of teachers' and pupils' psychological needs and more research is needed on the effects of building design upon pupils.

- Teachers, parents and pupils should be considered in the design and planning process - genuine consultation will improve the project and ensure that it is better used and cared for.

- Schools should be designed and built for a long service life and be kept in good condition in order to minimise deterioration and discourage damage by pupils.

- School grounds present an opportunity for environmental and other studies on which many schools are failing to capitalise.

- The school environment should have an impact on pupils and they must accordingly be allowed to take an interest in it.

- Students need to be able to identify with their school or at least with some areas of it. Participation in some of the decisions that affect them, such as redecoration or furnishing, will foster this sense of identity and can be expected to reduce vandalism.

Whereas the relationship to pedagogy was not really considered in great depth, a strong focus on learning environments is clear. The stakeholders are seen as important, consultation and dialogue should be fostered, and greater concern should be shown for the design of learning environments.

Broadening the Uses of Educational Buildings - Lyon

This seminar explored the relationship between school facilities and the community. Whilst significant attempts have been made, through innovative design in educational infrastructure, to provide ways and means of linking education more strongly to the community, more recent events in Lyon have shown that this is not a simple task. Indeed, Professor Derouet provided an insightful overview of the situation in France

159

observing that it had not followed the pattern of openness of schools seen in other western countries since the industrial revolution. "Thinking about this difficulty leads to an examination of the links between the ways of teaching, architectural style and political tradition". He suggested that 18th century schools were established to provide the community with a trained workforce to meet the needs of the newly industrialised world, and often included the practical means of training in the form of workshops. Whilst this tradition persisted until the 1970s, where technical schools were still separated from generalist schools, all schools became progressively isolated from the community. This was always the case in France, as Professor Derouet points out.

After the French Revolution, links within the community and relations between people were rejected as remnants of the feudal era. French people feel there is a basic incompatibility between community links and the pursuit of the general interest. It is a completely different story in English-speaking countries where the transition between the two systems took place more gradually. It is possible to be both an individual citizen and a member of the community.

Whilst this assertion may not hold in English-speaking countries, Derouet sees that the nation state was clearly more important than the local community in France. Perhaps the local is a key influence on the global for, as noted earlier, in Austria linkages of schools with the local community are now considered essential in both school design and curricular terms[21].

Derouet further observed that the goal of equality of opportunity required that the school be further isolated from outside interference of the church and other external and possibly questionable influences, such as business. This scenario is played out in the context of urban policy. In rural areas, community interaction is encouraged to provide a stronger sense of community, whereas in urban environments the dominant model is the school as a sanctuary, often surrounded by fences and surveillance, in contrast to the open, rural school.

There is also the paradox of designing for compulsory education for students below 15 years of age with a clear charge for teachers to provide adequate surveillance. This contrasts with training for employment in senior secondary schools where closer links with industry and community are desirable. Whatever the innovations, the real issue is how these are implemented.

First, in terms of the decision-making power. The fashion of integrating facilities was based on a model defined by national and international experts who wished to make the most efficient use of cultural facilities in the new cities. The rationality was imposed on the population. Nowadays, as Derouet points out, the major decisions lie with the elected representatives.

Communities were forced to integrate and open up but they resisted by a variety of means that, advised Derouet, "beyond the fact that the conditioning effect of space had yet to be proven, the resourcefulness of people in escaping this type of constraint knows no bounds".

As decision-making devolves increasingly to local government authorities, the local context, culture and environment will be the primary focus in deciding whether or not resources can be shared with the community. A new equilibrium between state and local community is yet to be found. However, Derouet notes that "the groups of individuals concerned must be conscious that the management of daily business puts into play principles at a high level of generality, and it is at this level that durable accords can be negotiated"[22]. The depth of interest determined another event in Sweden.

Under One Roof: the Sharing of Community Facilities - Sweden

In October 1996, Sweden's devolution of school management to local regions was is in its second year. The conference proceedings thus focused sharply on integrated service provision with local government authorities. This involved the collocation on school sites of traditionally separate services, such as adult education, community, social and welfare services. Collocation policies are usually related to the need to co-ordinate services more effectively or to maximise the efficient use of buildings, equipment, and other resources. As schools and educational facilities become more sophisticated and expensive, local communities increasingly demand wider access to them.

It has been suggested that past collocation initiatives have been driven primarily by resource managers and architects and, surprisingly, not by educators. Governments, concerned to improve efficiency, are reluctant to duplicate the provision of costly facilities. In the pursuit of the goal of lifelong learning, some educational authorities also see virtue in promoting greater integration of adult education, community services, and basic educational facilities on a single site. Many countries are decentralising the planning and administration of schools to local authorities or even to the governing boards of the schools themselves. Some local authorities anxious to promote schools as a focus for regenerating declining urban areas have seized upon the resulting increase in autonomy.

In other areas, integrating services such as child-care or sports and leisure activities within school campuses has proved popular and the traditional "closed door" policy of schools towards local communities has begun to change. As local communities become more involved in the provision of education, they also become more aware of the potential of schools as centres for a range of other services.

161

Conference participants challenged the assumption that the physical and organisational shape of schools can remain as originally designed for19[th] century societies. Schools are now seen not simply as buildings but as organisations and networks of relations and communications. It was thought that the "virtual school" based on information technology might permit new organisational forms that are more flexible and open to society and to local community needs. They may also be the site for a new partnership between teachers, children, adult learners and social and commercial organisations.

Perception about the benefits of integrated provision differ significantly between those responsible for planning and building schools and the principals and teachers who work in them. To some extent, this difference is an inevitable consequence of their contrasting functions: planners and architects, as well as education officials, have to look ahead, anticipate developments in the use of buildings and look beyond the school to the community it serves. Teachers focus on the "job in hand" and the needs of their current pupils. They are only forced to look beyond the horizons of their school, primarily in terms of accountability for the academic outcomes of their teaching. Generally, teachers are grappling with the life-world of diminishing funding, larger classes and other more immediate pressures, and do not understand how opening up to the community will necessarily help them in the classroom.

While there are encouraging signs that some schools are opening up to the community, at least in terms of use of their facilities, for J. Townshend, "If service integration is to become more widespread and serve the purposes of lifelong learning, then school principals and teachers will have to share this vision and become convinced of its educational value. This means involving them at an early stage in the consultation and planning process and building a community dimension into schools' mission statements".

It is clear that such developments will require support. OECD Member countries have committed themselves to policies promoting lifelong learning. However, the report notes that it is equally clear that central governments are not the best agency for implementing lifelong learning that requires sensitivity to local needs and flexible, diverse responses. Local authorities have an important role in promoting imaginative and innovative approaches to emerging local needs and in promoting greater integration between social and educational services.

In some countries, control over education has been further devolved to the institutions themselves. Whether local authorities are the controlling bodies or have only a supportive function in educational matters, their role as catalysts for greater integration of services and links with the world of work will grow in importance. What is not yet clear is how the representation of the diversity of local participants in lifelong learning can be instituted in the governance of schools and other educational institutions.

Despite these differences of approach, there is, in fact, a convergence around the notion of setting goals and standards at a national level and empowering local authorities and schools themselves to deliver the services. National governments are also acquiring or retaining responsibility for evaluating the performance of local systems. These developments form the political context within which integrated provision of services is occurring. However, without strong national goals and centralised measures to equalise funding and evaluate outcomes, some current developments could lead to greater inequality of service provision and educational outcomes. Lifelong learning requires a national framework within which local diversity can flourish without losing sight of common goals.

Producing a Secure Environment for Learning - Florence

As a logical sequel to the Sweden conference, the PEB Board thought that the theme of secure learning environments would be most relevant, given the then-recent violence in the UK and France of shootings, stabbings, and deaths in schools. The seminar was held in Italy in May 1997, and the depth of feeling was especially great, given that the school had always been regarded as a safe and protected place with the "clashes, dangers and inequalities of society kept beyond its boundaries". In this regard, the demands of families appeared to remain as high as ever. Parents expect public authorities to ensure their children are in safe and suitable places for education and training.

"The school must be defended" was the principal conclusion of the seminar. Most if not all conference participants, however, also said that the school should not be regarded as a sanctuary or turn into a stronghold but should remain "open", allowing trends in social life to permeate. It should remain in the "heart of the city" but also be protected against violence from outside. Suitable conditions for reconciling the apparently contradictory requirements of opening up and protection were spelt out: these represent considerable political and financial challenges for central government and local authorities alike.

The conference rapporteur, a French education directorate inspector, noted that the first task in prevention is to identify and assess every type of risk jeopardising the security of the school environment. Participants therefore opted for the development of observation and measurement tools consisting of indicators and the placement of observatories (developing standards and benchmarks and assisting in quality assurance) at the disposal of active prevention policy at all levels of school design, construction, and management. This was considered to be a necessity in view of the increased autonomy of schools and had the immediate impact of broadening the responsibilities of school heads.

163

The first step in providing a secure environment for learning was seen to consist in the strict application of the rules and regulations prescribing security standards, at both national and state levels, to provide effective protection against risks arising from the use of the premises, or installations against outside violence. Real consultation between all partners in the school was considered necessary. The partnership was seen to be as broad and continuous as possible, covering all stages in the life of a school from design to management. From the architectural standpoint, aesthetics were still considered to serve the school's main task and pedagogical objectives while taking into account security constraints. This was evident in the school visits in Bologna, Ferrara, Florence and Pistoia in very different contexts (schools located in historical buildings, town centres, or on outlying industrial land).

The proceedings note that such partnerships are also the expression of local policies that are not limited to establishing consultation procedures between education "actors" but should include all aspects of the training of management, education, service and health and surveillance staff in schools. Further, there must therefore be sufficient staffing, and education leaders should also work in co-operation with other public services, national and, above all, local, in the justice, police, and health fields.

The seminar showed that although the concept of the school is not endangered, slowly deteriorating physical conditions combined with urban violence may end in a severe crisis, possibly sooner than expected. The discussions held throughout the seminar showed that wherever political leaders took strong action, especially at the funding level, the effectiveness of the security measures was best expanded through long-term association of prevention policies based on consultation and partnership.

The key issue in the conference was probably the need to strike a balance between the "school as a fortress" and the "open school". The seminar did not focus on design specifically although some mention was made of defensible design. One UK speaker noted that the 19th century schools were much easier to fortify because they were very closed cells with forbidding exteriors! This fortress approach is a very real problem in some countries, particularly the UK, the US, and France.

Grounds for Celebration: the Use of School Grounds for Learning - Winchester

This seminar, which particularly complemented the Austrian seminar that examined the built form, was designed to explore the often overlooked issue of school grounds, the land on which schools are built and which surrounds them. School grounds can provide many opportunities to contribute to the educational process but they can also become a source of a variety of problems. The international seminar was organised to examine the crucial interface between schools and their community surroundings and the potential uses of school sites. It was intended to include in-depth analyses of four themes:

1. The influence of the school and its surroundings on student behaviour.

2. The use of school grounds, or "outdoor classroom" in the educational process.

3. Minimising the environmental impact of schools.

4. Eco-schools.

The seminar closely examined some recent initiatives in the United Kingdom and compared those with experience in 15 or so OECD Member countries. Participants visited six eco-schools in and around Winchester. The key conference issues of the outdoor classroom, student behaviour and Environmental Agenda 21 (from the Rio de Janeiro Earth Conference) were still seen to be critical. It was suggested that school sports grounds might also be a way of engaging with a broader agenda, which related to the community at large.

Ecologising Schools - Vienna

Once again CERI, under the aegis of the Environment and Schools Initiative (ENSI) sponsored a conference in Linz, Austria, with PEB and the Austrian Ministry of Education. The theme was related to the increasing awareness of the problem of sustainability, which has made environmental education more complex and demonstrates the connections to economic, social, and technological problems. "Greening" schools, in which the school is considered a holistic ecological learning place, is a growing international trend that could be considered part of a new environmental education paradigm.

Environmental education still tends to remain a marginalised and compartmentalised corner of most education systems, however. The OECD/CERI review of environmental education policies in six countries (Austria, Australia, Finland, Germany, Hungary and Norway) drew attention to many aspects of international developments, noting that:

While there were many examples of innovative practice in schools, a new paradigm of advanced teaching and learning with broad political legitimacy, solid scientific status and the funding to back up research and teacher training was required to truly change children's attitudes, values, behaviour and consumption patterns, and to ensure the integration of environmental education within the mainstream curriculum.

165

The seminar provided an overview of the OECD ENSI programme, addressed current issues in environmental education and focused on identifying the opportunities that exist for closer and stronger integration of environmental education curriculum with school grounds programmes such as Learning through Landscapes. The outcomes from this conference are expected to provide a focus on developing criteria, indicators and strategies for implementing school ecologisation and for environmentally-oriented teacher training.

Conclusions

These seminars share a theme of partnership, consultation and collaboration at all levels of society: the state, the school, and the community. Many of the studies illustrated that the success of schools is highly interdependent on relationships between parents, teachers, community leaders, local government agencies and government departments. These relationships are now being more closely scrutinised in theoretical studies concerned with "social capital". It might be useful to try to provide a better framework for understanding the inter-relationships between these levels. To do so, it is necessary to explore some theoretical developments.

From Theory...

These PEB seminars all have implications for the relationship of the school (any learning institution) and the community. Social capital means, in part, determining whether or not it is possible to derive performance measures that indicate a society's level of health and performance and whether these measures can be used as indicators to measure financial capital and human capital.

Social Capital as a Means of Performance Measurement

Defining social capital is not an easy task. Cox defines it as what underpins civil society; it is the binding civil society which itself is "the space between the government and the family". Putnam suggests that "networks of civic engagement are an essential form of social capital - the denser the networks in the community, the more likely that its citizens will be able to co-operate for mutual benefit". In simple terms, social capital seems to depend on values of *trust, reciprocity, networks and community co-operation* that are obviously linked to a communal rather than to a more individualised libertarian approach that is thus not necessarily conducive to collaboration.

The idea of social capital is not new but has been present for at least 1 000 years in northern Italy where economic strength depends largely on the stock of social capital. Putnam initiated extensive comparative studies of northern and southern Italy in an attempt to determine the key points of differentiation for the perceived vast gap in their social and economic health and wealth. He identified the means of communication, social interaction and organisation used in each region as major factors.

Putnam argues that social capital is built up over many centuries, but can be fostered or hindered depending on whether there is a horizontal, or vertical, hierarchical form of communication which, he argues, is a post-colonial structure left after the Normans in southern Italy. In northern Italy, by contrast, the key means of organisation is horizontal, reflecting the communal origins of the region. Horizontal communications foster trust, networks, communication and civic action, whereas vertical systems are more practically based on hierarchical differentials of power.

This polarity of view is evident in the school system in Bologna run by the communities and reflect their local needs in their horizontal arrangement. Not everyone agrees with this, however. As the OECD report on distressed urban areas remarked, "It is doubtful that familial, reciprocal and voluntary institutions, even in the north, will have sufficient capacity and resources to prevent the new urban poverty from consolidating its position in the southern cities and invading the northern ones on a large scale".

In Australia, school management is devolved to the states (equivalent to the German Lander) and there are some attempts at regional management, school clustering, and devolution of finances. At present, local government authorities are not responsible for schools as they are in the United States and Norway. In OECD countries, there is a diversity of arrangements among both hierarchical (devolved) and vertical (central) systems as well as hybrids of these.

Many, if not all, of the social capital attributes are non-material in nature and admittedly need to be "practised" constantly in order to avoid depleting the stock. The question raised here is whether social capital has a physical or material element and, if so, how can this be measured in the context of schools, colleges and universities and other learning environments such as cultural buildings?

Locating Social Capital

Sociologists continue to trace and analyse the evolution and phases or stages of society since the industrial revolution. Coleman argues that these phases or stages have evolved sequentially since the industrial revolution. "Firstly a change in the mode of production; secondly a change in locus of residence; thirdly a transcendence of place and lastly; the erosion of primordial institutions".

Not surprisingly, this transition can be also tracked in the development of school design. In the case of post-compulsory education, it can, in fact, be traced back to well before the industrial revolution and, in the specific case of universities, to the emergence of the first university in Bologna in 1088[23]. In terms of compulsory schooling, one way of following the transition may be through the evolution of the classroom, yet traditional classroom designs have evolved only to the extent that pedagogy has evolved and teaching is an inherently conservative profession, perhaps because culture is worth conserving.

This raises questions about the role and power of the state, however, and about the position of official knowledge and for whom culture and knowledge is "delivered". It also has to do with resourcing and the extent to which classroom teachers must resort to traditional means of teaching due to a lack of these resources. Suffice it to say the traditional 50-square-metre classroom for 25 to 30 students with rows of desks and chairs facing the teacher at the front, in vogue for some 200 years or so, is still all too common.

School designs have also remained virtually static and are commonly still quite strongly separated from the community, often with high fences to keep outsiders out. The concern for safety and security in society is seen uppermost in the design and placement of schools; the idea of trust, networks, reciprocity and collaboration appears to be deliberately designed out.

Opportunities for students, staff, parents and the community to "learn" social capital are thus extremely limited and, in fact, in many cases, almost physically impossible. However, some post-secondary institutions have developed significantly stronger links to community and employers and other tertiary educational institutions. But is this too late in the life of our young? Some claim that when the idea and practice of social capital are not developed in the early years of schooling, it is too late in the compulsory years.

Conversely, educational practitioners and theorists alike are now pursuing the idea of graduate competencies to measure performance. These key competencies include:

- Critical thinking.

- Problem solving.

- Teamwork.

- Organising research and study programmes.

- Communications skills in various modalities.

These competencies are being developed with new technology enhanced pedagogies, which the OECD is studying in its Information and Communication Technology (ICT) and the Quality of Learning Project and its Adult Learning in a New Technological Era Project. These studies note, amongst other findings, that the most powerful and flexible educational environments support four modes of learning:

• Real-time conversation by a pair of people or a small group of people.

• Time-delayed conversation (when conversational turns occur with gaps of hours, days or weeks).

• Learning by doing.

• Directed instruction (explanation to a large group of learners).

Social capital is said to be based on trust, norms, co-operation, reciprocity and civic "duty", and needs to be constantly nurtured and practised rather than be depleted as a working capital. It differs from financial capital in that it is primarily for, and by, the public good, whereas financial capital in the free market can be construed as being for the private good. Others might argue, of course, that a working market economy is good for all. What is clear, however, is that all of these activities must be practised in a social context: meetings, sporting activities, cultural events and the like. Similarly, graduate competencies must be practised in relation to the community to be of any worth. Where are these activities carried out? To a greater or lesser extent, they occur in learning and cultural establishments. And so the design of these venues becomes critical to either facilitating or alienating the process of civic interaction.

The Role of the Built Learning Environment in Social Capital

In addition to the fundamental and formal traditional institutional role of "facilitating" learning, educational and cultural buildings also have an informal role to play in relating to society. Schools in particular are increasingly taking the role, at least in compulsory education, of child rearing as two- (and increasingly single-) parent families work. Education is thus increasingly taking the role of parenting children so that they may take a positive and contributory role in life.

Some commentators, as Coleman points out, have taken a "return-on-investment" approach to this as a means of engaging in the quantitative debate. They argue that society will invest in children hoping that they will become contributing members of society as they mature. Should mentoring fail, the newly-graduated adult can become a drain rather than a contributor and might resort to criminal activity, will make no fis-

169

cal contribution, and will drain social welfare resources. It is therefore increasingly critical that students be educated to be a contributing part of society.

Italians in northern Italy support this view, as Giuseppino Fioravanti explains. They ensure that the new generation is exposed to the depth of their culture by embracing what society has to offer by nurturing, restoring and conserving their built heritage and using it as an omnipresent icon in order to demonstrate to the young how architecture and culture are inextricably woven into the very fabric of society.

It is not surprising that churches and other religious establishments are becoming available for reuse as learning institutions in our post-modern society of fragmentation. They are joined by factories and industrial "brown field" sites as the post-industrial age bites as we now seek to manufacture our goods in the developing world. But these sites, too, are embraced by the educational system in northern Italy. In fact, educational institutions are often used as a pathfinder in urban renewal and regeneration projects in many parts of Emilia-Romagna.

The OECD Territorial Development Programme, which examines social and regional planning issues, completed a study on distressed urban areas and it is worth quoting verbatim one of the findings, which begins to touch on social capital:

"The cities of the 20th century have also seen the emergence of new forms of architecture and urban planning. Reacting against tradition some architects, such as Le Corbusier, founded the modern movement. Their idea was to adapt cities to contemporary society. They thus wished to make architecture utilitarian and rational, and create buildings in harmony with the aspirations of modern man. Their response was however a naive one. Individual aspirations regarding the day-to-day environment were reduced to a few basic ideas. The psychological and sociological repercussions of urban planning on individuals were totally neglected... Ideas of social convention and situated rationality or even readability, studied by Kevin Lynch, were not taken into account. Beyond the functional aspects, urban planning and architecture must allow for the way the city is perceived by its inhabitants...the modernists deliberately ignored the geographical specificities of any given urban area. But the built environment where human beings live has an inherent meaning. The city has a soul and its specificities define its identity".

UNESCO is also looking at cultural and social well-being and at the role of educational and cultural buildings in sustaining it. It is primarily focused on developing countries. For example, it has a research and development programme which aims to understand the role of educational and cultural buildings to develop policies and strategies to implement built learning environments in disadvantaged, rural and remote countries and regions.

One such study is the community learning centre programme that is being implemented in many developing countries. This programme aims to engage with the entire community, not just school-aged children, to provide greater opportunities for improved literacy and numeracy. Of course, such centres are also likely to provide a strong physical cue as a community focus for the practice of social capital. Not surprisingly, these buildings are often constructed through community effort, drawing on the stock of social capital in those communities of trust, reciprocity, co-operation and networks.

The UNESCO programme also links to the World Health Organisation (WHO) healthy schools programme which aims to target school-aged students to develop habits and models of health and hygiene. School design also comes into this with the WHO saying that expected outcomes include "participation of children in discussion of how the school can be made healthy and in activities to improve the school environment, and the participation of parent and community organisations". This can be extended by looking at the view of the Campaign for Learning, a NGO seeking to sponsor alternative, non-formal educational alternatives and initiatives in the UK, that the range of learning environments includes the following.

OBVIOUS	LESS OBVIOUS	SURPRISING
Pre-school groups	Businesses	Retirement homes
Nurseries	Community centres	Homeless shelters
Schools	Sports centres	Sheltered housing
Colleges	Arts centres	Refuges
Universities	Museums and attractions	Prisons
Adult learner's centres	Health centres	Shopping malls/supermarkets
Homes	Post offices	Hospitals
Libraries	Cities	Churches
Television	Towns	Surgeries
	Villages	Trains and stations
	Internet	Football stadia
	Nature reserves	Bookshops
	The outdoors	Pubs
	Newspapers	Restaurants and hotels
		Cafés

The Impact of Universities on Regions

It is thus worth considering the economic and social impact of educational institutions on regions. For example, the OECD Programme for the Institutional Management of Higher Education found the following.

Universities, like companies and regions, are having to fundamentally reappraise their role and the way they govern themselves; in this process they cannot ignore their engagement with the regions where they are located. As in the other spheres, globalisation and localisation are complementary, not competing, logics. The challenge is to move the university agenda on from an exploitative relationship with the region – in it but not of it – to a resource development/stakeholder/investment model which highlights the mutual interdependency of the region and the university. Universities need to see the local arena of people and firms as having needs that can be turned into opportunities on which their own world class activity can build competitive advantage. The realisation of such aspirations does require a fundamental realignment of the perspective of many academics of their universities. Concerning academics it implies a greater sense of commitment to the institutions as a whole, to teamwork and to management. Engagement with the region is one way of beginning such realignment. If this realignment does not begin, public support for universities may be further undermined as we enter the 21st century[24].

A CVCP study, presented in 1995, found that a range of diverse local issues needs to be addressed:

• The significance of the university in the local community.

• The size of the student population in relation to the total population in the relevant age group.

• The participation of the local population in higher education.

• The local industrial structure – its sectoral and occupational composition, the balance between large and small employers, and the extent of local ownership of industry.

These factors might raise the awareness of the significance of the university in the local community, but they say little about the mechanism linking universities and their local community. Those which might elucidate this link include the following:

• The priority attached to such relationships by the university.

• Where the responsibility for management of these relationships lies.

• The range of public bodies with which the university regularly interacts.

• The extent and significance of public use of university facilities.

• The local component to university industry links.

It is quite clear that some property developers have noted the power of educational institutions to increase property values (*e.g.* the new Logan Campus of Griffith University) and see them almost as an anchor tenant of a new development. They recognise that new home buyers want learning opportunities at their doorstep, for lifelong learning, that is all sectors of education, and increasingly, in Australia, joint ventures are taking shape between developers, schools, vocational educational and higher educational institutions. Indeed shopping centre owner statistics show increased sales where there is a collocated educational institution.

Joint-use Libraries as Indicators of Social Capital

Participants at a recent conference of the Australian Library and Information Association examined the idea of joint-use libraries in some depth. It became apparent that these facilities are indeed wonderful opportunities to provide a bridge between parents, teachers, students, the community, shopping centres and industry. A Comedia study of their future role lists some indicators for the successful management of joint-use libraries that are very congruent with the ideas of social capital:

• Social bonding.

• Generating civic pride.

• Enhancing skills and being more educated.

• Employment opportunities.

• Relaxation through structured activities.

• New friends and relationships.

• Contribution to social harmony.

The joint-use libraries practice checklist includes the need for:

• Strong relationships.

• Mutual trust and understanding.

• Mutual need and benefit (reciprocity?).

• Leadership.

• Commitment.

- Sprit of co-operation, patience and flexibility.

- Recognition of the value of co-operation.

    In relation to the library buildings themselves the checklist includes the following key attributes. Is/are there:

- Spaces for separate programmes?

- Public transport?

- Universal design?

- Convenient toilets?

- Attractive design?

- Maintenance/cleaning?

- Appropriate furniture? A central site, walk-in?

- A separate and visible entrance?

- Sufficient parking?

    Are they:

- Close to classrooms?

- Visible from the street?

- Openable after school hours?

    Such concepts were also the focus of a two-day meeting of experts held in Paris in 1998 and convened by PEB [25]. Key findings included:

- The library sets an image: new and renovated libraries will provide a visible, identifiable and physical image for tertiary education institutions to attract students, teachers and researchers.

- The networked library and professional development: the new library is integral to learning by educating towards a critical use of networked resources. The need for staff and students to be trained or re-trained is recognised as critical and must receive adequate funding.

- The role of the library: protecting cultural heritage remains one of the fundamental roles of libraries. Librarians are faced with a new mission to guide students, professors and, whenever possible, the whole community in the digital world.

- Flexibility: new library facilities should include as much flexibility as possibility to meet the needs of today and the future, particularly with concern for rapid and unpredictable technological development.

For joint-use libraries, a number of criteria, suggested for their success, are more likely to work in small isolated rural centres where there is no economic justification for alternative public library services because of size or isolation. Technical and further education sectors, and senior and community colleges, where there are close parallels between campus students and the adult community, are also likely to be successful. Where there is genuine community interest in sharing a comprehensive range of resources and facilities at the local level, it can lead to the development of a community centre, which incorporates a joint-use library. Case studies have shown that in areas where the facility is adjacent to a retail area, most likely in growth zones of urban areas and new towns, a successful joint venture is likely.

Other possibilities are now emerging with universities, Technical and Further Education (TAFE), schools, government and "industry". Critical success factors include: the careful consideration of the institutional site and the position of the library to guarantee suitable access to all potential users; reasonable and convenient access for all users to the library building; adequate building size and design to cater for both groups of users and their specific and individual and group needs. Cost efficiencies are clearly related to the shared use of the library, teaching and learning areas, communication links, infrastructure services, student and other amenities and services.

Possible Spatial Measures of Social Capital

Measures of social capital are difficult to determine as they are essentially nonmaterial, however, the built environment provides a physical opportunity to explore some possible measures. Whilst performance indicators are generally quantitative, a greater understanding of how social capital works in the physical sense is likely to come from qualitative measures.

...To Practice: Three Case Studies from Australia

There is an increasing trend towards collocation of educational and other community services in Australia. The many examples across the country range from

175

shared-use community halls and community services in urban renewal suburbs, to major re-use of disused military bases. All share many of the issues discussed above and can demonstrate how social capital might be measured through joint-use facilities.

Case Study 1 - The Rockingham Campus, Perth, Western Australia

This collocated campus involves three partners: two post-secondary educational sectors (university and vocational education) and the local community. It is located some 60 kilometres south of Perth in a rapidly growing area with low tertiary participation rates. The local government authority was keen to develop a tertiary campus and to link it with both the city activities and the existing local TAFE campus. The project went ahead with some complications – another council was bidding for the joint campus, the University offered three possible sites, and the state government came in at a late stage to influence site location. Eventually, a site was chosen that included TAFE, the university, and the community and joint-use library.

• The City of Rockingham now has a major library for a significantly reduced capital outlay.

• The city has saved money by being able to close two of its libraries while still offering a better service.

• TAFE has a vastly improved library facility that is being utilised far more than was the old site.

• TAFE administration gained more space when it moved to the new premises.

• Murdoch University acquired a university library at half the normal cost.

• There is now a specialist Murdoch Engineering collection based on the existing TAFE collection.

• All three user groups have greatly improved stocks and costs in duplication have been minimised.

The Hervey Bay Case study notes that the joint-use library has also provided a variety of flexible learning study spaces. Culturally, lifelong learning is promoted through opportunities for interaction between the community and the academic sectors. From the marketing perspective, it also provides a shop front for the university. Based on this example in the debate on the efficacy of decentralised libraries to support the current imperatives of flexible delivery and massification of education, a joint-use academic public library offers a logical, cost-effective solution to the problem of providing information service and support to regional students.

Case Study 2 - The Music Conservatorium, Sydney, New South Wales

This project is a three-way partnership between the University of Sydney Conservatorium of Music, the Department of Education's specialist High School of Music and the Botanical Gardens. This site, originally the stables for the nearby Government House, is located on the Domain, one of Sydney's most illustrious sites dating back to the commencement of the Government House in the mid-1800s. It is very close to the Harbour Bridge, the CBD, the Opera House and the adjacent Botanical Gardens.

The site has been completely redeveloped with unsympathetic extensions demolished to restore the grandeur of the original stable buildings. The stable courtyard has been adapted to use as a music performance auditorium. Additional auditoria, practice rooms, administration, joint-use library and other facilities, located below ground with the addition of many light wells, surround the building. The High School is also located underground to the rear and can share the performance spaces, library, and Botanical Gardens.

Case Study 3 - The Nirimba Campus, Sydney, New South Wales

This is a major partnership between the University of Western Sydney, a Department of Education Vocational Training College (TAFE), two private high schools and the local community.

The site is an old, disused Naval Base that includes an airfield. The campus had many buildings that could be reused and included a number of sporting facilities such as an Olympic swimming pool. Joint-use agreements were struck between the schools, between the TAFE and schools, between the TAFE and University, and between all parties for some of the core areas.

This campus demonstrates how planning and design are critical to the effectiveness of the joint-use arrangements. Individual identities were maintained whilst shared spaces were still possible. The site offers shared opportunities with private institutional areas interspersed.

177|

Conclusion

There is clearly a move across the globe to looking to the social health and wealth of nations. The so-called "third way" which attempts to provide social security in an economically sustainable national context is indicative of this. It is, however, essential that both quantitative and qualitative measures be used to balance these two at times conflicting goals of economic and social wealth. Educational bricks and mortar represent a very tangible symbol of meaning in a community and this measure of importance has to be quantified and qualified to be more fully understood.

The idea of social capital may be a valuable way of furthering this balance and, in particular, "Making Better Use of School Buildings: Schools as Social Capital" is an important means to integrate both forms of measure as demonstrated in the case studies.

REFERENCES

COLEMAN, J. (1988),
"Social Capital and Human Capital", *American Journal of Social Sciences*, Vol. 94, p.7.
http://europa.eu.int/pol/reg/info_en.htm

COLEMAN, J.S. (1993),
"The Rational Reconstruction of Society", *American Sociological Review* 58.

COMEDIA, (1993),
The Future Role of Community Libraries, The Round.

COX, E. (1996),
ABC Radio Boyer Lectures.

CVCP (UK Council of Vice Chancellors and Principals) (1995),
Learning Cities Conference Proceedings, 20th and 21st April.

DEROUET, J-C. (1995),
"Opening up the School: Some Reflections on the Experience". Presentation at the
OECD Conference on Broadening the Uses of Educational Buildings, Lyon, May 1995.

FIORAVANTI, G.,
"Patterns and Strategies for Conversion of Existing Buildings into Schools", Office
of Educational Facilities, Regione Emilia-Romagna, Italy.

GODDARD, J. (1997),
"Managing the University Regional Interface", *Journal of the OECD Programme on the
Institutional Management of Higher Education* 9:3.

OECD (1996),
Review of Environmental-Education Policies in Six Countries: Austria, Australia, Finland, Germany, Hungary and Norway, OECD/CERI.

OECD (1997),
Final Report of the Project Group on Distressed Urban Areas, Territorial Development Division, Paris.

PUTNAM, R. (1993),
Making Democracy Work: Civic Tradition in Modern Italy. Princeton: Princeton University Press.

TOWNSHEND, J. (1998),
Under One Roof: The Sharing of Community Facilities, OECD.

Urban Planning Bureau of the City of Vienna (1996),
The New Schoolhouse: Schoolchild's Universe and Urban Practice, Vienna.

World Health Organisation (1995),
Building a Healthy City: a Practitioners' Guide, Geneva.

THE IMPACT OF SCHOOL BUILDING CONDITIONS, STUDENT ACHIEVEMENT, AND BEHAVIOUR

Glen I. **Earthman**
Virginia Polytechnic Institute and State University

Introduction

The influence of the built environment on student and teacher performance is one of the most provocative and compelling questions regarding school buildings. Educators and architects commonly hold that the building does indeed influence how well students and teachers perform: the important question is the degree of influence, and how to measure it accurately.

Over the past sixty years, considerable research has been undertaken in the United States to assess whether or not such a relationship exists. Researchers have investigated the influence upon student performance of various building components - wall colour, building configuration, the presence or absence of classroom windows, air conditioning, space allocation per pupil, carpeted floors, noise levels, thermal conditions, and furniture types. This research has generally proven very valuable to designers of new school buildings who have incorporated the best features of this list into most new school buildings in the United States. While students and teachers have obviously benefited from this infusion of research findings, however, the majority of students in the United States are not housed in new school buildings but rather go to school in older buildings, many of which are approaching 50 years of age. Few of these have the essential components found necessary for a good learning environment.

Research exploring the relationship between building conditions and student performance has an inherent problem: there are no predictable results. While predictability resulting from scientific investigation is almost a given in the hard sciences, it is very difficult to demonstrate in the social sciences. This paper discusses research that cannot produce predictable results; the examination and use of the findings in these studies remains, nonetheless, beneficial.

A major deficiency in school facilities research has been the lack of replication of sound studies. The studies presented here show the beginning of a progression in studies using the same methodology with different populations, and the beginning of discerning some generalities about the impact of buildings on student performance. Some recent research has shown a promising avenue of investigation, demonstrating a positive relationship between student achievement and behaviour, and the design and condition of school buildings. Others show a low to medium level of relationship between these variables.

Researchers differ in their opinions. Some claim that building influences are very insignificant and that if there is any influence, it results simply from chance; others claim that the built environment has a discernible influence upon the processes of teaching and learning, either inhibiting or helping them. More systematic analysis on a large scale is required before generalisations can be made, particularly since the issue evinces broad interest.

This paper focuses on the relationship between two variables relating directly to students themselves: the built environment and achievement, as measured by some form of standardised or normed test or examination administered to all students, and student behaviour, that can include a specific level of student activity or school climate that is a more general term. Educators tend to believe that student behaviour influences academic achievement and vice versa.

Building Age and Achievement

Conventional wisdom in educational facility planning and design seems to indicate that the physical environment does indeed affect the behaviour and performance of the students and teachers who occupy it. A significant relationship is difficult to demonstrate statistically, however. To explore this possible relationship, Bowers and Burkett (1988) investigated the differences in achievement, health, attendance, and behaviour of two groups of students in different physical environments: two elementary school buildings with students between the ages of 5 and 13 in the same school jurisdiction in rural Tennessee were used to differentiate physical environments for this comparison. One school was a recent, modern building in all respects. The other was constructed in 1939 and had very little improvement to the physical structure. The researchers reasoned that the students, faculty, and educational programmes in both buildings were essentially the same. Students in the fourth and sixth grades were tested to determine the degree of academic achievement. Students in the new school building significantly out-performed students in the older building in reading, listening, language, and arithmetic. Further, faculty in the new building reported fewer disciplinary incidents and health conditions than faculty in the old building. Attendance, likewise, was better among students in the new building. Bowers and Burkett concluded that a relationship did exist between the physical environment and student achievement, health, attendance, and behaviour.

In a very recent replication of the Bowers and Burkett study, Phillips (1997) found significant differences in the reading and arithmetic scores of students in new and old buildings. He found a definite relationship between the age of the school facility and student reading achievement scores as measured by the Iowa Test of Basic Skills, and a strong relationship between student mathematics achievement scores and building age. The mean mathematics scores for the treatment group (those students in new buildings) increased 7.63 percentile ranks after moving into the new facility. He found no significant differences in attendance patterns between the students enrolled in the old and new buildings.

Building Condition and Parental Involvement

Edwards (1992) investigated the relationship between parental involvement, school building condition, and student achievement in schools in Washington, D.C. She hypothesised that the condition of public school buildings is affected by parental involvement, which affects student achievement. She analysed these relationships by evaluating the condition of school buildings and determining the extent of parental involvement, and the amount of funds that parents raised for the local school, and compared these results with student achievement scores.

To determine the condition of the building, she used data from a self-evaluation of school facilities completed by a group of volunteers in each community. The condition of the sample buildings was classified into poor, fair, or excellent, as a result of the evaluation based upon the presence or absence of certain physical conditions. For instance, buildings that were dirty, had leaking roofs, classrooms with peeling paint, no air-conditioning, and needed repairs, were grouped in the poor category.

For parent involvement, Edwards used membership in the Parent-Teachers Association (PTA) on a per student basis plus the PTA budget at the school on a per student basis. Student achievement was measured by using average school scores on the Comprehensive Test of Basic Skills (CTBS) which was administered to all three levels of schools by the Washington, D.C. Public Schools. The average CTBS score of students in each school was obtained through standard published reports. He found that in schools where many parents were involved in the PTA and raised considerable funds for school purposes, the buildings were in better condition than where parents were less involved and raised less money. For every dollar increase in the PTA budget of the school, the building was seen to improve on the scale of building condition. In

183

this model of analysis, she found four variables that had significant results in predicting the changes in building condition: types of school (elementary, junior high, senior high), building age, student enrolment, and the mean income of the community in which the school is located. The first three variables have significant results in predicting the changes in building condition. Although the mean income factor was not significant, the parameter estimate was positive, indicating that as the mean income of the area increases, the building condition improves.

For building condition and student achievement, data analysis supported the hypothesis. Building condition had an effect upon student achievement scores. The analysis indicates that as a school moves from one category to another, the achievement scores can be expected to increase by 5.455 percentage points. If the school moves two categories from poor to excellent, for example, the achievement scores would be expected to increase by 10.9 percentage points in the average achievement scores. Conversely, based upon the analysis, the signs of the estimated building condition coefficients are negative, meaning that from the base of excellent schools, a building condition of fair or poor will reduce the average student achievement scores.

Building Condition and Achievement

In a similar study, Cash (1993) investigated the relationship between certain school building conditions, student achievement, and student behaviour in rural high schools in Virginia using basically the same hypothesis that Edwards employed. The condition of the building in this study, however, was the independent variable, and student achievement and behaviour were the dependent variables.

Local school system personnel evaluated the condition of the school building using an evaluation instrument developed by Cash based upon previous studies that had addressed certain building conditions, using elements showing a positive relationship between a particular building condition and student achievement and behaviour. The items in the Commonwealth Assessment of Physical Environment (CAPE) addressed conditions such as air conditioning, classroom illumination, temperature control, classroom colour, graffiti, science equipment and utilities, paint schedules, roof adequacy, classroom windows, floor type, building age, supporting facilities, condition of school grounds, and furniture condition. The presence or absence of these factors determined the overall condition of the building which was classified as substandard, standard, and above-standard.

In addition to these evaluative condition classifications, the 27 items on the CAPE were divided into structural and cosmetic factors. Thus, some items related to the structure of the building - classroom lighting, air conditioning, thermal environment, and

184

roof integrity, while others - painting schedules, wall colour, cleanliness, and graffiti - related to its cosmetic condition. These two major categories were used to analyse different sections of the CAPE with student achievement scores; however, student achievement scores were compared to the combined 27 items on the instrument to produce an overall building condition category. Therefore, three comparisons were made with student achievement scores: overall, cosmetic, and structural. Table 1 lists the items in the two categories.

Table 1. **Structural and Cosmetic Categories**
on the Building Appraisal Instrument

STRUCTURAL ITEMS	COSMETIC ITEMS
Building Age	Classroom Paint
Windows in Classrooms	Interior Paint Cycle
Floor Type	Exterior Wall Paint
Classroom Heating Type	Exterior Paint Cycle
Air Conditions	Floors Swept
Roof Leaks	Floors Mopped
Adjacent Facilities	Presence of Graffiti
Locker Conditions	Graffiti Removal
Ceiling Material	Classroom Furniture
Science Lab Equipment	School Grounds
Science Lab Age	Landscaping
Classroom Lighting	
Wall Colour	
Exterior Noise	
Student Density	
Site Acreage	

Within these categories, the evaluative classification of the building was used for comparison purposes. Inter-rate reliability for building evaluation was established by comparing building ratings completed by school system personnel and the results of the researcher's evaluation of a sample of the buildings in the study.

Student achievement was measured using scaled scores of students taking the Test of Academic Proficiency (TAP), administered to all 11th grade students in Virginia. The average school score for these high schools was used in the study and could be used to compare success on different sub-tests of the TAP. The ratio of students receiving free and reduced lunches was used to control for socio-economic status (SES) of the school attendance area, and in addition, Cash used the Virginia Composite Index, a measure of local fiscal capacity, to control for the wealth of the school jurisdiction.

Student behaviour was measured by the disciplinary incidents reported to the Virginia Department of Education, and by the number of annual student suspensions *185* and expulsions by local school administrators. These were converted to a per student ratio for comparison purposes and used to test the hypothesis that building condition affects student behaviour.

Data analysis was done by comparing achievement score means among building condition ratings using an analysis of covariance to adjust the means. The percentage of students who did not qualify for free or reduced lunch was the covariant. This factor served to adjust the means for students' socio-economic status. The adjusted mean scale scores in achievement and the behaviour ratios for each building were compared across the three levels of building condition and between the three levels of overall, cosmetic, and structural categories.

Results indicated a positive relationship between building condition and student achievement. In all of the TAP sub-tests, academic performance was positively related to school building condition. Cash found that student achievement was higher in buildings with higher quality ratings. Percentile rankings on the composite test score differed as much as 5% in all three categories. The comparison between the overall building category and achievement had higher levels of achievement in the sub-tests than when the cosmetic and structural building category was compared with achievement. Student achievement in the science section of the TAP was higher in those buildings with better quality science equipment than in those with poorer science facilities. Low and high rated schools varied by five percentile rank points. Table 2 shows the differences between the percentile rank of the school mean scores for students in substandard and above-standard buildings. Data are displayed for each category.

Table 2. **Carol Cash Study: Differences of Achievement Percentile Rank Scores of Students in Sub-standard and Above-standard Buildings**

Subject Areas	Overall	Cosmetic	Structural
Reading	+4	+3	+2
Mathematics	+4	+4	0
Writing	+2	+2	+1
Source of Information	+4	+4	+4
Basic Composite	+4	+4	+4
Social Science	+3	+3	+3
Science	+5	+5	+5
Composite	+5	+5	+5

There was a positive but inverse relationship between student behaviour and building condition. The better quality schools had higher ratios of disciplinary incidents, expulsions, and suspensions than did schools with low building conditions. The data did not explain the reverse relationship, but Cash theorised that the faculty in the better quality schools was perhaps stricter in applying disciplinary policy than faculty in lower rated buildings thereby resulting in a higher number of incidents reported.

Earthman, Cash, and Van Berkum (1995) conducted a similar study on a state-wide basis in North Dakota, using the same methodology as the Cash study, using all 199 high school buildings in the state. North Dakota was selected because students as a whole traditionally score among the highest in the nation on the Scholastic Achievement Test. North Dakota students also scored third highest in the International Comparison of 8th Grade Math scores in 1992 after Asia and Japan (*Leadership News*, 1994). Additionally, the state has a relatively homogeneous, mostly rural population. North Dakota therefore seemed like an excellent site for the logical extension of the Cash research.

The building condition rankings were done using the State Assessment of Facilities in Education, a modification of the original instrument from the Cash study. Again, a local self-evaluation methodology was used to obtain the rankings of substandard, standard, and above-standard buildings. In addition, the items of the instrument were categorised to create cosmetic and structural categories for comparison in the same manner as the Cash study. In this way, overall, cosmetic, and structural categories were compared.

Student scores on the Comprehensive Test of Basic Skills (CTBS) administered to 11th graders state-wide were used for student achievement. Again, scaled score means for each building were used for comparison purposes. In all but one CTBS sub-test, the students in standard buildings outscored students in substandard buildings. Social studies sub-test scores were identical for building conditions, but minus five points when the structural category items were used for comparison. Differences in all other sub-test scores between the two building conditions ranged from one to nine percentile ranks (Table 3).

Table 3. **Earthman, et al.**
**Differences Between Percentile Rank Scores of Students
in Substandard and Above-standard Buildings**

Subject Areas	Overall	Cosmetic	Structural
Reading Vocabulary	+7	+7	+7
Reading Comp.	+1	+1	+1
Math Concepts	+1	+1	+1
Math Application	+3	+3	+3
Language	+4	+4	+4
Spelling	+9	+9	+9
Social Science	0	+4	-5
Science	+7	+7	+7
Composite Score	+5	+5	+5

187

When the cosmetic building category was compared with achievement, the differences were exactly the same as for the other two categories, except in social science where a positive difference was observed.

Although composite score differences were exactly the same as in the Cash study, there are some noteworthy differences. The CTBS has more sub-tests than the TAP: reading vocabulary, mathematics concepts, and spelling. The differences in reading vocabulary and spelling are rather high, considering the differences in other sub-tests. The North Dakota study supports the findings of both Edwards and Cash who both found at least a 5% difference in composite achievement scores in their population. The North Dakota study resulted in a similar difference of percentile rankings in student achievement scores.

Student behaviour and the three building rankings were compared to explore a possible relationship between these variables. The total number of disciplinary incidents per school was very small in all schools state-wide. As a result, the comparison figures are extremely small and, in some cases, meaningless. Nevertheless, students in the above-standard buildings recorded fewer disciplinary incidents than those in the substandard buildings when comparisons were made on the overall and cosmetic conditions. When the structural building condition was used as a measure of comparison, however, the results were somewhat different. Students in above-standard buildings had more disciplinary incidents than those in below-standard buildings, confirming what Cash had found in her study. The first two comparisons, however, are the converse of her findings.

A third study (Hines, 1996) used large, urban high schools in Virginia. Hines used the same methodology and data gathering instrument as Cash (1996) used on small, rural high schools and his results in comparing building condition and student achievement were basically the same. The range of differences between substandard and above-standard buildings, however, was greater than that of rural high schools and in the North Dakota high schools study. Some of the differences were as high as 17 percentile rank points, which compares favourably with Edwards' results in her comparison between the worst and best school buildings. Edwards stated that the difference in mean achievement scores for her study population was as much as 10.9% between school buildings in the substandard and above standard categories[26].

The Hines study is an extremely valuable source of findings for differences in achievement between students in substandard and above-standard buildings. His analysis indicated that in five sub-tests, differences ranged from 11 or more points, while in each of the remaining sub-tests, the range of differences was nine points. The difference in composite scores was as much as 14 points (Table 4).

Table 4. **Eric Hines' Study: Differences of Achievement Percentile Rank Scores of Students in Sub-Standard and Above-standard Buildings**

Subject Areas	Overall	Cosmetic	Structural
Reading	+15	+5	+8
Mathematics	+17	+4	+9
Writing	+ 9	+4	+5
Source of Information	+13	0	-1
Basic Composite	+13	+5	+7
Social Science	+11	+4	+7
Science	+ 9	+5	+7
Composite	+14	+6	+9

Differences of this magnitude are very important to researchers. Not only do they corroborate the findings of previous studies, but they also severely challenge the proposition that the building makes no difference in student performance. These findings push the limit of variance of student performance attributable to the physical environment to a new level. Such differences in student scores are enough to account for student success or failure.

The Hines study is the latest and most dramatic in a series trying to explore the relationship between school building condition, student achievement, and student behaviour. All four studies used the same basic methodology and the results seemed to be consistent with the exception of the degree of difference in the mean scores of achievement examinations between schools in the lowest and highest categories. The building does contribute to the variance in student performance, albeit to a varying degree.

Comparison of Findings

Three of the six correlation studies cited above (Cash, Earthman, and Hines) used the same methodology and data-gathering instrument. Although the standardised test in the North Dakota study was different from the Test of Academic Proficiency used in the Cash and Hines studies, similar sub-tests can be used for comparison. Tables 4, 5, and 6 contain data regarding the differences in achievement percentile rank scores of students in substandard and above-standard buildings for the three studies.

Analyses of these data would indicate, first of all, that all three studies found a difference in the percentile rank scores of students in the various buildings. In each case, the differences were positive. Furthermore, the findings in these studies corroborate the findings in previous studies. Specifically, the findings indicate a difference in student performance in reading, mathematics, language/writing, and science.

Table 5. **Overall Differences of Achievement Percentile Rank Score of Students in Sub-standard and Above-standard Buildings**

Subject Areas	Cash Test of Academic Proficiency 1993	Earthman, et al. Comprehensive Test of Basic Skills 1995	Hines Test of Academic Proficiency 1996
Reading Vocabulary	—	+7	—
Reading Comprehension	+4	+1	+15
Math Concepts	—	+1	—
Math Application	+4	+3	+17
Language/Writing	+2	+4	+ 9
Sources of Info.	+4	—	+13
Basic Composite	+4	—	+13
Spelling	—	+9	—
Social Science	+3	0	+11
Science	+5	+7	+ 9
Total Composite	+5	+5	+14

Table 6. **Cosmetic Differences of Achievement Percentile Rank Score of Students in Sub-standard and Above-standard Buildings**

Subject Areas	Cash Test of Academic Proficiency 1993	Earthman, et al. Comprehensive Test of Basic Skills 1995	Hines Test of Academic Proficiency 1996
Reading Vocabulary	—	+7	—
Reading Comprehension	+4	+1	+5
Math Concepts	—	+1	—
Math Application	+4	+3	+4
Language/Writing	+2	+4	+4
Sources of Info.	+4	—	0
Basic Composite	+4	—	+5
Spelling	—	+9	—
Social Science	+3	0	+4
Science	+5	+7	+5
Total Composite	+5	+5	+6

All three studies used a factor of building condition to classify school buildings into sub-standard, standard, or above-standard categories; the building factor was made up of responses to questions relating to specific building attributes or conditions. Every question in the evaluative instrument was about building attributes and conditions that were individually identified in previous research studies as being directly related to either student achievement or student behaviour. For instance, studies were completed using such separate building factors as air conditioning, level of

Table 7. **Structural Differences of Achievement Percentile Rank Score of Students in Sub-standard and Above-standard Buildings**

Subject Areas	Cash Test of Academic Proficiency 1993	Earthman, et al. Comprehensive Test of Basic Skills 1995	Hines Test of Academic Proficiency1996
Reading Vocabulary	—	+7	—
Reading Comprehension	+4	+1	+8
Math Concepts	—	+1	—
Math Application	+4	+3	+9
Language/Writing	+2	+4	+5
Sources of Info.	+4	—	-1
Basic Composite	+4	—	+7
Spelling	—	+9	—
Social Science	+3	0	+7
Science	+5	+7	+7
Total Composite	+5	+5	+9

illumination, presence of windows in classrooms, availability of modern science equipment, floor material, or wall colour as a variable with which to compare student achievement. The next logical and higher level step in this research was to incorporate the important building conditions into a single building condition factor. Thus, the building condition classification stood for or represented a number of conditions that a school building in good condition possessed or would possess. This factor was then used to compare student achievement and behaviour with the condition of the school building. The building condition factor seems to be an important concept used in more recent research on the relationship between school building and student achievement and behaviour.

Conclusions

Each of the studies demonstrated a relationship between student performance (achievement and behaviour) and the condition of the built environment. The depth of the relationship varied, but the most recent study demonstrates a much stronger degree of relationship than previously imagined.

Some of the most important building factors that influence learning are those that relate to the control of the thermal environment, proper illumination, adequate space, availability of equipment and furnishings, especially in the subject area of science.

Differences in each of these four studies between the test scores of students in substandard and above-standard school buildings ranged between 1 and 17 percentile points, but nevertheless, there was a positive difference for students in the better build-

191

ings in almost all cases. These findings are of particular importance because of the large number of substandard school buildings across the United States. The factors which determined the condition of buildings in these studies are usually incorporated into new structures, but the vast majority of school buildings, according to the 1995 General Accounting Office study documenting the poor condition of public schools in the United States, lack these conditions.

There are difficulties, of course, in determining the degree to which school facilities can be the actual cause of student behaviour and achievement given the many variables that influence how much students can and do learn and how they behave. Obviously, the most important variables are genetic and home environments followed by community surroundings and conditions beginning from the day of birth to the day the student enters the school building.

School authorities and governing board members can improve the educational opportunities of students. If, as the studies strongly indicate, student test scores in above-standard school buildings are higher than student scores in substandard building by as much as 5 to 17 percentile points, there are ways of increasing student performance and test scores by improving building conditions. They can insure that buildings are in good condition and present the best possible learning environment or they can let buildings deteriorate to the point of influencing the educational opportunities of students under their charge. This is a very heavy responsibility to bear, yet the resulting condition of school buildings speak very loudly. These studies strongly suggest that spending funds to improve the built environment might produce greater student performance results than spending funds on instructional materials, textbooks, and even teachers.

The long-term influence of a poor building upon students adds a dimension to this issue that is difficult to measure and raises several questions. If students are housed in poor buildings for a number of years, will the effect on achievement be multiplied? Will students' aesthetic values be impaired? After long exposure to poor or marginal buildings, will students believe such conditions are normal? It is very difficult to conduct longitudinal research studies on the influence of a building but the research cited here is simply a photograph of conditions and relationships in a single period of time. There may be a cumulative effect upon this disparity in student test scores between poor and good school buildings that continues during the student's school years.

Equity of educational opportunity is also an issue when some students attend school in lower quality buildings than others. If students in poor buildings perform 5 to 17 percentile rank points lower than other students, they certainly are at a disadvantage, especially when future education relies so heavily upon past performance. Students in poor buildings will not have the same opportunity as those in better school buildings.

It has been demonstrated time and again that better-prepared graduates of a local school system are more productive citizens, have more productive jobs throughout their lives, and are happier. The corollary to this is that more productive citizens add to the prosperity of the state and support it more evenly through taxes. Consequently, anything that can be done to positively raise the level of achievement of students who are future citizens will greatly influence the economy over time.

REFERENCES

BOWERS, J. H. and BURKETT, C. W. (1988),
"Physical Environment Influences Related to Student Achievement, Health, Attendance, and Behaviour". CEFPI *Journal*, Vol. 26, no. 4: 33-34.

CASH, C. (1993),
A *Study of the Relationship Between School Building Condition and Student Achievement and Behaviour.* Blacksburg, VA: Unpublished Ph.D. Dissertation, Virginia Polytechnic Institute and State University.

EDWARDS, M. M. (1992),
Building Conditions, Parental Involvement and Student Achievement in the D.C. Public School System. Unpublished Master's Degree Thesis, Georgetown University, Washington, D.C. (ED 264 285).

EARTHMAN, G. I., CASH, C. S., VAN BERKUM, D. (1995),
"A State-wide Study of Student Achievement and Behaviour and School Building Condition". Presentation at Annual Meeting of Council of Educational Facility Planers, International, Dallas, Texas, 19 September 1995.

HINES, E. (1996),
"Building Condition and Student Achievement and Behaviour". Blacksburg, VA: Unpublished Ph.D. Dissertation, Virginia Polytechnic Institute and State University.

Leadership News. (1994),
"Performance-Based Funds to Finance Reform", 4, 15 August.

PHILLIPS, R. W. (1997),
Educational Facility Age and the Academic Achievement and Attendance of Upper Elementary School Students. Unpublished Ph.D. Dissertation, University of Georgia, Athens.

United States General Accounting Office (1995),
School Facilities: Condition of America's Schools. Washington, DC: GAO/HEHS-95-61.

Chapter Four

DESIGN AND EQUIPMENT
OF PHYSICAL FACILITIES FOR EDUCATION

ENVIRONMENTAL APPRAISAL
OF EDUCATION FACILITIES

Christopher **French**
Property Services Department, Essex

The Essex County Council has employed its own multi-disciplinary in-house property professionals since the 1940s. During this period, the Council has built up particular expertise in designing education facilities with an emphasis on environmental design. Like many local education authorities in the 1950s, Essex County Council
joined a consortium that developed a steel-framed industrialised system of building
(SEAC) to cope with the post war-boom in school building. This system was extremely
lightweight, compared to current building fabrics with heavily glazed fenestration,
lightly insulated wall panels and flat roofs. As a result, many of the schools built in
Essex between 1950 and 1975 had poor environmental performance: overheated in
summer and under-heated in the winter, they were very uncomfortable for both pupils
and teachers.

These buildings were also large users of energy given their relatively poor insulation standards. This went largely ignored until the energy crisis of the 1970s caused by
the precipitous rise in world-wide oil prices. The County Council's reaction was to abandon the use of the lightweight system of building for a home grown system using lightweight concrete exposed aggregate wall panels, pre-cast concrete columns, castellated
steel beams, and a lightweight concrete roof deck. The Property Services Department
also instituted a programme of energy saving measures to conserve fuel.

During the 1970s, most environmental appraisal and development concentrated
on the need to save fuel and to find alternative sources to fossil fuels. Experts genuinely believed that the world's fossil fuel resources would be exhausted by the end of
the century. Consequently, many projects involved reduced window sizes, increased
insulation standards, and a greater reliance on artificial lighting with daylight factors
of less than 2%. The energy conservation programme at this time was also influenced
by the political complexion of the County Council which emphasised value for money
and strict payback criteria for investments in increased insulation, double glazing,
draught lobbies, and boiler controls.

OECD 2000

A programme of development projects began during this period, many of which involved education facilities, exploring the use of alternative fuel sources, increasing insulation standards and making use of the natural warming effect of the sun by school orientation and fenestration patterns. Nuclear electricity was seen as the fuel source to replace fossil fuel, and Essex County Council designed and built several experimental schools heated by air-to-air, air-to-water and ground water-to-water heat pumps. Insulation standards of roofs, floors and walls were dramatically increased and ventilation rates decreased to reduce heat losses and thermal mass increased to reduce the variations in temperature throughout the school day and year. Several solar passive schools were also designed and built at this time with a predominantly south, south-east or south-west orientation for teaching spaces with supporting facilities on other elevations. Fenestration patterns were also designed to make use of the "free energy" from the winter sun, with large areas of shaded glazing on south elevations and small punch hole windows on the north. The opportunity was also taken to introduce solar collectors in the form of glazed atria, tomb walls and flat plate collectors to heat the school and/or provide hot water.

Technology was used a great deal during this period: heat pumps, electrode boilers, computer controls, air handling equipment, etc. Unfortunately, much of this technology was still in its infancy and has proven insufficiently reliable or adaptable over the years. Recently, some technology has been replaced with more conventional plant.

Sustainable, Environmentally-sound Design

The emphasis on environmental assessment and design has changed dramatically since the discovery of holes in the earth's ozone layer and the impending problems associated with a potential warming of the climate. The County Council's Energy Conservation Programme has therefore been replaced with a policy of sustainable development aimed at reducing the impact of its new buildings on the environment. The Rio Summit of 1992 set demanding reductions in production of CO_2 and CFCs by the world's industrial nations which have been adopted as the basis of our environmental design policy. Stringent CO_2 emission targets are set for every new school based on official standards as set out in Building Bulletin 87 (BB87) and insulation levels and fuel sources are carefully chosen to ensure these are not exceeded. Materials and refrigerants are also carefully selected to avoid releasing CFCs into the atmosphere.

The County Council has also tried to ensure that its new buildings reinforce its more general policies of sustainable development throughout the County across a wide range of issues such as the use of fossil fuels, impact on the ecology of Essex, and the use of materials from sustainable resources. The County Council also believes that it must set an example of sustainable development to the people of Essex through its own building programme by "thinking globally and acting locally" and disseminating information county-wide about the practicalities of sustainable development to schools and the media.

Every new education facility is subjected to an environmental audit during the design process using one of the currently available audit systems to score it according to various environmental factors such as CO^2 and CFC production, water use, insulation levels, fuel consumption, construction materials. The long-term aim is to raise awareness amongst designers of sustainability issues and to improve performance constantly.

Alternative Fuels

The use of alternative fuels has been increasingly emphasised over the last few years, but a recent development project has demonstrated that the technology is not yet sufficiently developed to make this viable. Calculations of pay back periods for wind generators, photo voltaic systems and solar water heating flat plate collectors still have a minimum payback of 40 years and some as much as over 200 years. It is increasingly difficult to persuade clients with limited financial resources to invest in such technology, even if it reduces the impact of their new building on the earth's resources.

Low Technology

There has also been a general dissatisfaction with the unreliable high technology systems of the past. Now, low technology systems are emphasised: opening windows and the stack effect of high ceilings have replaced many mechanical ventilation systems and simple on/off switches, and individual thermostatic radiator valves have replaced some of the more complex computer control systems.

The rise of the consumer society has increased client expectations of the environmental performance of education facilities and teaching staff now demand that space for learning be well lit, warm in winter, cool in summer, and have good acoustics. This has led to more auditing of environmental performance and much greater dialogue with the users of new buildings about how the fabric and services will control their teaching environment and the compromises which have been made during the design process.

Computer-modelling Techniques

The Property Services Department has developed computer-modelling techniques used during the design process to predict the environmental performance of new education facilities. These include a thermal-modelling programme called TAS that can

199

predict the temperatures in a particular space at different times of the day and year depending on orientation, insulation levels and fenestration patterns. It is particularly good at exploring the consequences of strategic design decisions and answering the design team's "what if" questions.

Lighting

Designs also place much greater reliance on natural daylight for teaching spaces, with daylight factors of 4-5% below the norm: several computer-based daylight prediction programmes have been used to check that acceptable lighting conditions can be achieved. Unfortunately, until recently, these have not been sophisticated enough to cope with the geometry of spaces with sloping ceilings, etc., and the department built a jointly-funded artificial sky at the local university to test scale models of new school building designs. It has proven to be very accurate when actual lighting levels are tested on site and has the added advantage of showing the visual effect of different fenestration patterns.

Environmental Audits

The Department has worked very closely to government standards for environmental performance contained within Design Note17 and the more recent BB87 for a number of years, and in many cases these have exceeded the minimum standards. The emphasis has changed from DN17 to BB87, however, from the saving of fuel to reducing environmental impact. Now, it is important to take a more holistic view of environmental performance by carrying out an environmental audit to ensure that any new school building has the least impact on the earth's environment. An auditing system developed by the Building Research Establishment called the Building Research Assessment Method (BREAM) attempts to score the various environmental aspects using a series of compensating formulas, etc. This method is rather complex and time consuming and carries a risk that design teams do not gain any real understanding of the issues confronting them. The School Environmental Assessment Method auditing system developed by the Department for Education (SEAM) is much simpler and most design teams can quickly score the effect of their strategic design decisions. It also has the benefit of making it easy for individual schools to score their own buildings to help them develop their own policy for future sustainable development.

Overheating

As insulation levels in new school buildings have continuously improved over the last 10 years, comfortable temperatures can now easily be achieved in new buildings with the minimum use of fuel. The increasing use of natural daylight in teaching spaces with larger windows and a desire for solar-passive orientation have increased the risk of overheating during the summer months; vulnerable glazing must be protected and sufficient ventilation provided. The worst effects of the over-heating problems have been avoided to date because most schools are shut during the months of July and August, but this may change when a four-term year is introduced. New schools need to avoid such conditions with remedial work possibly needed in the worst affected existing schools.

Allergies and Air Quality

Ventilation rates in some Essex schools were reduced to as low as one air change per hour during the 1980s in an attempt to reduce the loss of heat through excessive ventilation. This proved to be unacceptable to most teachers and pupils who complained constantly about uncomfortable, foetid air quality and minor illnesses amongst the occupiers. Ventilation rates have now been increased to a minimum of two air changes per hour.

Respiratory problems amongst British school children seem to be increasing, which many claim result from allergies aggravated by poor air quality. It is now necessary to demonstrate to teachers and parents that the internal air quality is the best obtainable within the resources available.

Alternative Energy Sources

The prophets of doom who predicted the demise of fossil fuel supplies in the 1970s tempted the Essex Property Services Department to experiment with new sources of fuel with limited success due to their reliance on technology. It is interesting that similar experiments with alternative fuel sources are now being carried out to avoid the generation of CO_2 that is harming the earth's ozone layer and leading to global warming. It would appear, however, that these technologies are still not sufficiently advanced to allow their economic use in main stream school facilities.

Interdisciplinary Teamwork

Essex County Council has always believed that the full potential of new school building can only be achieved through inter-disciplinary teamwork. This is where strategic design decisions are taken and owned by the whole design team, including the client at the beginning of the project. This is particularly important with environmental performance when many compromises have to be made during the design process among the different elements of construction and servicing.

Whole Life Costs

It is also important to base decisions about environmental control systems upon their whole life cost rather than on their initial capital cost only. This has proven very difficult, however, when clients with limited financial resources attempt to spread them over a demanding programme of work and many short-term decisions have inevitably lead to increased maintenance and running costs. The full impact of this short-term thinking has, however, been masked by the recent drop in fuel costs.

Conflicting Environmental Guidelines

The DfEE BB87 contains many recommendations on the various aspects of environmental performance: CO_2 emissions, insulation levels, day lighting, acoustics, artificial lighting, etc. These would appear to be achievable when considered in isolation, but many of them conflict with each other. For example, if greater glazed areas are introduced into the fenestration to achieve the required natural daylight levels, insulation levels will fall and fuel consumption will increase; if these larger windows face south, the interior may also overheat in summer. Conversely, if window areas are reduced, then greater use of artificial lighting may also lead to greater fuel consumption. Designers must, therefore, take a holistic approach to environmental design, balancing the various factors to achieve the lowest environmental impact consistent with the overall architectural concept and resources available. This is a very skilled and demanding process requiring an experienced multi-disciplinary design team.

Environmental considerations should not dominate the architecture of education facilities at the expense of such other factors as building form, character, materials and landscape, however. This was the case in Essex schools during the 1980s to the detriment of the teaching environment. Fortunately, environmental issues in more recent projects have proven to be more of a creative pressure, producing exciting architecture.

Many of the solar passive schools built in Essex during the last twenty years have featured a central glazed solar collecting atrium which has provided a dramatic focus to the design and inexpensive, covered space in the heart of the building for secondary activities such as libraries, craft work, coat storage and wet weather play areas. The schemes with highly glazed south-facing teaching spaces have also created sheltered outside teaching space where children are able to move freely from inside to outside in warmer weather, often sheltered by earth bunding and pergolas to shade pupils and glazing.

The need to provide good day lighting to the rear of classrooms and good natural ventilation has also encouraged the use of large volume spaces for halls and classrooms with exposed sloping ceilings which have also created very dramatic roofscapes. These issues are best demonstrated by looking at some of our most recent projects.

Lyons Hall C.P. School

This 210 place first instalment of a 360 place primary school built in 1996 serves a new housing estate in Braintree, has a solar passive design with all classrooms facing south with north lights lighting the rear of the bases creating an interesting wave-shaped roofscape.

Initial thermal analysis showed that such a design might overheat in summer and the original intention was to cool the building using the Thermodeck system by passing air through the hollow core of a suspended pre-cast concrete floor deck and exhausting the warm air at night. However, the cost of such a system exceeded the budget available and the project now relies entirely on the thermal capacity of the concrete roof to absorb excess heat during the day and to vitiate the warm air through high level windows at night.

Attempts at reducing electricity consumption by controlling lighting circuits with movement detectors have proven ineffective, however, due to staff resistance to the technology that removed their control of lighting. Traditional switch gear has now been installed.

Barnes Farm C.J. School

This 480 place junior school will replace an existing junior school on a new site in Chelmsford which has outgrown the current site it shares with its feeder infant school as a result of increased numbers. Unfortunately, the school is situated near a sewage treatment works. Care has been taken to ensure that the effect of obnoxious smells does not unduly affect indoor air quality.

The school has a solar passive layout with all classrooms facing in a southerly direction with views across the Chelmer Valley to Danbury Hill with other teaching accommodation including the two halls facing north. The cross-section through classrooms with their high north light windows is predicted to give good daylight and ventilation but much of the south facing glazing has to be shaded by external pergolas which also shelter pupils using the external teaching areas.

The school will serve its immediate neighbourhood. A decision has been taken to discourage parents from bringing children to school by car by restricting vehicular access and providing good pedestrian and cycle access. This will not only make journeys to school safer, but will also reduce the consumption of non-renewable fossil fuel oil and production of CO_2 in a small way.

Great Notley C.P. School

This school is a 180 place first phase of a 360 place primary school currently under construction and designed to be sustainable by consultants chosen by a competitive process to serve a new village development near the market town of Braintree.

The compact, triangular plan with its short perimeter and internal court is spatially very efficient and is predicted to have low energy consumption. All classrooms face in a southerly direction with north facing roof lights lighting their rear. The external walls are clad in cedar incorporating a breathing wall system using recycled newspaper as insulation. The flat, plywood roof deck is waterproofed with a single-ply membrane covered with a sedum growing medium to protect the membrane from UV degradation. All other materials, including finishes, have been chosen to be as sustainable as possible avoiding the use of PVC wherever possible.

The use of alternative fuel sources such as bio mass, wind generators, flat plate solar collectors and photo voltaic cells was also investigated, but quickly dismissed due to the excessive payback periods for these materials.

The design has also been the subject of an environmental audit using DfEE Building Bulletin 87 and SEAM and the design is predicted to be in the top band of performance.

Conclusion

The environmental appraisal of education facilities, which is currently a strong driving force in the design of new school buildings in Essex, is partly aimed at improving the learning environment and partly at setting an example of sustainable development to the people of Essex. It is difficult, however, to balance the many environmental factors influencing school design, some of which are mutually exclusive. With proper multidisciplinary design, sustainable development can, however, produce an exciting architecture with a comfortable environment for the next generation of teachers and pupils.

PATTERNS AND DESIGN STRATEGIES FOR NEW SCHOOL BUILDINGS

Rodolfo **Almeida**
Architect

Introduction

This paper takes a methodological approach to the process of planning educational buildings. It highlights topics that can be flexibly applied as checkpoints to appraise design and project proposals according to specific country situations. It addresses the design and equipment of physical facilities for education in order to highlight key issues for appraising investments in educational facilities. In particular, it deals with those issues that can facilitate the design appraisal. These include building quality and relevance to education; the introduction of new information technology (IT); the provision of services to and integration with the surrounding community, the quality of the architectural space; furniture, building suitability and its impact on its urban, suburban, or rural location, and the adequacy of building materials, costs, and standards.

An overview of the entire process of planning educational buildings must precede the discussion of design, which can be directly or indirectly affected by individual components of the process. Concepts will vary from country to country and from local authority to local authority and project to project.

A well-designed educational building improves educational quality. Architecture must be well adapted to the pedagogy and particularly to the rapidly evolving information technology. A good architectural building is also well adapted to local conditions and regional cultures within reasonable construction, operational, and maintenance costs. Architecture is also a pedagogical tool in itself through its shapes, spaces, volumes, colours, building materials, textures, relations to the outdoor learning spaces and to the environment, by using alternative sources of renewable energy and, above all, by inspiring users to learn in a beautiful physical environment. Sam Cassels, in the OECD publication on the impact of new technology on school buildings, aptly said that "The language of design should reflect and enrich

205

the evolving language of education. To walk into an educational building, even an empty one, should be an experience that increases understanding and enthusiasm about learning".

Quantity and Quality

Education was in great demand from the 1950s until the 1960s-1970s. Massive construction programmes of educational buildings were implemented throughout most of the world; quantity was the problem. In the early 1960s, UNESCO established a School Building Section at its headquarters, and three Regional School Building Centres: ARISBR, started in Indonesia and ended in Bangkok to cover the Asia and Pacific Region; CONESCAL, located in Mexico, covered Latin America and the Caribbean, and REBIA, in Sudan, covered Africa. With these four Units, UNESCO began to work at regional and country levels in several ways. It began training government staff, carrying out badly needed R&D studies on space norms, use of local building materials and techniques, safety, community participation, etc., started organising regional and national seminars and workshops, establishing documentation centres, disseminating technical documentation, and providing technical assistance to Member States. Of the Regional Centres, only CONESCAL survived beyond the 1970s, until 1984; they were integrated with the respective Regional Education Offices to carry out the same functions.

Central units in Ministries of Education, or units shared with the Ministries of Public Works, or specialised government school building bodies were responsible for designing educational buildings.[27] These central units were typically well financed, and well staffed with professionals, architects, educators, and engineers. They developed their own national norms and typical schedules of accommodation and design that were applied nation-wide with more or less consideration for climate and geography and generally without consultation or dialogue with the communities. The important task, however, was to respond to the increasing demand for education, and to enrol as many students as possible, even in remote areas. Thousands of very similar schools were built, therefore, and the majority of these continue to be used. When the central units were closed, much of the trained staff disappeared, and experience was lost along with valuable technical documentation.

The focus has now shifted to quality. The ongoing process of decentralisation beginning in the late 1970s and in which many countries are just now engaging has radically altered the situation. Local authorities are now responsible for financing, design, construction and maintenance of educational buildings for pre-school to upper secondary level whereas tertiary education is usually overseen by the central government. The objectives include providing more adequate schools better adapted to their com-

206

munities and to their cultural values, to the climate and geography, and to a respect for the environment. Local communities tend to participate more in planning, designing and maintaining their schools. There is also some flexibility in some countries of local adjustments to national timetables and curricula, and to introducing new courses. Educational buildings tend to be schools and to provide services to the community such as sport facilities, library, day-care centres, technical workshops, etc. Education also occurs outside the school in public libraries, theatres, museums, and public markets. Increasingly, the use and development of information technology is having and will continue to have an impact on building design; there is increasing interaction between communities and schools.

Problems continue to exist, depending on the human or financial resources of each local authority to define a sound educational and social project and translate it into architecture with local means or by appealing for assistance to regional or central government. Can local authorities develop local inputs to curricula or do they need to resort to the compulsory national curricula? Flexible norms that can be applied at local level are lacking. In some countries, the old national norms have not yet been updated, or new norms are not formulated with a new perspective in light of educational, social, and technological changes. All of these aspects will have an impact on the design of new premises and for remodelling or reconverting existing ones.

Designs are often submitted for approval, either to local authorities or to the central government, based on norms, for financing or a green light for construction. Often, the impulse of a highly motivated architect and educator brings good designs into existence, leading to a variety of different types of new school designs to satisfy the needs of different communities. This complicates design evaluation.

Methodological Overview of the Planning Process for Educational Buildings

An effective approach to educational buildings should take several objectives into account.

- Educational and community requirements, climate, and geography.

- Location according to priorities, to ensure equal access to education and other social and cultural community uses.

- Implementation of a well-structured building programme within a coherent timetable and allocated budget.

- Making use of national and local resources for manpower, materials, and finance.

OECD 2000

UNESCO uses an educational building process that includes four cycles. This process highlights evaluation checkpoints and criteria to improve design quality:

- Analysis and diagnosis.

- Research and development.

- Plans and programmes.

- Implementation and evaluation.

Analysis and Diagnosis

This cycle is intended to identify deficiencies, estimate required expenditures for meeting the school building network needs - repairs, maintenance, remodelling, extensions, replacements, new facilities - and to define priorities. The cycle begins with an inventory of educational buildings and school furniture so that national, regional, or local levels are fully aware of the educational buildings network and can determine requirements. It makes it possible to undertake micro-planning in which specialists, local authorities, and community participate. The inventory interprets the available information on existing educational resources so that a specific plan can be prepared for each community.

The inventory can be carried out in two stages of educational mapping. In the first stage, the location, condition, and use of existing educational facilities are defined; in the second stage, proposals are made of plans or programmes for new projects, substitutions, expansions, repairs, and maintenance of facilities. This makes it possible to define the needs of local populations: school age population, handicapped, adults, other community needs. Translating these needs and problems in terms of local educational facilities could point to poor location, poor building conditions, high construction costs, lack of maintenance, climatically ill-adapted designs, low use of space, lack of community spaces, etc. This information lets local authorities define their priorities among actions to be undertaken.

Research and Development (R&D)

The R&D cycle is central to this paper. It defines parameters, norms, and prototypes of educational facilities that serve as the basis for formulating projects, plans, and programmes, as well as for architectural programming, designing, implementation, maintenance, use, and evaluation of educational buildings and their integration into the community.

The link between educators and architects should be systematic and continuous. Architects need the collaboration of educators who, in turn, need the experience of architects and engineers for physical environmental matters. Currently, IT developments, growing environmental awareness, energy conservation, safeguarding historically important buildings, etc. require the involvement of a range of professionals in the design state. However, the basis and beginning of the work lies in defining educational specifications.

Educational Specifications

Educational specifications could be defined as the systematic and detailed description of the requirements of the educational system as a whole and of its adaptations to local educational and community requirements. This information serves as a basis for defining the type of centre and number and type of facilities that best respond to needs.

Defining the type of educational centre requires specifications.

- Type and level of education, student age group, duration of studies of each type and level, other types of non-formal education that the community might desire.

- Curriculum and activity schedule for each subject by type, level and grade, and use factors.

- Teaching methods and didactic material for each subject, analysis of possible alternative spaces for these studies or activities.

- Enrolment by type and level of education.

- Possible future modifications in the educational system: content, teaching methods and materials, information technology, new uses, enrolments, etc.

- Community participation in decisions on building use for school and after school hours, school and public facilities-sharing, integration of school and community services (social, cultural, sports, etc.)

- Educational activities need close analysis and typology.

- Curricular: direct teaching/learning according to curricular and study programmes, via lecture, seminar, independent study, tutorials, computer work, out-of-school study.

- Research: Study that benefits institutional teaching that may also be useful beyond the classroom.

- Extension: activities linking the educational institution culturally and socially with the community.

- Supplementary: activities meeting basic needs of the educational community: board, recreation, food, sports, transportation.

- Service: basic support for administrative activities - cleaning, maintenance, supplies.

Space Norms

Standard rates for space, more commonly known as space norms, vary in meaning and value according to the country. In all countries, however, space norms derive from educational specifications. Generally speaking, educational space norms are quantitative and indicate the requisite area for properly carrying out an activity within an educational space, including its furniture, teaching materials, new IT, etc., or the total activities in a school for a given number of students.

Norms are expressed as net area per student (excluding project wall area) and vary with educational level and type of teaching, location, climate, and resources. Space norms must be flexible and indicative and should take into account educational and cultural activities. A careful analysis of the area per student helps optimise investments: cost per student is the cost per unit area multiplied by the space standard. The closer the relationship between area and user, the more productive the investment in cost-effectively reaching objectives.

A compromise exists between educational/social/cultural requirements and country/local financial capacity to address "ideal" norms. In many countries, minimum space norms were defined in terms of pedagogical needs within budgetary limits; these norms evolved as national wealth grew.

A functional analysis procedure helps define those educational requirements involved in determining spatial needs:

- Subjects and activities taking place in the space.

- Type and number of participants: students, teachers, behaviour.

- Furniture and equipment: quantity and occupied and influence areas.

210

• Dimensions: possible layouts and their corresponding dimensions.

• Installations: electric, video, computer, sanitation, water, gas, etc.

• Physical comfort: light (electrical, natural), ventilation (mechanical, natural), acoustics, thermal, climate, etc.

Alternatively, an empirical procedure, consisting of analysing similar or comparable educational facilities elsewhere in the country, is also feasible. It may be supplemented with an analysis of information available on similar cases from other countries to serve as a reference for the results of the functional analysis.

Comfort and Health Norms

Comfort or environmental well-being in educational buildings refers to acceptable or suitable lighting, heat, ventilation, acoustics, psychological and other conditions that should be present in a school so that educational activities may be carried out in the most appropriate manner. The same holds for health norms hygiene (laboratories, kitchens, dining halls), choice of building materials, and furniture design. Comfort may be classified into thermal, visual, and acoustic, with different degrees or ranges of tolerance. Comfort must also be analysed for the entire building and for individual spaces: *e.g.* lighting requirements differ in an electronics workshop and a general classroom, some large facilities may require special acoustic studies to prevent reverberations or echoes, sunlight may be desirable in Winter and require protection in Summer. Most countries have developed specific health and comfort norms.

Safety Norms

While space and comfort norms are determined on the basis of everyday use of the educational building, safety norms are established to prepare for potential natural disasters that cause direct damage and secondary effects such as fires or collective panic, requiring speedy evacuation.

The most familiar natural disasters include:

• Floods caused by rains, melting snows, or dam ruptures.

• Tsunamis and coastal floods caused by seismic activity and tropical cyclones.

• Earthquakes.

- Land, rock and snow slides.

- Fires and conflagrations.

- Volcanic eruptions.

- Droughts.

The national building codes of most developed countries are compulsory for all building types. In some countries, specific norms have been issued for educational buildings, hospitals, and other public buildings in which large numbers of people gather. In many countries, school buildings are also designed as shelters during natural disasters. Buildings are therefore equipped with communication systems, food and water storage, and built to resist the damage of mass occupancy. UNESCO has designed several manuals for building design in developing countries to withstand cyclones and earthquakes. This influences architectural design and can also be evaluated.

Furniture

Furniture should be functional, economical, aesthetically pleasing, and locally manufactured. It is part of the building and should facilitate the function for which the building was built - in this case, learning. Work furniture, to be differentiated from storage furniture, is intended for teaching aids, books, computers, printers, CD-ROMs, etc. It usually includes tables, chairs, and benches, serves directly, and depends on position and movement; its efficiency is measured in terms of comfort. To ensure suitability, a country wide anthropometrical survey should be undertaken to fit furniture to students.

Once furniture type, dimensions, and quantities are defined, it can be designed or purchased. Design should reflect use, given the local industrial context; work furniture should be multi-purpose, sturdy, and mobile for easy storage or transfer. Design would allow student groupings for different learning situations, from individual, to small group to discussion seminar. Specifications should be supplied to the designer.

If ready-made furniture is purchased, technical performance specifications should be prepared to launch the bid. Such specifications provide functional characteristics and basic dimensions, and refer to life span, resistance, cost, production, assembly, joints, stackability, storage, transport, distribution, maintenance, etc. Different industries could thus bid with different materials: timber, metal/timber, plastic, etc., but each would need to meet the performance requirements and produce, test, and evaluate prototypes before awarding the final contract. Offers would be evaluated on the basis of performance specifications independently of materials. Industry would thus contribute to the R&D of the furniture of each school.

Equipment

Equipment includes the set of elements through which knowledge is transmitted and is therefore eminently instrumental. Some equipment serves as an end in itself such as a film projector that is studied to learn how it works. This is therefore also a teaching aid. New technologies are changing the equipment needed in school buildings and also creating new types of spaces and internal arrangements, and installations: telephone, video, internet, computers. The design team must work closely with the furniture designer to include alternative layouts and their equipment.

Cost Limits

Cost limits can be defined as the base or reference costs making it immediately possible to quantify a project to an acceptably reliable degree. This is a work parameter that makes the cost planning of a project possible during the design stage and makes control possible during construction. It provides the architect/builder with information for quantifying investment.

Cost limits can be established at the overall level as cost per student or cost per unit area for specific educational levels: cost per square meter for a primary school or cost per building element. Whatever the parameter, the design team must try to examine the building's use rate to see if a high rate will be planned to optimise investments. Similarly, the use rate of individual spaces should be determined, to see if they are to be highly used or can become polyvalent: internal circulation spaces are being used in many countries as "streets" on which different activities take place: recreation, reading, social gatherings, cafeterias.

Accommodation Schedule

An educational establishment includes several types of space, reflected by space norms:

- Academic and community facilities: classrooms, laboratories, workshops, multi-purpose areas, resource centres, libraries, multimedia centres (that are increasingly becoming the centres of learning), dining facilities, kitchens, cafeterias, youth clubs, spaces for community and cultural activities, etc.

213

- Administrative and service facilities: offices, teachers' rooms, parents' waiting rooms, health services, store rooms, machine rooms, maintenance rooms, etc.

- Student housing.

- Teachers, caretaker, and night watchman residences.

- Circulation spaces.

- Outdoor facilities: outdoor teaching spaces, sports fields, playgrounds, parking lots, green areas, etc.

Once educational specifications and other uses are defined, space typology and quantities can be determined. Educators, architects, and community representatives can begin to work as a team until the final design is defined.

- Subject: the activity, its requirements, numbers of users at different times (students, teachers, and the ratio of the two); space(s) for teaching, depending on contact hours and needs, furniture, equipment, requisite water, electricity, video installations.

- Space Typology: space and definition of activities taking place within the space and schedule of activity; numbers of users at different times, furniture, equipment, installations.

- Quantification: summarises subject and space typologies, providing the number and type of spaces, the number of hours used weekly, a 'use factor' per space. If the use factor is too low, the space is costly and decisions need to be made to make the space available to the community when it is empty, for parents' meetings, family planning lectures, or for reviewing the subject to increase space use. Community requirements can be integrated here: use of already specified spaces or the creation of new spaces. This gives the total area needed in the facility.

In this permanent dialogue among these three issues, different teams can come to vastly different conclusions depending on their makeup, ranging from traditional to innovative uses of space. All conclusions must be verified against budget and revised accordingly.

Some countries are still centralised or are becoming decentralised, and still have typical schedules of accommodation for a given level of education and number of students. A central government unit may simply transmit these to the team, and list spaces that may or may not resolve local problems if the schedule is not directly tied to the local context. Once conclusions have been reached, through dialogue among involved parties, co-ordination with the local community and respectful of budgetary constraints, a final schedule of accommodation can list all spaces, their use rate and total net area.

Survey

A survey of eleven colleagues (8 from Europe, 1 from Latin America, 1 from an Arab country, 1 from Israel) gave a range of replies concerning the definition, understanding, and application of space norms or guidelines from rigid situations. Particularly in former Eastern European countries where a central government issues compulsory, nation-wide standards, space norms are not adapted to the local context. As decentralisation proceeds, this situation is changing.

There is a large range of freedom exercised by local authorities concerning norms and definitions of buildings; the use of standardised, and ill-adapted designs seems to be diminishing as a trend towards local definitions emerges. What emerges is the clear importance, on the one hand, of the committed engagement of the design team in the entire design process from definition, through schedules of accommodation to construction. At the same time, there is a need to develop handbooks using examples to complement and illustrate central and local norms that are usually expressed solely in figures and tables. These would offer different methods of design teamwork involving the community in the design process and illustrating alternatives to the educational specifications and their resultant accommodation schedules. They would provide visual examples of alternative functional relationships and spatial arrangements, variations on internal arrangements, forms, sizes, and relationships to outdoor teaching areas, alternatives for users to better use and manage. These would be many ways of stimulating the local authorities to solve their educational/social/cultural needs with an architecture tailored to their context. Moreover, these handbooks would include indicators for evaluating architectural designs overall.

The design process at local level could also be simplified by establishing space norms per student per level of education, giving the design team the flexibility to develop the project within space and budget allocations. The project could thus be evaluated more realistically.

Design Guidelines and Architect's Brief

Handbooks complementing space norms could become design guidelines that include illustrations of alternative designs for different spaces, serving as procedural indicators to facilitate design and evaluations. They should focus on the following issues: *215*

- Determining the organisation, operation, and present and future characteristics of educational buildings.

- Obtaining the greatest degree of building efficiency with regard to their community services: education, social, cultural, recreational, health.

- Achieving the greatest possible economy in building and operation costs

- Ensuring conditions related to comfort and health, equipment, installations, building orientation to benefit from climate.

- Taking into account the specific site conditions (location, geography, topography) possibilities for future expansion, infrastructure services, environment, climate.

- Providing concepts of spatial organisation for making the educational building form an operationally efficient and functional complex: grouping facilities into related study areas; locating common learning facilities, separating quiet and noisy areas, ensuring easy access for the community to shared spaces such as gymnasiums, auditoriums, cafeterias, sports areas.

Conclusion

Educational architecture is moving towards more collaborative designs that better integrate the local context in all ways. Concerns for the environment, the ecology, and energy resources are growing, and imaginative solutions are being found to scarce land availability. Local materials and architectural vocabulary are part of the respect for the local environment as schools open to the community at large and function not only as schools, but with enough flexibility to adapt to community needs as well as new educational concepts and needs, many of which are brought about by changing technology.

This paper has sought to emphasise the importance of architecture to improve the quality of education and has outlined a method for identifying the checkpoints for design appraisal, and the need for creating design handbooks and guidelines attuned to local contexts.

REFERENCES

ALMEIDA, R. (1988),
Centro Educativo Communitario del Sur (CECSUR), Mission Report to Mexico,
Puebla (unpublished).

Ministry of Education, Chile and UNESCO/ Santiago (1004),
Seminario "Espacios Educativos en Chile y America Latina", Educational Building
and Equipment No. 21.

INVESTING FOR FLEXIBILITY

Sam **Cassels,** Architect
and Peter **McLennan**

Investing for flexibility is about responding to new economic drivers. A flexible design must meet the strategic business objectives of different users; a truly flexible design addresses the key operational requirements of alternative, but targeted, uses and markets.

Time is Money

Today the most important variable in determining the impact of change is the shortening investment cycle. Time is now measured in milliseconds, and physical products have to compete for resources in a marketplace where time is money. The time horizon for the economic appraisal of buildings now resembles that for consumer products. Most commercial business cases look for paybacks of 18 to 36 months or, exceptionally, 36 to 60 months. However, we continue to consider buildings as fixed investments over 60 years or more even though we know that in the long term they will almost certainly not be used for the purpose for which they were designed.

Knowledge is quickly outdated. For it to remain economically viable, a knowledge base needs to be continually refreshed. At the post-graduate level, intellectual capital must be quickly capitalised upon by getting educational return back within one to three years to avoid wasting the investment.

This is an increasingly important issue in tertiary institutions where leading research work is being undertaken. In the UK and in the US, the costs of refurbishment, renovation, or replacement of sections of building are very high. In one UK university known for its successes in winning government sponsored research, the governing council was told that the greater the university's success, the greater the adaptation costs would be, thus creating a "crisis of success". This situation is similar in the US, at many of the leading tertiary institutions.

219

In today's world, technology reinvents the art of the possible every few years. Yet much of what we do in our schools, offices, and homes remains defiantly familiar: only a few significant things do change beyond recognition. The key to investing for flexibility is to spot the significant details in our lives from which these fundamental changes will come. This requires a very specific knowledge of how an organisation works in the short to medium term rather than a generic model for long-term universal change.

Liquidated Assets

Fixed assets are often a liability for organisations, especially those dependent on demographic demand. However, by design, these buildings have only a single use that makes them exceptionally vulnerable to changes in demand. This is exacerbated by the fact that tertiary institutions tend to own the vast majority of their buildings or have long inflexible leases, resulting in an inevitable legacy of obsolescence. The buildings yield no economic benefits and can actually remove value and utility from the institution.

Traditionally, yields for educational institutions are not directly measured in the UK where most were and still are government funded at all levels. PFI (Private Finance Initiative) changes this. If retail space yields 5%, commercial offices 7%, and, industrial buildings 10%, what should be the yield for an educational facility? The fundamental fact is that PFI is about the transference of risk. Since the higher the risk, the higher the required yield, it is of real economic importance that the perceived risks involved in educational PFI projects be understood and managed.

Not surprisingly therefore a particular problem with PFI has been the reluctance of banks to cover risk on specialised design investment when maintaining the asset value is so problematic. Here, the importance of facility management may provide a means of achieving long term asset value. One of the best models for achieving this in the UK would be the Broadgate office development in London. Although there are different owners and corporate tenants, the basic principles established for maintaining the fabric and utility of the stock are carried out by Broadgate Estates on behalf of the landlord.

Even if buildings are capable of major change in use, there are statutory barriers to flexibility of a radical nature. One of the main problems in the UK is development control as exercised by local planning authorities and central government. These policies often conflict with one another in terms of gauging the changing social requirements for land and its use, and can completely ignore medium term economic forces. Furthermore, the laws governing buildings and their use are based on a codified and historical "Use Class" system that is difficult to untangle or interpret creatively for any mixed-use development[28].

Briefing for Flexibility

How does one brief and design for this? Under the UK's PFI programme, new educational buildings are being provided and maintained by the private sector for periods of over 25 years. It is naive to assume that a conventionally flexible design will anticipate all of the major changes that will occur over that period of time. And yet the purpose of PFI is to transfer this risk to the private sector. This paper is based on a successful PFI bid for a college in Scotland which incorporated fundamental concepts of flexibility and which satisfied both the educational requirements of the College users and the commercial requirements of the consortium bidding for the contract. (See Appendix).

West Lothian College required a design that would address a wide range of possible scenarios and yet would be economically viable. The following five key issues arose for the college's statement of requirements' and illustrate the radical nature of the long term changes being contemplated and the importance of the short-term economic drivers which had to be respected:

Delivering the Business Case. The business case for the new campus will require delivery of two objectives.

• Successful *rationalisation* of current facilities without disruption to existing revenues and the generation of capital on schedule.

• Accurate *translation* of business case needs into architectural reality and the identification of measurable educational and financial criteria for its success.

Targeting Markets. The College will be attempting to integrate two quite different markets by:

• Attracting and retaining *technology based customers* with highly customised programmes providing access into and from the wider College as a social and technological centre of excellence.

• Providing magnet facilities which address the needs of *the community* to improve their employment prospects and also generate links and synergy with the marketplace.

Supporting Competitive Advantage. The College's conventional means of delivering services will be supplemented by two methods of acquiring competitive advantage.

• Forming *strategic alliances* with complementary organisations to give access to new markets and allowing the College to exist in many places.

- Using more *flexible and open techniques* to respond to market demand, widen the potential take up, and create more opportunities for learning within a European benchmarked and mature environment.

Exploiting Space. Space will be an asset to the College rather than a liability by controlling two factors.

- Minimising the *amount of area* per FTE which constitutes a fixed overhead.

- Avoiding unnecessary complexity and *simplifying* the types of space in order to ensure high space use and flexibility.

Generating Income. The College will maximise its revenue potential by addressing two time scales:

- Short-term, by listening to *what the customer wants* and providing it within adaptable accommodation in terms of layout and image.

- Long-term, by planning for future growth and decline with full capacity site development strategies and marketable *building types*.

Flexibility usually relates to the variety of arrangements that are possible within the building shell, given its servicing and structural systems. In this case, however, flexibility was about challenging the conventional building typologies. The solutions adopted were as equally responsive to the commercial needs of a business park as they were to the educational needs of a college. Indeed, it highlighted to what an extent this split no longer applies in today's educational marketplace. Just as the business corporation needs increasingly to consider itself as a learning organisation so the educational institution needs to regard itself as a commercial organisation.

The Invisible Hand

Virtual environments are certainly an increasingly realistic response to providing flexibility for change: better perhaps to invest in technology than in buildings. This has already happened at the Open University and other establishments. Cornell, for example, is one of the few "wired" universities in America and it seems to be paying huge dividends. The late Carl Sagan lectured to 700 students in the introductory astronomy lectures at Cornell. Seats were impossible to come by in one of the most popular first year classes on the campus. Today, Cornell has one of the most sophisticated video classrooms in the US and a strong sense of place. The Open University needed a "site" to make it work as an institution.

222

Building costs are a very small percentage of the overall operational, maintenance and replacement costs for a building. PFI both demonstrates that this has been recognised and that its consequences are not yet fully appreciated. Whilst the promise of innovation using PFI has been fulfilled to some degree, in areas such as prison design and operation, it has not yet been seen to do so in educational buildings. What PFI does present is an opportunity to think beyond conventional building typologies, which are to some degree a product of the late industrial age, and not particularly relevant to the new Information Age with its continually changing technology and spin-offs. Indeed the relevance of traditional flexibility in such a context now needs to be questioned. Flexibility is less about projecting into the future than it is about listening to the forces around us today.

Taking the Risk

The key to designing for flexibility lies in risk management. The audit trail from business strategy to operational requirements to design brief needs to be a short-term scenario tested equally against bankruptcy and success. The alternative is to travel hopefully in the face of experience. The challenge is to create a much more diverse stock of building types whose richness will protect us from the folly of pretending to know all the answers.

223

APPENDIX

West Lothian Mission Statement:

To provide education and training to stimulate and satisfy the needs of employers, inward investors and individuals in the community.

KEY FACTS

- 150 staff.

- 1 800 student FTEs.

- GBP20 000 000 in capital building costs.

- GBP2 000 000 in annual operational costs (GBP50 000 000 contract value).

- 15 200 total square metres for the College development, comprising 8 540 total square metres for college buildings, for future changes to core business requirements; 3 540 square metres for Research and Development buildings, potential for speculative initiatives; and 3 120 square metres for a support facility that creates an opportunity for leisure requirements.

CONCLUSION

In many industrialised countries, the accumulation of human capital has been acknowledged as an important policy to sustain economic growth and to stimulate technological innovation. In its original version, the human capital framework conceived an investment in education as a cost-benefit analysis carried out by individuals. The decision to invest in human capital in this model was based on the evaluation of the costs and benefits of this investment. This evaluation rests on the comparison of direct and opportunity costs with the additional expected earnings associated with the individual's consequent increase in productivity. But the benefits of education are neither solely individual ones nor wholly captured in this private investment framework. Education develops productive resources beyond those accruing to the individual or the employer. These 'externalities' are essentially of two kinds. First, the higher the average educational level of the labour force, the better information can circulate amongst firms or other productive units, the more effective is learning, and thus the easier becomes the diffusion of innovation. These types of benefits are positive externalities linked to the increased cognitive abilities induced by education. Second, education also enhances the individual's ability to integrate into society and contributes to social cohesion. Cost-benefit analysis, with its focus on the perspective of society, is an appropriate method of appraisal to incorporate these various externalities.

The appraisal of the investment in human capital is affected by the nature of the educational process. The final outcome of the educational process is the result of an interaction between factors related to the educational environment and those related to the social background of the individuals. However, if there is a general agreement on the fact that the outcome of the educational process is multi-dimensional, the underlying factors remain imperfectly defined. The final output is affected by inputs such as the inherent ability of the student, the family and the social environment. In addition, even if we can measure the quantity of educational inputs (teachers' and pupils' time, buildings and equipment); it is hard to measure the quality of such inputs.

The European Investment Bank takes an active role in the development of new facilities for education across the Member States of the European Union. Investing in new educational facilities will provide an important input for the production of a highly

225

skilled society. However, new appraisal methodologies have to be implemented to evaluate investment in educational buildings. The question of the design of these methodologies was at the heart of the discussion in Luxembourg in the conference organized jointly by the Projects Directorate of the EIB and by the OECD Programme on Educational Building.

Some general guidelines can point the way forward in project appraisal. **First**, project definition. What is an educational project? It is a blend of equipment, buildings, and human resources. **Second**, comes the issue of project effectiveness and evaluation. As the EIB finances projects in various countries, it will discern, from local experience, what defines good practice. This, in turn, can support a process of 'benchmarking', by indicating where and how resources are most or least effectively used. It is important to learn from local experience and to collect practical data which can help to improve monitoring mechanisms, and help define what makes a project most effective. The **third** factor relates to project management. Human capital is about people and about competencies embodied in people. There is a need to make sure that the people who manage education resources – including capital expenditure - are capable of controlling and delivering results. It is important to find the best way to improve the capacity of local, regional and national managers to set their own priorities and to make the best possible investments to meet those priorities.

The following sections review in more detail various issues related to the appraisal of educational investment, making reference to the conclusions drawn in the course of the Conference.

Education Projects and the Evaluation Process

Investing in human capital covers a number of different aspects. First, on the benefit side, it means a more skilled workforce leading to potentially a higher productivity level. Investment in human capital also includes a wide range of externalities. Second, investing in human capital normally implies providing new facilities.

Any reliable appraisal of investment in human capital must consider the full set of costs and benefits attributed to schooling. Different categories can be identified:

• Marketed and non-marketed effects.

• Individual and social or public goods effects.

• Effects that enter the economy as intermediate inputs or investment.

However, the majority of existing studies measuring the effect of additional schooling have focused on the labour market outcome as indicated by additional earnings.

Robust appraisal of investment requires that the various alternative means to achieve the desired objective have been addressed and carefully considered. For instance, the answer to specific building needs can be achieved either by refurbishing existing buildings or building new ones.

During the conference, different types of methodology to evaluate investment in educational buildings were discussed. These different methodologies are briefly reviewed below, with emphasis on their most important shortcomings.

Performance indicators

The evaluation of investments in the education sector can be based partially on a system of international, national or regional performance indicators. In several countries, systems of school evaluation have been established with the aim of measuring the added value of different schools. This enables a comparison of schools at the national level, but should also help the further development of international indicators. However, because performance indicators tend to be at an aggregate level they do not reveal regional variation. Neither do they capture institutional discrepancies between different countries. There is, therefore, a need for greater insight into the economics of education in a very detailed manner, for example, to evaluate the performance of urban versus rural areas, and of depressed compared to richer regions.

OECD has developed indicators on regional differences in unit costs and student/staff ratios, but this research encountered severe conceptual difficulties in defining comparable regions. Whilst some regions look administratively comparable, or appear comparable in terms of being urban and rural, they are clearly not comparable when the education decision-making process is examined. Such conceptual problems have hampered the further development of indicators.

Cost-benefit analysis approach

Cost-benefit analysis is appropriate for projects with external effects where costs and benefits can be evaluated in monetary terms.

The estimation of the rate of return to schooling can basically be realised through two different methods: the net present value rule (or the internal rate of return) or the

227

earnings function. The computation of the NPV/IRR should include external costs and benefits in order to have a complete evaluation of a project. The ability to take into account such external effects will depend on the availability of data and on the ability to convert outcomes of the project in monetary terms. In addition, the observed rate of return will also depend on labour and social policies which influence employment and earnings opportunities.

The *earnings function* approach estimates the rate of return by regressing the log of annual earnings on schooling and other explanatory variables, with the rate of return corresponding to the estimated coefficient on years of schooling. Recent empirical studies have tried to address the impact of ability and socio-economic factors on the estimated rate of return. The implementation of such an empirical analysis requires a comprehensive database for each European country and corresponds more to an *ex post* evaluation of the investment, which is not a reliable predictor of the future rate of return in forthcoming projects. Typically, results from this *earnings function* model deliver similar results to those of discounted cash flow NPV model.

Great care is required in inferring recommendations for investment using either estimation of the rate of return to schooling. First, investment in education is typically a long-term investment affecting lifetime earnings. Moreover, investment decisions are taken on the basis of imperfect information. Second, the outcome of such decisions will depend on the market for the educated and trained individuals. More generally speaking, the observed rate of return will be notably affected by the demand and supply for skilled labour, on the existence of labour market rigidities and barriers to entry in some occupations, and on technological change. Third, the evaluation of the rate of return is generally computed at the national level. Finally, estimation of the rate of return very often does not include the various externalities associated with the investment.

Cost-effectiveness approach

Cost-effectiveness analysis is an appropriate methodology to evaluate educational projects where the benefits do not have a readily accessible market price or are not easily measurable in monetary terms. In this approach, inputs are usually measured in pecuniary terms whilst outputs are evaluated in non-monetary units such as test scores, number of graduates, number of research papers.

In cost-effectiveness analysis the costs and the effects of a given educational project can be evaluated and basic questions considered, for example:

• For a given level of effectiveness, which projects are the less costly?

• For a given level of costs, which projects maximise effectiveness?

• Which projects maximise the cost-effectiveness ratio?

One problem of this approach is how to find appropriate measures of quality using physical unit measures of output. In other words, when a product is homogeneous, the physical unit adequately conveys the attributes of the output but education is not often like this. In addition, for valid comparison, the different projects have to produce the same type of outcomes, i.e. if one programme is designed to deliver efficiency benefits whilst a second is focused on equity and access, the comparison between the two projects becomes more complex. To take into consideration multiple outcomes of the educational process, we can apply a weighted cost-effectiveness analysis and attach different weights to each outcome. Dividing the weighted scores by the cost of the corresponding intervention gives the weighted cost-effectiveness ratio. Clearly, a limitation of such an approach is the subjective nature of the choice of the weight attached to each dimension.

In the education sector, one additional difficulty is the notion of intermediate versus final effectiveness. The effectiveness of a project, for example, could be defined either in terms of the number of graduates produced or in terms of individuals for whom the labour market provides a job corresponding to the level of qualification they have acquired. In the first case, we consider some intermediate notion of effectiveness and in the second case, the final effectiveness of the educational project. A related issue encompasses the consideration of external benefits in cost-effectiveness evaluation. To the extent that non-cognitive effects can influence a person's performance in the workplace or the quality of life after school, it has to be included in the analysis. Schools may be internally efficient in raising test scores of students, but externally inefficient in preparing students for their adult life including preparing them for the requirements of the labour market.

Building Projects

The design of buildings can be seen as an input to the educational process and as such can affect the educational achievement of pupils or students. School effects will be manifest through the pupil/teacher ratio, the quality of teaching and the quantity and the quality of other inputs such as library, laboratory, computing facilities. School and class size can also affect school performance. However, existing empirical evidence on the impact of such an educational input is not persuasive: we do not know whether investing in new buildings, or buildings of a certain type, improves educational performance or attainment.

The evaluation of the impact of the building *per se* requires data on the physical educational stock. In addition, building new educational facilities can generate posi-

229

tive external effects. Data on the level of utilisation of space provides useful input in designing strategies for educational buildings. Overall, buildings are used very little after core school hours, but information about the utilisation of school buildings in OECD countries remains incomplete. The number of instructional hours provided in schools has been evaluated, but it has not yet been possible to draw conclusions about the issue of overall utilisation of facilities.

The Programme on Educational Buildings has undertaken qualitative studies of the utilisation of school buildings over the years, and has done research on the integration of community services on school premises. But this does not mean that quantitative data are available. This is one area in which PEB would like to develop performance indicators; the Luxembourg meeting is part of this effort. The question is even more important in developing countries, where schools tend to be used for adult education and other community purposes. This raises the theme of community learning centres, and of the joint use of buildings. How should different types of utilisation be evaluated? And what level of utilisation should be regarded as not desirable?

The evaluation of the costs and benefits of building new schools or new higher education institutions requires that we take into account the obsolescence of the buildings. This aspect is rarely accounted for but raises many questions. Two principal issues arise. The first concerns the costs attached to obsolescence, and the second concerns the timing issue: how should rapid obsolescence be addressed and what are the implications for equipment? Ten years ago, a debate took place on the impact of information technology on schools and how to provide computer rooms. Today, the debate revolves around wireless technology. A more serious effort has to be made to address these changes and how they relate to long-term capital investment.

A further aspect is how to take the interior and exterior design of educational buildings into consideration. The environmental appraisal of education facilities is currently a strong driving force in the design of new school buildings in OECD countries, and is aimed at improving the learning environment and at setting an example of sustainable development. It is difficult to balance the many environmental factors influencing school function, but proper multi-disciplinary design should enable the question of sustainable development to be fully integrated in the appraisal of educational investments.

Finally, another issue related to the previous ones and common to all projects, be they new buildings or refurbishment of old ones, is the choice of building materials. Indeed, the appropriate choice of materials is directly part of the correct costing of buildings.

Project Management and Political Constraints

A link must be established between the themes raised in the conference and the decision-making process. What process leads to the decision to build a new school on the one hand, and to the estimate of the relevant budget on the other? The implementation process for a project can influence the final outcome of the investment. Investment decisions by local decision-makers are based on a number of considerations including political, social and economic aspects. The interaction between these different dimensions can lead to the construction of a school in a particular location, even though a cost-benefit or cost-effectiveness analysis would suggest that a different one is preferable.

From an economic point of view, when investing in a school, an addition is made to the capital stock which will involve a greater value of operating resources than the cost of the capital item alone, i.e. the major part of an educational budget consists of subsequent outlays on personnel. How can indicators be used to guide the choices of investment to take into account the respective magnitude of capital and operating expenditure?

The question of prioritising investments is crucial here. Recently, given the emphasis and resources spent on education there has also been an increase in the research undertaken in this area. So far the results mainly consist of performance indicators and the provision of data. Some research is concerned with what defines a good educational building. Notwithstanding the attempt to pull together these strands of information, it appears still to be the case that there is no way to discriminate between different projects other than through the detailed, individual scrutiny of individual investments. The question of whether investment in educational buildings is a better alternative to other forms of investment in human capital warrants further research. Once progress has been made on this issue, a still more problematic one remains on the horizon: the design and application of monitoring instruments for education sector projects. Applied research in the economics of education, therefore, appears set to offer good labour market prospects for some years to come!

Some final thoughts

The EIB has been involved in finance for general education facilities for only a short time. The OECD has a longer track record but much of its work is on other aspects of the education system than the issue of capital choice and appraisal of educational facilities. The Conference held at the EIB in November 1998 has perhaps produced a larger number of questions than precise answers. This is inevitable given the complexity of the subject. We hope, however, that the Conference has moved the subject on at least a little. At the same time, both institutions are committed to a continued exploration of the problem. We look therefore to a dialogue with other actors in this area.

1   UNESCO Statistical Yearbook, 1997.

2   OECD *Economic Surveys, United Kingdom*, 1996, *p.* 82.

3   OECD *Economic Surveys, Portugal*, 1995.

4   OECD, *Netherlands: Reviews of National Policies in Education*, 1991.

5   OECD, *Denmark: Reviews of National Policies in Education*, 1995.

6   OECD, *Sweden: Reviews of National Policies in Education*, 1995.

7   OECD, *Austria: Reviews of National Policies in Education*, 1995, *p.* 37.

8   OECD, *Greece: Reviews of National Policies in Education*, 1997.

9   OECD *Education Indicators*, 1997.

10 Murnane and Levy, *Teaching the New Basic Skills: Principles for Educating Children and Thriving in a Changing Economy*, 1996, *p.* 40.

11 OECD, *Human Capital Investment: an International Comparison*, 1998, p. 9.

12 Alfred Marshall *Principles of Economics: An Introductory Volume*, eighth edition, 1992, p. 216

13 It will be said that the political decision process already considers non-market outcomes when deciding public education budgets, and therefore these non-market outcomes are already included in these education expenditures in measured GNP and should not be valued separately. Although true, public expenditures on education (which are the factor-cost basis for valuing education outcomes in standard social accounting) exclude the foregone earnings costs borne largely by parents, a major part of the economic cost of education investments. Indeed, these are larger than direct costs, at least at secondary and higher education levels which of necessity will be the focus on most increments in education investments in the OECD countries where primary and junior secondary education are universal.

    Therefore, measured GNP by standard social accounting methods grossly undervalues the outcomes of education, to the extent, using Wolfe and Zuvekas' (1997) measures, that it leaves out the value of all of the non-market returns.

14 World Bank, 1998, p. 193.

15   Healy in *Human Capital Investment: an International Comparison*, p. 113.

16   For detailed information on definitions, sources and methods, OECD, Education at a Glance (1998). All indicators cited are taken from this publication.

17   Ideally, this table would cover both direct private costs (tuition and other education-related fees, textbooks, uniforms and transport) and indirect private costs (lost output when employees participate in on-the-job training). Many private costs are difficult to measure and to compare internationally. This indicator focuses on public and private expenditure on educational institutions. Private payments other than to educational institutions (column 6 of Tables B1.1a, b, and c) include direct purchases of personal items used in education or subsidised expenditure on student living expenses. Public subsidies to households that are not attributable to payments to educational institutions (column 7 of Tables B1.1a, b, and c) include subsidies for student living costs and the value of special subsidies provided to students, either in cash or in kind, such as free or reduced-price travel on public transport, or family allowances that are contingent on student status. (also included in column 5 of Tables B1.1a, b, and c).

18   Tables B4.1 and B4.2 calculate expenditure per student by dividing the total expenditure at that level by the corresponding full-time equivalent enrolment. The only types of educational institutions and programmes that are taken into account are those for which both enrolment and expenditure data are available. Enrolment data are adjusted by interpolation to match either the financial year or the calendar year of each country. The result in national currency is then converted into equivalent US dollars by dividing the national currency figure by the PPP index. The PPP exchange rates used pertain to GDP and are derived from the OECD National Accounts Database for OECD countries and from the World Bank database for OECD non-member countries. The PPP exchange rate gives the amount of a national currency that will buy the same basket of goods and services in a country as the US dollar will in the United States. The PPP exchange rate is used because the market exchange rate is affected by many factors (interest rates, trade policies, expectations of economic growth, etc.) that have little to do with current, relative domestic purchasing power in different countries.

19   The capital expenditures reported here represent the value of educational capital acquired or created during the year in question - the amount of capital formation - regardless of whether the capital outlays were financed from current revenue or by borrowing. Neither current nor capital expenditure include expenditure for debt service. Expenditure per student relative to GDP per capita is calculated by expressing expenditure per student in units of national currency as a percentage of GDP per capita, also in national currency. Where the educational expenditure data

233|

and the GDP data pertain to different reference periods, the expenditure data are adjusted to the same reference period as the GDP data, using inflation rates for the country in question. Calculations cover expenditure by public institutions or, where available, those of public and private institutions combined. Only expenditure on educational institutions is considered. The proportions of current expenditure allocated to compensation of teachers and other staff, total staff compensation and other (non-personnel) current outlays are calculated by expressing the respective amounts as percentages of total current expenditure. In some cases, compensation of teaching staff means compensation of classroom teachers only, where in others it includes heads of schools and other professional educators.

20 Average expenditure per student by resource category is calculated by multiplying expenditure per student in PPP by the respective proportions of teacher and staff compensation in total expenditure for educational institutions. Current expenditure other than for the compensation of personnel includes contracted and purchased services such as support services (*e.g.* building maintenance), ancillary services (teaching materials, preparing student meals, for example), and rental for buildings and other facilities obtained from outside providers as opposed to education authorities or personnel.

21 Urban Planning Bureau of the City of Vienna, The new schoolhouse: schoolchild's universe and urban practice.

22 In outlining this conclusion, Derouet is clearly taking a post-modern position in terms of the individual-local superseding the global.

23 The university was built in order to "coerce" the nomadic monks and their students to stay in one place as a means of providing a regional competitive advantage in northern Italy at the time. See "The History of the University in Europe", CRE, 1996.

24 J. Goddard, "Managing the University Regional Interface;" Journal of the OECD Programme on the Institutional Management of Higher Education, 9:3, Nov 1997, p. 27.

25 http://www.oecd.org/els/edu/peb/els_pebn.htm#Programme on Educational Building (PEB)

26 Edwards, p. 24.

27 In Chile, the Sociedad Constructora de Establecimientos Educacionales, created in 1939 was closed in 1987; in Mexico, the Comtité Administrador del Programa Federal de Construccion de Escuelas (CAPFCE) was created in 1944 and today is

decentralised. It was responsible for 22 000 schools in 1944 and 170 000 in 1994. In Colombia, the Instituto Colombiano de Construccion de Escuelas (ICCE) was created in 1969 and closed in 1987. In Bolivia, the Consejo Nacional de Construcciones Escolares (CONES) was created in 1971 and closed twenty years later. In Venezuela, the Fundacion de Edificaciones y Dotaciones Educativas (FEDE) was created in 1976 and is currently decentralising. France had a Direction des Bâtiments in the Ministry of Education until 1970, and many Eastern European countries have also had central units.

28 RICS valuation methods and appraisal practices are based on the five aggregate use categories: retail, industrial/warehouse, residential, commercial and other (general catch-all category, there are 17 formal categories under the Use Class Order 1987). The system was devised in the post war era and suffers from an emphasis on manufacturing and a belief that this can all be neatly controlled.

OECD 2000

OECD PUBLICATIONS, 2, rue André-Pascal, 75775 PARIS CEDEX 16
PRINTED IN FRANCE
(95 2000 01 1 P) ISSN 92-64-17036-7 – No. 50647 2000